Varieties of Exile: The Canadian Experience

VARIETIES OF EXILE
The Canadian Experience

Hallvard Dahlie

University of British Columbia Press
Vancouver
1986

VARIETIES OF EXILE
The Canadian Experience

©The University of British Columbia Press 1986

This book has been published with the help of a grant from the Canadian Federation for the Humanities, using funds provided by the Social Sciences and Humanities Research Council of Canada, and a Grant from the Endowment Fund of the University of Calgary.

Canadian cataloguing in Publication Data

Dahlie, Hallvard, 1925-
  Varieties of exile

  ISBN 0-7748-0252-9
  1. Canadian literature (English)—History and criticism.* 2. Literature—Exiled authors—History and criticism. 3. Exiles in literature. I. Title.
PS8101.E95D34 1986   C810'.9   C86-091171-3
PR9185.5.E95D34 1986

International Standard Book Number 0-7748-0252-9

Printed in Canada

To my parents,
who brought me from the Old World to the New,
and taught me to love both.

Contents

Acknowledgments   ix

1. The Ambiguities of Exile: Shaping a Definition   1

2. Roughing It in Exile   10

3. Between Two Worlds   34

4. The New World Triumphant   59

5. Tourists and Expatriates   87

6. From the Old World: A Canadian in Paris   115

7. Birds of Passage   144

8. Emigrés and Academics   183

9. The Legacy of Exile   199

Notes   203

Bibliography   207

Index   215

Acknowledgments

I wrote the first drafts of this book in 1981-82, during my Fellowship in the Calgary Institute for the Humanities, and during the fall of 1982, when I was a Killam Resident Fellow at the University of Calgary. I wish to thank the Institute and the University of Calgary for these awards and accompanying facilities for research and writing. In particular, I should like to thank Dr. Harold Coward, Director of the Calgary Institute for the Humanities, his administrative assistant, Mrs. Gerry Dyer, and the secretarial staff, Mrs. Wynne McLelland, Miss Saida Din, and Mrs. Gloria Eslinger, for the typing of the early drafts.

I owe a strong thanks, too, to the Department of English, to Dr. James Black, its head during the period in question, to my many colleagues, and to the graduate students in my seminars on the literature of exile, all of whom gave freely and richly of their ideas. I am grateful to members of the department's secretarial staff, particularly to the late Mrs. Betty O'Keeffe, who worked patiently and skilfully on my many revisions, and I wish to communicate a special thanks to Mrs. Freda Adams, who typed the final manuscript and handled the correspondence and the many other details pertaining to its final preparation.

The librarians and their staffs where I conducted my research were unfailingly generous and helpful, and I extend to them a special thanks: Mr. Donald D. Eddy, Department of Rare Books, Cornell University, for permission to publish material from the Wyndham Lewis Collection; Ms. Anne Yandle, Special Collection Division, University of British Columbia Library, for permission to publish material from Malcolm Lowry Collection; Ms. Sue Hodson, Assistant Curator, Literary Manuscripts, the Huntington Library, for permission to publish some Lowry items from the Conrad Aiken Collection; Ms. Apollonia Steele, Special Collections Division, University of Calgary Library, for permission to publish material from the Brian Moore Papers;

and Mr. Richard Landon, Thomas Fisher Rare Books Room, University of Toronto Library, for access to the Mavis Gallant and Josef Skvorecky Collections. I also wish to thank Mr. Cy Fox, Executor of the Wyndham Lewis Estate and the Wyndham Lewis Memorial Trust, for permission to publish excerpts from Lewis's unpublished letters, Mr. Peter Matson of Literistic Ltd., for permission to publish excerpts from Lowry's unpublished letters, copyright The Estate of Malcolm Lowry, and Mr. Brian Moore for his permission to publish excerpts from his unpublished work.

I wish to acknowledge the help given me by the editors and readers of the University of British Columbia Press, especially Jane Fredeman and Jean Wilson, and by the Canadian Federation for the Humanities, both for its provision of assessors' comments on my manuscript, and for its grant in aid of publication. My thanks, too, to the University of Calgary for its grant from the Endowment Fund to aid in the publication of this book.

My strongest personal thanks go to my wife Betty and my family who gave me strong and consistent encouragement, and helped in so many ways to make the research and writing of the book a pleasurable task.

H.D.
Calgary, 1985

1

The Ambiguities of Exile: Shaping a Definition

If study of any subject ideally should go back to beginnings, then a convenient starting-point for an examination of exile is the dawn of the Christian era, for it was in the year 8 A.D. that the Emperor Augustus exiled the Roman poet Ovid to Tomis on the shores of the Black Sea. As far as I can determine, the precise reasons for his exile have never been established and are being debated among classical scholars to this day, with speculation even spilling over into the more imaginative area of fiction.[1] But at the very least, Ovid was regarded as something of a threat to his society, possibly because of the nature of his controversial and highly popular *Art of Love;* it is further possible that he was singled out as an appropriate scapegoat for indiscretions committed within Augustus's own family. Whatever the reason, the pattern established was the exile as outcast, as threat to the prevailing order, and as dangerous thinker whose ideas were potentially subversive, all of which tendencies have characterized the exile from that day to this.

The edict proclaiming Ovid's exile was never repealed, in spite of the poet's ceaseless exhortations and flatteries to both Augustus and his successor, Tiberius, and he died in exile some nine years after his banishment. During those years his output was prodigious, but of chief interest here are his *Tristia* and his *Epistulae ex Ponto,* the two books of lamentation widely regarded as the earliest consistent expression of an exile's attitude towards his world. The two books contain countless passages that reflect this vision, many of which bear striking resemblances to the exile literature pertaining to the New World; indeed, the following laments could, with little modification, have been expressed by several of the exile figures I will be examining in this book:

> I shall continue to dwell at the edge of the world, a land far removed from my own . . . . No interchange of speech have I with the wild

people . . . . They hold intercourse in the tongue they share; I must make myself understood by gestures. Here it is I that am a barbarian, understood by nobody.[2]

Ovid here touches on a number of characteristics that recur in the literature of exile over the ensuing centuries: isolation, remoteness from one's native land, the juxtaposition of metropolis and hinterland, the threat posed by barbarous and strange people, the loss of language, the difficulty of communication. As long as exile was an enforced condition or punishment— and until relatively recent times this has generally been the case—the direction of the banishment was always from the centre of one's world towards its edges, to a region where one's native language was no longer of any use. Not surprisingly, perhaps, the idea rarely surfaced—except occasionally in some of the Anglo-Saxon poems, like *The Seafarer* or *The Wanderer*—that the region of exile possessed in itself any intrinsic value, that it could inform the exile with experiences and perspectives that might compensate for the culture of which he had been deprived. But one has only to alter the perspective, to regard the exile from the point of view of those among whom he has been banished, to detect the ironic truth of Ovid's lament that it is he who is the barbarian. And near the end of his exile, he did in fact begin to integrate himself into the alien Getic culture, to learn its language, and even to write some verse from that new perspective, as he explained, with some alarm, in one of his *Epistulae ex Ponto:*

Nor should you wonder if my verse prove faulty, for I am almost a Getic poet. Ah! it brings me shame! I have even written a poem in the Getic tongue, setting barbarian words to our measures; I even found favour— congratulate me— and began to achieve among the uncivilized Getae the name of poet.[3]

His comments are not without the arrogance and condescension bred of a culture always regarded as superior, and readers of early exile literature pertaining to the New World undoubtedly will find remarkably familiar the tone and attitude revealed in these confessions.

One could easily multiply quotations of this nature from many of the literatures of the western world: from the Anglo-Saxon poets, from Dante, and above all from Shakespeare, whose *Richard II* contains one of the classic articulations of the exile's dilemma, the familiar lamentation that Mowbray utters upon his banishment. To "turn me from my country's light / To dwell in solemn shades of endless night" has come to represent a universal and timeless lament of exile, though, as we will see, the last century or so has brought about a significant modification of this attitude, particularly on the part of exiles in or from the New World. Quite clearly, any definition or description of a term as elusive or as protean as exile must take into consideration these historical derivations and manifestations, but my emphasis will be on the many modulations of this term that are applicable to Canadian exile literature of the past 200 years or so. What will emerge is evidence showing that though many of these traditional characteristics remain relevant, particularly for the earlier exiles to Canada, the situation of exile during this period has, on the whole, become both a more complex and a more pragmatic experience, with its negative or punitive characteristics increasingly disappearing.

The conventional concept of exile as I have briefly been discussing it conforms quite faithfully to its commonly understood meaning, as reflected, for example, in the first of two definitions cited by *The Oxford English Dictionary:* "enforced removal from one's native land according to an edict or sentence," a condition that applies without reservation to both Ovid and Mowbray. Within this perspective, the exile was perceived as a threat to the well-being or unity of his society and therefore had to be disposed of; whatever social, religious, or political structures have controlled man throughout history, from the early tribal and Christian orders through to the collectivist ideologies of the twentieth century, this principle governing exile has been in operation. For example, in a persuasive article entitled "The Exile as Uncreator," a recent critic demonstrates how this pattern operated in Anglo-Saxon times, arguing that within the Christian analogy of the community as a whole body, the exile was "naturally seen as a kind of amputation, the cutting off of a sick and infectious member who poses a menace to the body and the ideological system that holds it together."[4] The operating principle here is that the exile, once cleansed and purified by God's love, would want to return and rejoin the community; as is apparent in the works of such contemporary writers as Henry Kreisel and Josef Skvorecky, this concept has undergone a total reversal among today's ideological exiles, who believe it is not they who require cleansing, but rather the societies that banished them in the first place.

This traditional concept of exile normally had the elements of compulsion and punishment about it, and its expressions in literature characteristically emerged as lamentations of loneliness, homesickness, and, not infrequently, self-pity. But there is another concept which is more relevant to a modern examination of this phenomenon, and again I turn to the *O.E.D.* for its second definition: "expatriation, prolonged absence from one's native land, endured by compulsion of circumstances *or voluntarily undergone for any purpose*" (my italics). Both definitions contain the obligatory proviso of "absence from one's native land," a condition that today is by no means accepted by all critics who discuss exile, though I stress here that aside from

two exceptions in Chapter 4, it is a *sine qua non* of my study: I will be
examining not only those writers from the Old World who became exiles to
Canada, but also a number of indigenous Canadians who have exiled themselves for varying periods from Canada. The two Oxford definitions are
broad enough to cover all the commonly used synonyms of exile that my
dual perspective involves: expatriate, émigré, immigrant, emigrant, refugee,
evacuee, displaced person, outcast, remittance man, and that term peculiar
to a certain class of British settlers in Canada, gentleman emigrant. Small
wonder that little agreement on terminology has been shown by the major
critics who have addressed themselves to this phenomenon: the titles alone
of such books as Malcolm Cowley's *Exile's Return* (1934), Ernest Earnest's
Expatriates and Patriots (1968), Terry Eagleton's *Exiles and Émigrés* (1970),
and Thomas Farley's *Exiles and Pioneers* (1975) reflect the ambiguities and
flexibility of this term.

Because "exile," "expatriate," and "émigré" are the most established, and
the most respectable, of this long list of synonyms, it is not surprising that
many critics frequently interchange them or define them in sufficient breadth
to satisfy most subjective interpretations of these terms. But though it would
be little more than pedantry to insist on absolute distinctions among them,
some qualifications are relevant to the exile pattern that I will be applying to
the writers I am concerned with in this book. Exile, as opposed to the other
two terms, suggests an obligatory decision on the part of the writer, induced
by circumstances that can be either external or internal, though its Ovidian
dimension of enforced punishment has for all practical purposes been lost.
Exile is a step which both in its genesis and in its unfolding is irreversible, for
there is a self-fulfilling paradox which attends this term: as long as the
dislocated individual continues to be at odds with both the world he has
rejected and the one he has moved into, he remains spiritually and intellectually an exile; if he returns permanently to his homeland, he can in retrospect
be seen as having been either an expatriate or an émigré; and if he becomes
totally integrated into his adopted society, he would in that respect become
indistinguishable from that country's indigenous writers and thereupon
cease to be an exile. Strictly speaking, however, these are all theoretical
situations, for in practice the exile never goes home and he never attains a
completely total integration: genuine exile is a permanent condition characterized by dislocation, alienation, and dispossession.

Expatriation, on the other hand, is a less permanent situation: it evokes its
logical as well as its verbal corollary, repatriation, for as a rule it derives from
a situation which, when eliminated or otherwise resolved, can quite easily
reverse the direction of the pilgrimage. Up to a point, though this is not a
crucial criterion, the time spent outside one's native land is a governing
factor, and in this respect, Earnest's definition of an expatriate as "anyone

who has lived abroad for a considerable length of time"[5] is not sufficiently accurate. I agree with him that most of the writers he discusses are expatriates, though I would label Henry James as exile, while all the lost generation individuals of the 1920's that Cowley calls exiles I would classify as expatriates. In practice, the expatriate is little more than an extended tourist, who leaves his country temporarily because he believes that certain possibilities for living or for art are more favourable elsewhere. Cowley points out, however, that many of his group, "having come [to Europe] in search of values, found valuta"[6] instead, and in this respect, many expatriates quickly return home once the artistic and / or monetary conditions there make it attractive to do so. True exile derives from a much more profound and lasting impulse, and is essentially a more lonely and vulnerable position to assume than expatriation, which is frequently attended by some kind of public attention, and whose exponents at times seem to be playing for the home crowd.

The term "émigré" has less relevance to my study than the other two, and though it originally had a precise denotation (a French royalist emigrant who fled the French Revolution), it is frequently used today in reference to any emigrant or refugee. Eagleton in his book, for example, applies the label to writers like Joseph Conrad or Henry James, emigrants who adopted England because they liked that society better than their own, while he uses "exile" to define indigenous writers like George Orwell and D.H. Lawrence, who felt alienated from that society.[7] In today's world, however, "émigré" is more accurately applied to political exiles, driven out of their native countries by totalitarian repression, and prepared to return once the political conditions make it morally and intellectually proper to do so. In practice, however, such émigrés to the New World have not infrequently been transformed into permanent exiles, or even into sudden and total converts to their adopted land, so appealing do they find their new freedom. Josef Skvorecky, for example, an émigré-turned-exile from Czechoslovakia, recalls that on his first night in Canada he could not get over "the feeling of security, of an utter absence of that central European nightmare called the Doorbell-Ringing-At-Four-a.m."[8] Sometimes, a new life for an émigré evokes a kind of superior indifference, as reflected, for example, by Vladimir Nabokov, who recalled in his *Speak Memory* how he and his Russian colleagues in western Europe viewed their new countrymen as "perfectly unimportant strangers... in whose more or less illusory cities we, émigrés, happened to dwell.... It seemed at times that we ignored them the way an arrogant or very stupid invader ignores a formless and faceless mass of natives."[9] As we will see in the next chapter, this attitude is essentially no different from that reflected by many early British exiles to the natives they encountered in Canada, manifested fictionally, for example, in such characters as Colonel Rivers in Frances Brooke's *Emily Montague*.

Within the Canadian context, both Farley's *Exiles and Pioneers* and John Matthews' *Tradition in Exile* are almost exclusively concerned with developments in poetry, Matthews contrasting Canada's poetic traditions against Australia's. Though not specifically defined, exile in his book involves the juxtaposition of the particularities of these two literatures not only against each other, but also against their common English derivation and base.[10] Farley uses "exile" as a term in antithesis to "pioneer," and to each category he attaches a number of attitudes towards the world. Thus, the exile feels displaced, aristocratic, alienated, pessimistic, fearful, and so on, in contrast to the pioneer, who feels at home, democratic, solidary, optimistic, and daring. Farley's subsequent deductive application of this "content analysis" method to selected works from English- and French-Canadian poetry leads him to his sociological conclusion that the two solitudes of exile (English) and pioneering (French) must eventually coalesce, so that we will "stop fearing the pull of the North American frontier which is our home."[11] Both Matthews and Dennis Duffy, in *Gardens, Covenants, Exiles,* differ from Farley in that they emphasize the loyalty of the exile, whether English or Loyalist, to the strengths of their original homeland, though Duffy sees a larger patterning arising "out of a communal trauma of defeat, exile, and beginning again."[12]

This discussion of the concept of exile and of the critical approaches to it suggests that it is far more important to recognize the rich ambiguities of this term than to force upon it a precise definition. In the larger sense, it may be true, as Andrew Gurr argues in *Writers in Exile,* that "in varying degrees the normal role for the modern creative writer is to be an exile,"[13] but such an all-embracing interpretation of the term would unduly expand my approach, which is basically quite uncomplicated and straightforward. I intend to examine selected works of a number of writers who constitute the two streams of exile I referred to earlier, that is, those who have physically moved to or from Canada, as long as they have communicated a substantial imaginative or artistic perception of the realities and / or myths about Canada.

In its earliest manifestations, exile from the Old World to Canada can be seen quite simply and accurately as part of the larger pattern of westward migration that has characterized the Northern Hemisphere over the past two centuries or so. Works by such writers as John Galt, Catharine Parr Traill, and Susanna Moodie in the nineteenth century, and by Frederick Niven, Laura Salverson, and Ethel Wilson in the twentieth, dramatize this historical situation, and though the Old World remains a strong force in their articulation of their vision of the realities of Canada, they on the whole reflect an optimistic response to the situation of exile. Frederick Philip Grove has much in common with this group of writers in that he too sees the New World as a potential paradise, or at least as a territory that man can transform by commitment and hard work, but he and his protagonists, in the psychological crises they experience, also anticipate such later Old World exiles as Wyndham Lewis, Malcolm Lowry, and Brian Moore. Of these writers, only Lowry saw Canada's physical reality in paradisal terms, but his vision was a unique one, predicated on the land retaining its natural and primal state and not, as with the earlier writers, on it being transformed into an increasingly civilized state.

But the New World has for some time, too, been characterized by reverse pilgrimages, as the books by Cowley and Earnest thoroughly document. Not surprisingly, this phenomenon came later and in less pronounced form in Canada than in the United States where, paradoxically, it was many whom we consider to be the most American of writers—Irving, Cooper, Hawthorne, James, Wharton, Hemingway, Fitzgerald—who embarked on this pilgrimage to the Old World. All of them, however, maintained consistently their proprietary interest in what James called the "complex fate [of] being an American," a position which for virtually all of them was strengthened rather than threatened by their Old World experiences.

Whether or not the question of being Canadian is less complex than that of being American (all that is certain is that it is not precisely the same thing), Canadian expatriates and exiles on the whole have been less concerned with this issue than their American counterparts. They are not of course as numerous, and they have not emerged in the popular imagination as a homogeneous group, or as having any readily graspable cause behind their peregrinations. Expatriation out of Canada has been essentially a solitary undertaking: only John Glassco, and to a far lesser extent, Morley Callaghan, belonged in spirit to the lost generation group of the 1920's, and after World War II, individuals like Mavis Gallant, Norman Levine, and Mordecai Richler found their way independently to the European continent. Both the world and the spirit behind expatriation had changed between the wars, a point wryly made by Brian Moore in his review of Cowley's *Exile's Return,* where he remarked that "the difference between the artist's pilgrimage to Europe in the Twenties and in the Sixties is the difference between first love and the obligatory initial visit to a brothel."[14]

As one of these later generation pilgrims, Richler recalled the absence in the early 1950's of any large, unifying cause behind their expatriation: "It would be nice, it would be tidy, to say with hindsight that we were a group, knit by political anger or a literary policy or even an aesthetic revulsion for all things American, but the truth was we recognized each other by no more than a shared sense of the ridiculous."[15] What Richler is implying here is that the expatriates of the 1920's were sufficiently homogeneous to be categorized as a fairly exclusive *generation*; except in a chronological sense, no such labels could be applied to those of his own day. Ironically, what had come to pass for them was precisely the state of affairs reflected in Amory Blaine's famous lament near the end of Fitzgerald's *This Side of Paradise*: "Here was a new generation . . . grown up to find all Gods dead, all wars fought, all faiths in man shaken," but with the significant difference that this situation was a verifiable reality for Richler's generation, whereas for the young men of Princeton, it was, we see in retrospect, merely a fashionable cry. Richler may, like Fitzgerald, have felt "the faint stirring of old ambitions and unrealized dreams," but that lament did not move his generation either to admiration or to pity, as it once had done. Writers of Richler's time found they could no longer take refuge in popular causes or clichéd responses to their problems, and increasingly they assumed positions of psychological exile from their world.

As my comments to this point have implied, I am concerned with the exile theme only as it is expressed in the literature pertaining to English Canada; its exceedingly rich manifestations in French-Canadian literature clearly need to be examined in its original language, and others are more qualified than I to do that. Another omission from my study is the literature of the Loyalists, in large part because most of the major first-generation Loyalists, like Jonathan Odell and Joseph Stansbury, expressed themselves in poetry, a genre I do not cover in my study, while the prose writers of importance, like Thomas Haliburton and Joseph Howe, were indeed of Loyalist stock but were born in Canada and are therefore excluded. In a very important sense, too, the Loyalists as a whole did not really move from one country to another, but rather from one part of British North America to another part of it, and though this fact does not militate against the worth of their literature, it does explain why the tensions and sense of alienation are not so pronounced in their works as in the other exile literature I examine in this book.

Quite clearly, the total number of writers in the categories of exile that could be examined is very large, and indeed is growing steadily as I write, but I am restricting myself here to fifteen or so who have come to Canada from the Old World, and some half dozen indigenous Canadians who have exiled themselves from Canada. I am concerned mainly with novels and short stores, ranging chronologically from Frances Brooke's *The History of Emily Montague* (1769) to Josef Skvorecky's *The Engineer of Human Souls* (1984), but I will also be examining a number of important non-fictional expressions of the exile phenomenon, like Moodie's *Roughing It in the Bush* and Levine's *Canada Made Me,* and letters by a number of nineteenth- and twentieth-century exiles, notably those by Lewis and Lowry. My emphasis lies with writers of the twentieth century, but as Chapter 2 illustrates, a number of works from the eighteenth and nineteenth centuries reflect attitudes towards the New and Old Worlds that help explain the modulations of the exiles'

responses in this century. In effect, my major concern is more to demonstrate that the phenomenon of exile has been a frequently recurring element
in Canadian literature, than it is to attempt a discussion of all the works that
exploit this component.

2

Roughing It in Exile

As might be expected, the variations of the term "exile" that I discussed in Chapter 1 were manifested in fairly predictable and uncomplicated patterns in the literature of colonial and nineteenth-century Canada. As long as Canada remained a colony, most of her writers were temporary transplants or grudging visitors from the British Isles, whose cultural superiority was a natural and automatic assumption that very much controlled the responses these writers made to the New World. In their books, therefore, which in some cases were little more than travel accounts or guidebooks for potential emigrants, the theme of exile constituted a relatively unsophisticated and undeveloped component, quite frequently expressed merely as conditioned and obligatory observations about the New World as paradise or wilderness, or about its deficient society and unformed culture. But occasionally echoing through even some of the more practical and prosaic of these books was the note of desolation so common to the literature of exile, and which essentially sounds modulations on the Ovidian lament, "of what am I to write save the evils of a bitter country, and of praying that I may die in a pleasanter region?"[1]

Literally, of course, exile from Great Britain to the New World meant, as did Ovid's exile, removal from the centre of civilization to its periphery, to a region of strange people and unfamiliar customs, and it took some time for the belief to develop that residence in a hinterland could constitute anything more than an exotic, fearful, or dangerous interlude in one's life. A somewhat affected articulation of this dilemma was expressed by Anna Jameson, a woman of letters and a Shakespearean scholar in England, but in the late 1830's a colonial administrator's estranged wife in Canada. "I am in a small community of fourth-rate, half-educated, or uneducated people," she lamented in 1837. "The place itself, the society, are so detestable to me, my own domestic position so painful and so without remedy or hope, that to remain here would be death to me."[2] There is an echo here of Juliet's "I long to die /

If what thou speak'st speak not of remedy," but her complaint was not entirely theatrical; her descriptions of Toronto and its society in her *Winter Studies and Summer Rambles* clearly reflected aspects of her unpleasant experiences in that city, and interestingly, quite aside from their own intrinsic value, they anticipate the similar laments of that later Toronto-imprisoned exile, Wyndham Lewis.

Because many writers of this period found themselves in what has become known as a garrison situation, their attitudes towards the New World quite likely stemmed both from exclusiveness and superiority on the one hand, and from fear and insecurity on the other. For by definition, while a garrison ostensibly guarantees the isolation and exclusivity of those inside, it also emphasizes the fact that there are threats, real or imaginary, from without, and except for the more insensitive of its inhabitants, a great deal of rationalizing about their vulnerable situation must have gone on inside. In simplified terms, the two prevailing European views about Canada during this period undoubtedly contributed to this rationalizing process: from one point of view, it was regarded as an intolerable place to live, and from another, as part of the New World celebrated in utopian thought, it was seen as a potential paradise where one might live, if not as a noble savage, then even more advantageously as a gentleman in proper estate.

This concept of the New World as a paradise, emanating originally from the thinkers, writers, and explorers of the Renaissance, was given more immediate manifestation in the works of such later writers as Rousseau and Chateaubriand, who celebrated, with more theory than actual experience, the simplicity and primitiveness of this world's inhabitants. And because removal to the New World for the early exiles from Great Britain lacked the component of an enforced banishment, it was relatively easy for them to use this "noble savage" concept in interpreting their own pilgrimages in paradisal and positive terms. This perception of the New World as a paradise remains quite constant in the vision of most of the Old World exiles from the eighteenth through to the twentieth century, and, indeed, it receives some of its strongest manifestations in writers like Grove, Wilson, and Lowry in the middle decades of this century. But at the same time, particularly in writers like John Galt and Anna Jameson, a note of parody occasionally sounds, deriving from the discrepancies between the theoretical paradises of myth and literature and the realities of the New World. For most of the writers of this period, the world of exile which they in anticipation had feared emotionally and intellectually was transformed experientially not into paradise lost but, rather, into paradise *manqué*: though it fell short of its originally conceived and ideal possibilities it became, nevertheless, a world eminently inhabitable, both physically and morally.

The earliest of the exile literature of this period, notably Brooke's *Emily Montague,* gave only superficial attention to the potential inherent in New

World characters and moral situations, for initially these realities were rarely
viewed as offering any experiential alternatives to the culture of the Old
World. By the middle decades of the nineteenth century, however, the
residual Ovidian note of complaint or lamentation started to give way to one
of anticipation and possibility, as individuals stopped regarding the New
World merely as a route to social or artistic stagnation. Writers like Galt,
Traill, and Moodie began to exploit the dramatic possibilities residing in the
clash of social, cultural, or psychological oppositions that their two worlds
generated, though fictionally this development was not very rich until well
into the twentieth century.

There was initially in some of these early exiles—with Susanna Moodie at
any rate—something of the superiority that Nabokov spoke of concerning
his own exile, but their attitude towards the New World soon manifested the
experiential expansiveness required of the genuine exile mind. In this respect,
the comment that Margaret Atwood makes about exile in the "Afterword" to
her *Journals of Susanna Moodie* can stand as a tribute to the strength of
character not only of Susanna but also of many of her fellow exiles:

> We are all immigrants to this place even if we were born here: the
> country is too big for anyone to inhabit completely, and in the parts
> unknown to us we move in fear, exiles and invaders. This country is
> something that must be chosen—it is so easy to leave—and if we do
> choose it we are still choosing a violent duality.[3]

As we will see, there is no "violent duality" implied in Brooke's *Emily
Montague:* her Canadian world was simply a secure Augustan world trans-
posed in its entirety to the British garrison in Quebec. Any incidental
physical or psychological forays into the surrounding territory were little
more than social games whose rules and outcomes were all predetermined.
But with Moodie and her literary descendants, whose writing careers coincided with the growth of a distinct Canadian consciousness, this duality
began to constitute a significant aesthetic component.

The theme of exile in the literature of nineteenth-century Canada is
manifested more in non-fiction than in fiction, a phenomenon undoubtedly
related to Canada's emergence as a territory seen as well worth exploiting
and settling. Frances Brooke could write relatively lighthearted fiction
because Canada in her day was not really taken seriously, a situation which
had altered significantly by the time Canada had both constitutionally (1791)
and militarily (1812) demonstrated a new reality about herself. In the course
of the nineteenth century, therefore, Britain sent out her explorers, her
settlers, her administrators, many of whom contributed to the massive
documentary reportage that has become part of the mythology of Canada so

conveniently and accurately designated by the title of Susanna Moodie's mid-century *Roughing It in the Bush.* For the most part, the voluminous residue of letters, settlers' guides, travel accounts, and the relatively few novels of literary worth all add various dimensions to the "roughing it" theme, and in the process they provide us with interesting opinions on what it meant to be an exile in an emerging land.

Not surprisingly, exiles have always been prolific letter-writers, for aside from the tangible link provided with their homeland, this means of expressing oneself constitutes a subjective and, at times, a defensive response to the state of exile. Though letters are ostensibly a private form of communication, they not infrequently end up as published diaries and journals, exemplified in the nineteenth century, for example, by John Howison's *Sketches of Upper Canada* (1821) and Traill's *Backwoods of Canada* (1836). As Patrick Dunae observes in *Gentlemen Emigrants,*[4] British travellers and settlers were anything but reticent in documenting their impressions of Canada, even in some cases where their contact with a region was so fleeting they could scarcely see it, let alone explain it. John Howison, at any rate, had no hesitation in tackling this anomaly as he writes his first letter to his friend in England:

> You may remember . . . when I promised to present you with occasional sketches . . . after I reached this side of the Atlantic, I did not include Lower Canada in my engagements, as the rapidity with which I expected to pass through it, would, I supposed, prevent one from becoming much acquainted with what it contained . . . . However, before I enter into any details connected with Upper Canada, I shall give you a superficial account of my journey from Montreal to Glengary . . . .[5]

This "superficial account" consists of some sixteen pages of observations and opinions justified, apparently, by Howison's belief that his reader must be gently conditioned to meet what is coming next:

> This will enable me to introduce you gradually to the barbarisms of Upper Canada; for were I to plunge suddenly into the woods, and bring you among bears, Indians, and log-huts, your nerves might receive such a shock as would render you timid about continuing longer in my company. (2)

One is perhaps not surprised to learn that Howison is somewhat offended, as Moodie is to be, at the growing sauciness and republicanism of the ordinary person, particularly at the suddenly lapsed manners of two Scotsmen who "merely nodded . . . with easy familiarity" at him rather than "pulling off their hats, as they had invariably done before on similar occasions" (47). Often throughout his letters he berates the Scots, perhaps justifying to himself his early observation that "a seven weeks passage across the Atlantic did not appear to have divested them of a single national peculiarity" (4). Like Brooke's Colonel Rivers, Howison can never forget he is an English gentleman; on one occasion he has the opportunity to study closely the morality and behaviour of Scottish peasants, New Englanders, and native Indians and, like Rivers, he sees the Indian as possessing "a sort of negative superiority over both parties, having no absolute vices, and being exalted by the virtues that generally belong to the savage" (181). As is also true for Rivers, the Indian poses no threat to Howison; because the Scots are by historical deed his subjects, and the Americans his military victors, he can, therefore, neatly rationalize that unlike the Indian, they are both "destitute of any sort of principle, either moral or religious" (181).

Howison's letters, like Traill's in *The Backwoods of Canada,* constitute both a practical guidebook for the potential emigrant to Upper Canada and a moral comment on the New World, though in both cases the subjective involvement that characterizes the writings of Moodie and Jameson is largely missing. Howison, for all his travels, still occupies a society which, like Traill's, is one "well acquainted with the rules of good breeding and polite life," but he recognizes the advantages the New World holds for emigrants of proper education and sufficient income to allow some mitigation of the prevailing hardships. And near the end of his *Sketches* he offers perhaps one of the lingering reasons for exile to the colonies (very much like that offered by Colonel Rivers), while at the same time giving Upper Canada the back of his hand, so to speak:

> Another circumstance tends to make Europeans partial to Upper Canada. They find themselves of much more importance there than they would be at home; for the circle of society is so limited, and the number of responsible people in the Province so small, that almost every person is able to obtain some notice and attention. (265)

Small wonder that he chooses to illustrate his final observations with the Miltonic quotation, "Better to reign in hell than serve in heaven," though to his credit he stops short of implying that such exiles, therefore, are fallen archangels.

Catharine Parr Traill was familiar with Howison's book, and though she agrees with much of his practical advice to would-be emigrants, she subscribes much more fundamentally to the intrinsic worth of the New World. Never deviating from her belief in good taste and good manners, she nevertheless recognizes the authority of *autres pays, autres moeurs,* though she is somewhat impatient at those of her fellow exiles who try too early to emulate the democratic spirit of the New World. She imposes a moral injunction in her proclamation about who has the appropriate "energy of character" to undertake a life in exile, warning would-be emigrants that "Canada is not the land for the idle sensualists." As she makes clear in the "Introduction" to *The Backwoods of Canada,* Traill anticipated a total integration of the exile into the fabric of the New World, though she acknowledges the pain suffered by the emigrants who have been compelled to leave their native land "to become aliens and wanderers in a distant country."[6] Unlike Moodie, she has no moral or cultural hesitation in granting the supremacy of certain components of the New World—the democratic notion that the label of "gentleman" is one to be earned rather than bestowed by birth; the intrinsic value even for gentlemen and gentlemen's wives of learning a useful trade; the everyday conversation of the "lower order" of Yankees: "they speak better English than you will hear from persons of the same class in any part of England, Ireland, or Scotland; a fact that we should be unwilling, I suppose, to allow at home" (83).

In this positive attitude towards the New World, Traill illustrates how substantially perspectives had changed in the relatively short time since Brooke had toyed with Canada in *Emily Montague.* That novel's Arabella Fermor, we will see, despaired of any cultural development whatsoever; Traill asserts the very opposite, though it must be conceded that her didactic assertion—"Canada is the land of hope; here everything is new; everything going forward; it is scarcely possible for arts, sciences . . . to retrograde" (258)—has none of the literary grace or memorableness of Arabella's condescending summation. It does sound a note, however, that is increasingly to be heard during the remainder of the nineteenth century and into the twentieth, not only in such non-fiction works as her sister's *Roughing It,* but also in such fictional characters as Duncan's Hugh Finlay, Grove's Philip Branden, and Moore's Ginger Coffey.

Even in those moments during her otherwise prosaic descriptions of the country where the plaintive note of the universal exile is sounded, where in literal terms she has every right to bemoan her isolated state, Traill derives spiritual strength rather than lapsing into self-pity or despair. During the journey through the bush from Peterborough to the Strickland farmstead, the wagon driver becomes lost, and Traill, sitting "on the cold mossy stone in the profound stillness of that vast leafy wilderness," speculates calmly on her situation. Though the imagery is standard gothic, her resolution is highly personal:

> It was a moment to press upon my mind the importance of the step I had taken, in voluntarily sharing the lot of the emigrant—in leaving the land

of my birth, to which, in all probability, I might never again return. Great as was the sacrifice, even at that moment, strange as was my situation, I felt no painful regret or fearful misgiving depress my mind. A holy and tranquil peace came down upon me, soothing and softening my spirits into a calmness that seemed as unruffled as was the bosom of the water that lay stretched out before my feet. (118)

Like one of her fictional descendants, Wilson's Topaz Edgeworth, Traill exhibits a childlike curiosity about her world and a spontaneous acceptance of whatever she discovers; the long, fulfilled lives of these similar figures reflect a state of spiritual and physical assimilation with the New World, and in effect, of all the characters looked at in this book, they are the only two who rapidly cease to be exiles. Though Traill's book is more a practical guide to emigrants than an example of imaginative exile literature, it is nevertheless useful here in that it offers this kind of experiential verification of the exile issues confronted by fictional characters not only in Wilson, but also in Galt, Niven, and Salverson. It raises an important question, too, about the relationship between non-fictional literature and the purely imaginative literature that deals with exile: how frequently does the writer alternate between being totally factual and becoming a kind of imaginative protagonist? The reverse problem, of course, obtains with works that are declared unequivocally to be fiction—Galt's *Bogle Corbet,* Lewis's *Self Condemned,* or Moore's *The Luck of Ginger Coffey*—a reminder that a recurring characteristic of exile literature is its highly subjective nature, a tendency that in not a few cases formally leans very close to pure autobiography.

Susanna Moodie's *Roughing It in the Bush* (1852) on one level constitutes an affirmative answer to the question she posed in an otherwise dispensable poem: "Oh can you leave your native land, / An Exile's bride to be?" But on a more important level, it is a highly ambivalent record of her hopes, doubts, and fears, for hers was not the easy and comfortable affirmation of her sister. Her subsequent *Life in the Clearings* (1853) reflects the complete integration of the Moodies into their New World, and probably for that reason it is a lesser work, emotionally and intellectually, lacking the tension of *Roughing It*, where the exile is always looking both ways. Only in the various prefaces and introductions to subsequent editions of this book does Moodie attain rationally a positive view towards Canada, even though she is ultimately unable to deny completely her prejudices in favour of the well-born. Nevertheless, by 1871 she is able to proclaim that her attachment to Canada is so strong "that I cannot imagine any inducement, short of absolute necessity, which could induce me to leave the colony where . . . some of the happiest years of my life have been spent."[7]

It is in these preambles, too, that she offers various justifications for their

exile, which in the first instance was a "matter of necessity, not of choice," a
condition true, apparently, for all "persons of respectable connections, or of
any station or position in the world" (xv). Such people, we are told, emigrate
to better their economic condition, but since they "cannot labour in a menial
capacity in the country where they were born and educated to command,"
Moodie invests this pedestrian reason with something more elevated: 'there
is a higher motive still, which has its origin in that love of independence
which springs up spontaneously in the breasts of the high-souled children of
a glorious land" (xvi, xv). Clearly, Moodie here is closer in spirit to Brooke's
Colonel Rivers than to her sister, who saw nothing demeaning, for example,
in a naval officer's son learning how to wield an axe. And like Rivers, too, she
occasionally reflects a condescension towards Canadian women, opining
that the greatest proof of their beauty and dependability lay in the fact that
so many British officers chose them as wives and found no "cause to repent
of their choice" (11). No record presumably exists to indicate whether any of
the wives in question had "cause to repent" *their* choice!

But in the text proper of *Roughing It,* she is far less dogmatic than Brooke
or Traill, and her tentative explorations of New World realities offer more
dramatic tension than do either Brooke's conditioned observations or her
sister's uncritical certainties. The conflict between her attitudes shaped by
the Old World and those generated by the New receives its initial shaping in
the Grosse Isle scene, where her conditioned response—"it looks a perfect
paradise at this distance"—is quickly modified as she steps ashore:

> Never shall I forget the extraordinary spectacle that met our sight the
> moment we passed the low range of bushes which formed a scene in
> front of the river. A crowd of many hundred Irish immigrants . . . were
> running to and fro, screaming and scolding in no measured terms. The
> confusion of Babel was among them. All talkers and no hearers—each
> shouting and yelling in his or her uncouth dialect . . . . We were
> literally stunned by the strife of tongues. (30-31)

Ovid, we recall, complained about not being understood by the barbarians
among whom he had been banished; here it is the exiles from Moodie's own
part of the Old World who are the barbarians, rather than the indigenous
people, for "the Indian," she argues later, "is one of Nature's gentlemen—he
never says or does a rude or vulgar thing." I suspect that Moodie would not
have been so offended had the dialects of her fellow exiles not been so
"uncouth," and she goes on to deplore the fact that even the "honest Scotch
labourers and mechanics from the vicinity of Edinburgh" were transformed
into barbarians the moment they set foot on shore.

It is at this point that her moral re-education begins, for from here on pragmatic necessity begins inexorably to undercut many of her a priori convictions; for the first time, something other than class or social status takes on a directing force in her life. As Ovid had discovered many centuries earlier, there was a reality in the world of barbarians that was quite distinct from and independent of, the reality that governed the civilized and cultured world. One could ignore this, as Brooke did, or like Traill, embrace it with childlike affirmation; Moodie met it directly, but with a strong psychological aversion, and it is the resolving of this conflict that provides so much of the tension of *Roughing It*. Her knowledge that she could never see her native land again undoubtedly made her somewhat equivocal, and even defensive, in her responses to the New World, but she was able, up to a point, to exploit her artistic talents to help her come to terms with her new landscape, a point enlarged upon by the critic Carol Shields:

> The Canadian experience was a liberating one for Mrs. Moodie. Though she accepted her landscape as inevitable, she found, mainly through her writing, the means to overcome natural restrictions. She was not insensitive to the comparisons between cultures, nor did she ignore the changing social conditions of her time. Her work, in fact, reflects the times, moving from her early moralizing, sentimental tales to sketches which reflect a broader more generous acceptance of life.[8]

On its immediate level, "acceptance of life" is frequently a painful experience for Mrs. Moodie, for among other things it involves acceptance of a reduced social status for both herself and her husband, a process which her ingrained snobbery rendered more difficult than it need have been. At times her homesickness for England becomes almost overpowering, but only occasionally does she allow herself to indulge in self-pity, choosing instead to maintain a stoical bearing towards her lot. "After seven years' exile, the hope of return grows feeble," she muses at one point. "Double those years, and it is as if the grave had closed over you, and the hearts that once knew and loved you know you no more" (150). She is not unlike the conventional Ovidian exile here, exploiting the obligatory grave imagery to underscore her desperate plight, a point she shortly reinforces by equating herself with a condemned prisoner in a cell, whose "only hope of escape [is] through the portals of the grave" (166).

But there is a persistent reality in her new land which compels her to abandon self-pity and to turn to more practical exigencies, not the least of which involved her overcoming the skulduggeries of the various Yankee women she encounters—Satan's daughter Emily, Old Betty Fye, and both the mother and wife of Uncle Joe. The exchange of words between Mrs. Moodie and these saucy women contributes some dramatically rendered scenes of narrative suspense, wherein both protagonists and antagonists take shape and substance as the arguments proceed. But it also draws attention to the nature of the gulf that separates some extremes of the Old and New Worlds—inbred superiority against a pragmatic vulgarity and struggle for survival. That there might be a middle ground, or a meeting point, is a possibility that at this moment neither Mrs. Moodie nor any of her tormentors is prepared to accept. Though Mrs. Moodie wins these particular battles, her adversaries get in some telling points, and it is this kind of artistic and moral courage that reflects the fundamental honesty with which Mrs. Moodie was learning, with some pain to herself, to view her place of exile. She never, of course, comes even close to accepting the democratic spirit so grossly distorted by these viragos, and to the end of her long residency in Upper Canada she clung to all the pretensions and vestigial remnants of gentility that she could muster—even to the naming of two of her sons after high-ranking administrators. Perhaps Margaret Atwood is correct in insinuating that to this day, the city of Belleville, from Moodie's perspective beyond the grave, "is still no place for an English gentleman."

The equivocal nature of Moodie's responses that I referred to earlier derives in part from the ambivalence within herself that *Roughing It* dramatizes: the cultural or social obligation she feels, on the one hand, to discourage any further British emigrants from settling in Canada and her own growing psychological conviction, on the other, that she at any rate would not want to leave this country. Her concluding statement in the book is precise and unambiguous:

> If these sketches should prove the means of deterring one family from sinking their property, and shipwrecking all their hopes, by going to reside in the backwoods of Canada, I shall consider myself amply repaid for revealing the secrets of the prison-house, and feel that I have not toiled and suffered in the wilderness in vain. (563)

But in her preamble to the 1871 edition of *Roughing It* (the first Canadian edition), she dissembles a bit and berates "the many who have condemned the work without reading it," assuring them that they "will be surprised to find that not one word has been said to prejudice intending emigrants from making Canada their home" (6). This dissimulation she neatly rationalizes in the way many exiles have done—Wyndham Lewis in a number of his letters, for example—by shifting her own emotional confusion to others: "Unless, indeed, they ascribe the regret expressed at having to leave my native land, so natural in the painful home-sickness which, for several months, preys upon the health and spirits of the dejected exile, to a deep-rooted dislike to the country." (6-7)

In fairness, Moodie had no hesitation in encouraging the lower classes to emigrate, for they really had nothing to lose; it is the gentleman she is concerned about, for he "can neither work so hard, live so coarsely, nor endure so many privations as his poorer but more fortunate neighbour" (563). The irony of this statement is not lost upon the reader, for in spite of the incompetence of Moodie's "gentleman" husband, he did much better than his "more fortunate neighbours," and Moodie herself stands as a powerful contradiction to her own observations. Though clearly she was not happy in doing so, she did personally suffer and endure "many privations" and, like her sister, turned these hardships into positive contributions to her new country. If Traill, in her easy assimilation into Canadian life, anticipates Wilson's Topaz Edgeworth, Moodie, in her psychologically more inconsistent and disturbing integration, prefigures such fictional descendants as Grove's Philip Branden, Lowry's Sigbjørn Wilderness, and Lewis's René Harding, for they too, cut off from the protection of the social and institutional authority of the Old World, had increasingly to rely on self, and on a pragmatic testing of the possibilities of the New World.

In both Traill and Moodie there is a strong moral injunction implied in their attitudes about who could be suitable emigrants to Canada, with something like "energy of character" emerging as a crucial ingredient. For one of the important temporary visitors, however, this prerequisite took on a different meaning, for with Anna Jameson it became a means of personal adventure and indulgence; indeed, in some respects, she is not unlike "the idle sensualist" that Traill warned us would never do well in Canada. Jameson's attitude to the New World reflects a humorous skepticism that on the whole was absent in the other two: "This is the land of hope, of faith, ay, and of charity, for a man who hath not all three had better not come here; with them he may, by strength of his own right hand and trusting heart, achieve miracles."[9]

This could of course be said quite flippantly by one who was not required to remain in Canada forever, like Moodie and Traill, and indeed, Jameson's visit lasted barely nine months. Yet she reflected the attributes of an exile spirit in a somewhat different fashion than the other two, though as Clara Thomas observes, this could in part have been an act of self-dramatization, for "to a considerable extent she was guilty of playing the Ennuyée all her life."[10] In some respects—her familiarity with many worlds, her adventurous spirit, her sharp eye for significant detail—she anticipates Sara Duncan, though in her particular outrage at the ugliness and shortcomings of Toronto, her relationship is more with Wyndham Lewis, who, like her, also found himself in Canada against his will.

Like Arabella Fermor in *Emily Montague,* Anna Jameson is somewhat mercurial in her attitude towards Canada, with seasonal and climatic factors often colouring her responses. The quotation cited above is from the "Summer Rambles" portion of her book, and through its ironic texture, one can detect an observer who is on the whole comfortable in her contact with the country. During the previous December, however, she lamented that she was "like an uprooted tree, dying at the core," though even here she is conscious that she possesses "a strange unreasonable power . . . mocking at [her] own most miserable weakness" (I,4). This vacillating tendency characterizes many writers in exile, but particularly those who are exiles out of personal or domestic necessity rather than out of personal volition. But Jameson can also be bluntly forthright and realistic, as in her deflationary description of Niagara Falls, which ranks in honesty with that offered by Mrs. Corbet in Galt's *Bogle Corbet*. Perhaps her best-known description is the one she gives of the bleak Toronto she finds herself in on a cold day in December 1836:

> A little ill-built town on low land, at the bottom of a frozen bay, with one very ugly church, without tower or steeple; some government offices, built of staring red brick, in the most tasteless, vulgar style imaginable; three feet of snow all around; and the grey, sullen, wintry lake, and the dark gloom of the pine forest bounding the prospect; such seems Toronto to me now. I did not expect much; but for this I was not prepared. Perhaps no preparation could have *prepared* me, or softened my present feelings. (I, 2)

A passage like this helps us understand how Ovid might have felt at Tomis on the Black Sea some eighteen centuries earlier, and Jameson, too, finds the society of her new residence as appalling as its physical characteristics. "We have here a petty colonial oligarchy, a self-constituted aristocracy, based upon nothing real, nor even upon anything imaginary," she asserts at one point (I, 98), though she nevertheless feels obliged to treat this society as though it *is* the real thing: "All the official gentlemen have called, and all the ladies have properly and politely left their cards: so yesterday, in a sleigh, well wrapped up in furs and buffalo robes, I set out duly to return these visits" (I,13). Undoubtedly, Mrs. Jameson was somewhat bewildered as to how she should behave in this world, and a certain inconsistency characterizes her impressions. She is gratified that it is only "gentlemen" she is obliged to meet, though a bit shattered that there was no one "to introduce them," and in her contrasting of this society with that of the Old World, the New World seems to have a moral edge:

> In London society I met with many men whose real material of mind it was difficult to discover—either they had been smoothed and polished down by society, or education had overlaid their understanding with

stuccoed ornaments, and figures historical and poetical—very pretty to
look at—but the coarse brickwork or the rotten lath and plaster lay
underneath: there being in this new country far less of conventional
manner, it was so much easier to tell at once the brick from the granite
and the marble. (I, 20)

Throughout this book, notably in the "Summer Rambles" section, Jameson is genuinely taken up by the intrinsic qualities of the land and its people,
and she is particularly moved and enlightened through her intercourse with
the native peoples. By the time the winter of her discontent is over, she is
preparing herself for her long voyage to the far reaches of Lake Huron, and
here she exhibits a spirit not unlike that of such early exiles as the Anglo-
Saxon wanderers and seafarers: "Though no longer young, I am quite young
enough to feel all the excitement of plunging into scenes so entirely new as
were now opening before me; and this, too, with a specific object far beyond
mere amusement and excitement—an object not unworthy" (II, 36).

Jameson's three-volume work is a rich, though uneven, record of personal
observations, opinions, and questionings, reflecting, as she admits, "the
impertinent leaven of egotism which necessarily mixed itself up with the
journal form of writing" (I, vii). Sometimes this egotism leads her into
illustrating immoderately her vast knowledge of Goethe and other European *littérateurs,* and these digressions all too frequently disrupt the narrative flow of her journal. But her singularly advanced opinions about the
position of women seem less disruptive not only because, as she states in her
"Preface," her book is "particularly addressed to my own sex" (I, vii), but
also because these observations are frequently derived from the tangible
problems of women in the New World. "I never met with so many repining
and discontented women as in Canada," she observes at one point (II, 133),
reflecting a domestic situation that is fictionally verified in numerous realistic novels of the twentieth century. And in a comment that might have
disturbed Susanna Moodie had she read it, she touches on a form of vanity
that particularly affects discontented exiles:

I have observed that really accomplished women, accustomed to what is
called the best society, have more resources here, and manage better,
than some women who have no pretensions of any kind, and whose
claims to social distinction could not have been great anywhere, but
whom I found lamenting over themselves, as if they had been so many
exiled princesses. (II, 134)

In her interpretation of the realities of Canada, Jameson is clearly closer
to Moodie than to Traill, and her observation that there is enough tangible

evidence in Upper Canada to define it either as "a place of exile for convicts" or as "an earthly elysium" (II, 236) reinforces not only Moodie's vacillations but also the basic contradictions about Canada in general that have emerged in the writings of the Old World exiles over the past two centuries. The non-fictional treatment that this duality receives in Moodie and Jameson is to be picked up again in such twentieth-century works as Grove's *In Search of Myself* and Levine's *Canada Made Me,* but it is clearly in the fictional form that it receives its most varied development, from the relatively simplistic treatment in Brooke's early novel to the complex discontinuities that characterize Lowry's works.

Though Frances Brooke was one of the least committed of the exiles I deal with in this chapter, her *History of Emily Montague* (1769), though interpretable in a number of ways, can with considerable justification be viewed as the first fictional treatment of the exile theme as it applies to Canada. In structure, style, tone, and informing philosophy, however, this epistolary novel is thoroughly Augustan, and reflects an attitude, therefore, that is totally colonial towards Canada. We are not surprised to discover that its more lively protagonist bears the same name as the lady who occasioned Pope's *Rape of the Lock,* and it is fitting that it is Arabella Fermor's father who pronounces the dictum that suggests the novel's ethical centre: "there are no real virtues but the social ones."[11] Since at that time there was no indigenous society in Canada of any import, this pronouncement effectively cancels out any abiding relevance of the New World; Canada emerges in this novel quite simply as a tolerable place to visit, provided one is not required to remain too long.

Emily Montague constitutes, of course, on one level a transatlantic working-out of the "husband, husband, who's got the husband" fictional dilemma, for its 228 letters reflect the marriage theme much more consistently than the exile theme. Colonel Rivers and Arabella Fermor in Canada, and Lucy Rivers in England, emerge in this international exchange of letters as the novel's major dramatic agents: the former two write well over two-thirds of all the letters (154), and of these over half (88) are sent to Lucy, who serves therefore as a kind of moral sounding board. Lucy in turn is virtually silent, writing only five letters in all, but she is neither as psychologically or as emotionally detached from these amorous games as her silence and geographical distance might suggest. Indeed, she and he brother express a warmth to each other that not infrequently transcends sibling loyalties, and one suspects at times that if they could only marry each other perfection would be achieved. Rivers addresses her in one of his letters "as a sister endeared to him much more by her amiable qualities than by blood" (#62), and Lucy in turn laments that "the only man I perfectly approve, and whose disposition is formed to make me happy, should by my brother" (#67). That they both ultimately marry for love cannot be doubted, but it seems to have helped that their respective spouses bear striking resemblances to each other.

Like Lucy, the title figure of this novel is also relatively silent, though she constitutes the main subject-matter of the letters of both Rivers and Arabella, wherefore, presumably in keeping with the epistolary tradition, the reason for Brooke's title. With Augustan appropriateness, Emily Montague is consistently the most rational, level-headed, and moral of the six youthful participants, though, in the process, she acquires a certain degree of abstraction and blandness. Her propriety renders her even more static when juxtaposed against the lively and occasionally indecorous spirit of Arabella, who in turn becomes dull and conventional only when she returns to the Old World. Indeed, the action of the novel as a whole slows irrecoverably once the participants begin their return to the Old World, in spite of the brief drama supplied by the Fanny Williams episode. Emily, it is true, supplies a momentary Old World-New World intrigue in the first part of the novel, as she vies with Madame des Roches for the hand of Colonel Rivers, but given Brooke's Augustan vision, the outcome is never really in doubt, and a potentially rich and dramatic conflict quickly assumes a conventional and morally proper resolution.

Arabella Fermor is the most mercurial of all the marriage-seekers in this novel, but she is also the most realistic both in her judgment of other characters and in her own attitudes towards the world she temporarily occupies. In a sense, she stands in counterpoint to both Lucy in England and Emily in Canada; she is essentially pragmatic in her assessments to Lucy of the realities of the New World and to Emily of the realities of marriage. When she herself falls in love with Captain Fitzgerald, she possesses him completely, almost jealously, thus assuming a moral position midway between what she regards as the convention-free Indian marital relationships and the convention-bound system operating in England, represented most accurately by the attitudes of Mrs. Melmoth. Like Rivers, but without his self-pity, Arabella is at times self-centred and flirtatious, though only when courtship assumes the nature of a game, as illustrated in her whimsical lament to Lucy about the nature of Canadian beaux:

> they appear to me not at all dangerous, and one might safely walk in a wood by moonlight with the most agreeable Frenchman here. I am surpriz'd the Canadian ladies take such pains to seduce our men from us; but I think it a little hard we have no temptation to make reprisals. (#10)

Her views of the New World fluctuate on the one hand according to her coquettish successes and failures, but also, more realistically, according literally to the seasons. Writing to Lucy in June, she concedes that, all in all, "the manner of living here is uncommonly agreeable," and argues that Quebec is superior to all English towns except London (#157). Yet in an earlier January letter, she gives a more pessimistic response, one of the many variations that have come down to us of Voltaire's famous *arpents de neige* assessment of Canada:

> I no longer wonder the elegant arts are unknown here; the rigour of the climate suspends the very power of the understanding . . . . Those who expect to see *"A new Athens rising near the pole"* will find themselves extremely disappointed. Genius will never mount high, where the faculties of the mind are benumbed half the year. (#49)

And perhaps as well as the indigenous Canadian, she communicates the sense of isolation brought on by the onset of winter and voices a lament that poignantly evokes a situation that exiles undoubtedly have experienced throughout the ages:

> I have been seeing the last ship go out of the port, Lucy; you have no notion what a melancholy sight it is: we are now left to ourselves, and shut up from all the world for the winter: somehow we seem so forsaken, so cut off from the rest of human kind, I cannot bear the idea: I sent a thousand sighs and a thousand tender wishes to dear England, which I never loved so much as at this moment. (#45)

But though she is more adaptable to the New World than Emily or Edward, she by no means reflects the complexity or profound confusion of the exile mentality, and her mercurial temperament is manifested most characteristically in a kind of of superficial inconsistency. As she revealed herself in her contradictory advice to Emily about the relative merits of Clayton and Rivers, so in her first letter to Rivers upon once again landing on English soil, she seems to contradict much of what she had consistently written from Silleri:

> What could induce you, with this sweet little retreat, to cross that vile ocean to Canada? I am astonished at the madness of mankind, who can expose themselves to pain, misery, and danger; and range the world from motives of avarice and ambition, when the rural cot, the fanning gale, the clear stream, and flowery bank, offer such delicious enjoyments at home. (#202)

What induced Colonel Rivers, of course, was a combination of opportunity and opportunism: his free land grants in Canada would elevate him, if all worked out, to an achievement that could never be possible in England. He explains his mission in some detail in the novel's opening letter to the rakish John Temple, who is eventually to become his brother-in-law:

> What you call a sacrifice, is none at all; I love England, but am not obstinately chain'd down to any spot of earth . . . ; love of variety, and the natural restlessness of man, would give me a relish for this voyage, even if I did not expect, what I really do, to become lord of a principality which will put our large-acred men in England out of countenance . . . . [In] thus cultivating what is in the rudest state of nature, I shall taste one of the greatest of all pleasures, that of creation, and see order and beauty gradually rise from chaos. (#1)

Even allowing for the anticipation and possibilities that a first voyage to an unknown land involves, this is ambition indeed; but of course it reflects not so much the vision of the genuine exile as it does the arrogance of the secure Englishman who takes his country and his culture with him wherever he goes—the perfect representative, in other words, of the garrison attitude.

Appropriately, therefore, Colonel Rivers has both the first word and the last word in this novel; it is his code that frames it and defines its moral vision. As manifested in him, the garrison mentality implies a persistent imperviousness to the ideas, customs, and attitudes of the people of the occupied territory and an unwillingness or incapacity to entertain the possibility of error. His association with the Canadian people is limited to the female sex, a behaviour consistent with the master-subject social structure wherever it has existed. "I have been making some flying visits to the French ladies," he confides to his sister. "Tho' I have not seen many beauties, yet in general the women are handsome; their manner is easy and obliging, [and] they make the most of their charms by their vivacity." But his greatest compliment to them derives appropriately from his own ingrained sense of superiority: "I certainly cannot be displeas'd with their extreme partiality for the English officers," he concludes; "their own men, who indeed are not very attractive, have not the least chance for any share in their good graces" (#6). That this attitude towards the French-Canadian is shared by other English exiles, particularly those from the officer class, is suggested by Susanna Moodie's comments about the "shrivelled-up Frenchman" she encounters at Grosse Isle, whom she equates with "hopeless decay" in contrast to the "vigorous health" of his companion, "a fine-looking, fair-haired Scotchman" (21).

At the outset, like many of his European counterparts who emigrated to the

New World, Rivers saw the shores of America in terms of creation: "I felt a kind of religious veneration, on seeing rocks which almost touch'd the clouds, cover'd with tall groves of pines that seemed coeval with the world itself." He quickly gets through the platitudes about landscape, however, and moves on to his abiding concern: "I have just had time to observe, that the Canadian ladies have the vivacity of the French, with a superior share of beauty" (#2), though with his first glimpse of Emily Montague he is quick to reflect a condescension springing from his belief in the superiority of things English: "only think of finding beauty, delicacy, sensibility, all that can charm in woman, hid in a wood in Canada!" (#6)

Almost in anticipation, as it were, of Stephen Leacock's spoof on instant transatlantic experts of the New World scene, Colonel Rivers modestly assures us that he is not "one of those sagacious observers, who, by staying a week in a place, think themselves qualified to give, not only its natural, but its moral and political history" (#2). He reflects in his letters an appreciation of the native Indians of Canada, though in large part his attitude can be seen as a manifestation of the "noble savage" concept widely held throughout Western Europe. In a sense, he praises them from a position of assumed superiority; they are no threat, for example, to his design upon the local ladies, as the Canadian men are; these latter, significantly, he describes in terms of "bigotry, stupidity, and laziness" (#8). He appreciates the fact that the indigenous Hurons have preserved their identity and independence in the midst of a European colony, and in an early letter to his friend Temple, he communicates what is perhaps the first indication of a threat to the garrison mentality that he so well represents:

> An old Indian told me, they had also songs of friendship, but I could never procure a translation of one of them: on my pressing this Indian to translate one into French for me, he told me with a haughty air, the Indians were not us'd to make translations, and that if I chose to understand their songs I must learn their language. (#4)

Colonel Rivers' views of Canada as a place to make a permanent life are predicated both on his deeply ingrained sense of class and superiority, and on an occasional concession that the new land itself has possibilities not realizable in England. Fittingly, his vanity must first be satisfied: "What man of common sense would stay to be overlook'd in England, who can have rival beauties contend for him in Canada?" (#6), he asks his sister; and later to Temple he expresses yet another lingering cause for exile: "I cannot live in England on my present income, though it enables me to live *en prince* in Canada" (#36). And though one is hard-pressed to imagine Colonel Rivers plowing a field, he nevertheless makes an observation about the New World that is shared by many later observers of the Old and New Worlds: "the pleasure of cultivating lands here is as much superior tó what can be found in the same employment in England, as watching the expanding rose, and beholding the falling leaves: American is in infancy, Europe in old age" (#7). Interestingly, this observation reflects a view of the New World almost identical to that made, in a different metaphor, by the contemporary Canadian novelist James Bacque, whose protagonist in the *The Lonely Ones* proclaims upon his return to Canada: "Everything here suddenly seems possible again. Canada after Europe is like hearing Beethoven after Brahms."[12]

It is important to stress, however, that none of the participants in Brooke's transatlantic chronicle ever considered seriously the prospect of permanent exile in the New World. Though Rivers, as we saw, admitted he could live royally on his income in Canada, marriage to Emily Montague on that income was impossible "without reducing her to indigence at home, or *dooming* her to be an exile in Canada for life" (#38, my italics). Only in his brief visit to the hermit does he experientially recognize a justification for exile, as an atonement for an unbearable loss of a loved one: the hermit here reflects, perhaps, a manifestation of what the critic David Williams saw as the classical paradox: a banished man who is truly moral and virtuous can never be an exile "for his true home is within himself."[13] On the whole, Rivers held a low opinion "of those who fly society; who seek a state of all others the most contrary to our nature" (#32). Fortunately for Rivers, of course, the question of income and dowry is generously settled: he and Emily, like the other marriage partners, can reside forever in England without the threat of further exile to disturb them.

Relatively few letters written by Rivers, Arabella, or Emily are specifically or exclusively about Canada or Canadians, and the tone of those which do exist characteristically alternates between contempt and bemused tolerance, between patronizing praise and outright ridicule. Very early on, Colonel Rivers expresses a lament about Canada that in one form or another is to echo through the exile literature of the ensuing century or so:

> The scenery is to be sure divine, but one grows weary of meer scenery; the most enchanting prospect soon loses its power of pleasing, when the eye is accustom'd to it: we gaze at first transported on the charms of nature, and fancy they will please for ever; but, alas! it will not do; we sigh for society, the conversation of those dear to us; the more animated pleasures of the heart. (#5)

Though he modifies his views towards Canada according to the fluctuations in his relationship with Emily, the outcome of the novel dictates the centrality of this attitude in Brooke's overall vision. And it is reflected, too, in the letters of Arabella's father who, since he is presumably beyond the vagaries of human passion that afflict the novel's younger protagonists, emerges as a kind of objective reporter on the state of things in Canada. Characteristically, his thirteen letters to his friend the Earl of _____ contain platitudinous observations, like "nothing can be more true, my Lord, than that poverty is ever the inseparable companion of indolence" (#117), proof of which injunction is invariably some flaw he perceives in the moral or living habits of the Canadians or natives. And while he concedes in another letter that "the English are the worst settlers on new lands in the universe," it is not because as a people they are incompetent, but rather, since the best of the English remain at home through love for their country, only the worst, "the dissolute and the idle, who are of no use anywhere," become permanent settlers in Canada (#123).

Ironically, what has happened in terms of the characters and societies juxtaposed in this novel is that the larger indigenous world has triumphed over the garrison within it, and Rivers' earlier astonishment can of course be seen chiefly as a manifestation of his own superiority: "Nothing astonishes me so much as to find their manners so little changed by their intercourse with the Europeans" (#11). For in effect, while Rivers and his society were in the ascendancy in Quebec, the Hurons for the moment constituted the garrison, and in that position, they rejected the influence of the surrounding colonial rulers, just as the British remained impervious to *their* surrounding larger world of Canadians. In one of his letters to the Earl, Arabella's father explains at some length how this process works in reality, though it must be kept in mind that Fermor shares Rivers' hostility towards the French in Canada:

> I believe I have said, that there is a striking resemblance between the manners of the Canadians and the savages; I should have explained it, by adding, that this resemblance has been brought about, not by the French having won the savages to receive European manners, but by the very contrary; the peasants having acquired the savage indolence in peace, their activity and ferocity in war; their fondness for field sports, their hatred of labour; their love of a wandering life, and of liberty. (#152)

At best, the juxtaposition of opposed cultures in *Emily Montague* is not much more than a literary exercise or convention whose rules are all predetermined and operative on one side only. The arguments that are adduced about the nature of the respective societies and values must either be accepted or rejected without debate, for there is no empirical or analytical evaluation made of either side, and the frequent moral pronouncements are never measured against the psychological or social predicaments of the

characters involved. It is clearly one of the limitations of the epistolary
structure in fiction that it does not allow for a dramatic illumination of
contrasting worlds; its formal nature allows at best only an incremental
accumulation of impressions and details, without providing the opportunity
for convincing juxtaposition or dialectics.

The infusion of the exile theme into the conventional epistolary novel
allowed Brooke an opportunity to investigate more thoroughly the conflicts
experienced by her characters, but on the whole she failed to exploit this
possibility beyond the superficial. Like many other components in *Emily
Montague,* that of exile seems to serve merely a decorative function: Rivers
in exile in Canada is indistinguishable from Rivers in England, even though
he strikes the occasional pose in Canada as one afflicted with the horrors of
exile, and can also offer the platitudinous sentiments about the transformative power of exile: "If [Emily] loves as I do," he writes to his sister, "even a
perpetual exile here will be pleasing. The remotest wood in Canada with her
would be no longer a desert wild; it would be the habitation of the Graces"
(#71). Brooke comes close on occasion to exploiting the latent ironies and
possibilities of this platitude in her tentative juxtaposition of the society of
Rivers and the "remote wood" of Mme des Roches: one or two letters from
the latter to Rivers might have led to a little more drama in his ultimate
decision. As it is, the platitudes reflect the pallid nature of the narrative, and
one can readily see the application to *Emily Montague* of Johnson's comment about Richardson—that we read him not for the story but for the
sentiment.

Within the perspective not only of exile fiction in Canada but of Canadian
fiction in general, *The History of Emily Montague* remains an isolated work,
for there is no evidence I am aware of that it had any influence on subsequent
writers. Given Brooke's literary and social background, her novel was of
more interest in England than to readers in the New World, for as we have
seen, it consistently supported the conventional attitudes that English society held towards the colonies, and Canada, in those pre-American Revolution
days, enjoyed relatively little prestige. Historically, as far as this book is
concerned, the novel is significant in that it reflects the first manifestation
of the exile theme in literature dealing with Canada, which was exploited
later, as we have seen, not in further epistolary novels, but in such related
forms as travel letters, journals, and diaries. As William New points out,[14]
Brooke's novel is on one level concerned with the tension inherent in the
complementary actions of searching for a paradise and being threatened by
eviction from it, and this kind of conflict is central to much of the exile
literature produced in the two centuries since, particularly in Lowry, but
also in Moodie, Salverson, and Grove. Unfortunately, Brooke's exploitation
of these tensions was not always as powerful as might be expected, given the

cultural and social distinctions of the worlds she was observing, and aside from her artistic limitations, this failure undoubtedly reflects the lack of serious commitment on her part to the New World she inhabited for some five years.

Of a different nature, but on the whole not as satisfying aesthetically as in Brooke, is the expression of the exile theme in Galt's *Bogle Corbet* (1831), or more accurately, in the concluding book of this three-volume novel, where the protagonist leads a group of settlers from Scotland and England to make their new home in Upper Canada. Clearly reflecting the experiences that John Galt had with the Canada Company in the 1820's, this work reads at times more like a documentary report than an artistically shaped novel, but in Bogle and Urseline Corbet we find attitudes towards the New World reflecting a realism that was totally missing in *Emily Montague*. Not for Bogle are the conventional responses to Canada's scenery so frequently uttered by Brooke's characters: as a practical planner, he is more interested in "the warlike and glittering aspects" of [Quebec] city[15] than in the Falls of Montmorency. And not to be outdone, Urseline, described by her husband as "not distinguished for a poetical temperament," prefers water pouring from a tea kettle to that of Niagara Falls, of which she says "there is certainly an unaccountable and extravagant waste of water about them" (160). At times, Galt steps over the line between realism and parody, as in the scene where the Corbets listen to the Americans comment on Niagara, or where he dramatizes the deflation of the learned but painfully affected Cambridge student, Mr. Clavis. But there is always a compassionate charity in Galt's creation of characters, for they are never abandoned as mere caricatures, whatever national idiosyncrasies they might at first exhibit.

The novel begins, however, in much the same tone as in Moodie's "Introduction" to the third edition of *Roughing It*, by setting out the reasons for emigration, in which respect Corbet's settlers provide a fictional verification of Moodie's opinions. "All who consulted me," Bogle recalls, "were individuals in impaired, or desperate circumstances, unable to preserve their caste in the social system of this country, wrecked and catching at emigration as the last plank" (11). And like Moodie, too, Corbet ascribes higher motives than mere financial survival to the better classes, in whom "the mingled and combined feelings of necessity, interest, and sorrow are found" (11). But his comments are not merely isolated platitudes about human self-deception and pretense, for later in the novel they apply with some pertinence not only to such defecting settlers as Peddie and Gimlet but also, more importantly, to his own uncertainties about the exile he has chosen for himself.

From the outset, the sea voyage into exile is characterized by difficulties and threats rather than by the standard benevolent harbingers of paradise.

Violent storms, increasing cold, the looming iceberg, the near shipwreck off
Anticosta, referred to as the "forbidden isle" and the "dismal island," all
evoke thoughts of death rather than a new life, as myth and superstition are
aggravated by the harsh realities of the world they are entering. Only after
their safe landing at Quebec and the beginning of their overland voyage to
Upper Canada does the vision of these exiles become more optimistic,
reflected in such conventional imagery as "the arborous wall of Paradise"
and "the green Eden of new settlements beyond" (45). Nevertheless, the
illness and near death of Mrs. Paddock, which on one hand in Galt's
presbyterian world are a reminder of the "sins" of her family, reflect the
difficulty, as we will see again in the works of Niven and Salverson, that the
older exiles have in assimilating themselves into the fabric of the New World.
And the novel appropriately ends on a similar note of irresolution, as Corbet
himself, like Moodie and Traill, leaves the reader with a moral observation
about the situation of exile:

> the tale of it may not be unprofitable to those who may glance at these
> pages for amusement, and find them in many respects as much devoted
> to information. But though so many days are here blank leaves in the
> book of life, let me not be misunderstood; I have no cause to regret my
> emigration; I have only been too late. The man must indeed be strangely
> constituted, who above fifty emigrates for life, with the habits and
> notions of the old country rivetted upon him, and yet expects to meet
> with aught much better than discomfort. (198)

In his realism, his humour and scepticism, and in his creation of ordinary
characters, Galt has moved a long way from Brooke's Augustan vision of the
world, and has presented a convincing interpretation of at least some aspects
of "roughing it in exile." His vision and attitudes to the New World are closer
to those of Jameson and Moodie than to Traill's, but in terms of any
nineteenth-century fictional analysis of the exile situation, he, like Brooke in
the preceding century, really has no descendants, though stylistically, in his
subdued realism and tendency to understatement he evokes both McCulloch
and Haliburton. He does, however, introduce a minor theme in his novel that
is to receive considerable attention by later novelists concerned with an exile
situation, and that is the question of the distinction between a Canadian and
an American and between the values and ideas of their two societies. It is not
a pervasive theme in *Bogle Corbet* and is dramatized mainly in the conflict
between Corbet and some of the settlers who were being enticed to settle in
America rather than in Upper Canada. Galt's objectivity in the matter is
reflected in the neat irony that informs the resolution of this conflict: the
rebel leader, James Peddie, who does choose the United States, eventually

returns to Corbet's settlement—"I did na find myself in my element yonder" (153)—while Andrew Gimlet, who persuades most of the settlers to stick with Corbet, leaves Canada during the first winter to take up residence in the United States. That Gimlet is a youthful carpenter looking for constant work and Peddie an older man homesick for his own kind of people does much to explain their decisions, but Corbet's analysis of the emigrant attitude in general is also relevant:

> A constant yearning for something new in scene or occupation is pecu-
> liar to emigrants, whether industrious or dilatory. The same spur in the
> side which impels them from their native land, goads them wherever
> they go, and is the main cause of that restless irritation characteristic
> more or less of them all. (72)

Corbet's appeal for the emigrants to remain united so that he can proceed with the construction of his community (which the settlers themselves name Stockwell after a street in Glasgow) on one level assumes a continuation of the kind of garrison structure that protected the British society in *Emily Montague*. It is, in a sense, an anti-exile appeal that hints at one of the distinctions between the Canadian and the American experiences of settlement and that offers a rational, classical interpretation of man's nature as opposed to that propounded by Rousseau and the romantics: "by beginning with a town, you follow the course of Nature, but in scattering yourselves abroad in the forest, you become, as it were, banished men. You will take upon yourselves a penalty and suffering, such as only rejected culprits should endure" (66). Moodie, as we have seen, echoes this notion of exile as a punishment for society's outcasts, and for neither her nor Galt was there anything romantic or idyllic about roughing it in the bush: it was only a temporary hardship one had to endure before once again assuming an appropriate place in society.

Galt's novel implies, as Brooke's did not, a permanent reality about Canada, and it is the first work with protagonists whose involvement with an exile situation begins to display a psychological credibility and tension. It points to a number of later novels, by both indigenous and non-native writers, whose attitudes to Canada and whose responses to exile reflect, both intellectually and experientially, much more complexity and genuine questioning than was the case with most of the other writers examined in this chapter.

3

Between Two Worlds

With the gradual consolidation of a distinctive Canadian consciousness and the attendant dissipation of the garrison mentality, we find by the closing decades of the nineteenth century the exile theme being played out within an increasingly complex cultural pattern. Not surprisingly, of course, as the New World gradually became settled and understood, it began to lose some of its exoticism and wonder, and its inhabitants began at the same time to sense more acutely its cultural shortcomings in contrast to the richness of the Old. Within Canada, this residual attraction of the Old World was particularly strong for those exiles from the British Isles who, as we saw in the last chapter, regarded this country largely as a temporary residence or, if they had to remain, as a place where they could exploit their British connections to achieve the success that was denied them in their homeland. In neither case did Canada win out, and in many respects these later transplanted exiles from the British Isles had modified their vision very little from that reflected by Brooke's characters in *Emily Montague* a hundred years earlier.

But as we saw earlier, this attraction of the Old World has always remained strong, too, for the native-born residents of the New World, even for the most loyal and nationalistic of American writers and artists. It is important to remember, however, that a qualitatively different relationship existed between the United States and the Old World than was the case for Canada. Americans were, in a constitutional and a pragmatic sense, foreigners in the eyes of the British, and they could therefore visit their cultural sources and at the same time expatiate on their own uniqueness and achievements with total confidence in themselves as distinctive individuals. But Canadians had emotional ties and quasi-constitutional links with Great Britain that were not so easy to deny; and indeed, it was not only Europeans but Canadians themselves who perpetuated the notion that they were on the whole Britishers coming "home" rather than a separate and distinct component of the New World. The question posed by Lady Doleford in Sara Duncan's *Cousin Cinderella*—"can one be at home out of England?"—represented a widely held opinion of the day in both Great Britain and Canada, and it undoubtedly reflects the kind of encumbrance that has helped delay the total emancipation of Canadians.

Alternatively—and this situation crops up in much of the fiction being discussed in this and succeeding chapters—Canadians were merely regarded as Americans, for from the European perspective to this day, "America" means all of North America, especially everything north of the Rio Grande. Again, this confusing of national labels was not always discouraged by the Canadians themselves, and in writers from John Galt to Clark Blaise this note is sounded in many contexts, reflecting attitudes which range from benign amusement to sarcasm and outrage. But whatever the stance of the writer, Canada is rarely taken for granted or presented as a universally recognized and understood cultural reality in the manner that holds true for the United States or England. Duncan's Lorne Murchison reflects this situation when he decides for the sake of convenience to agree with the perverse Londoners that he is "an American, 'but not the United States kind,'" resenting the necessity to explain to the Briton beside him that there were other kinds."[1] This kind of compromise, coupled with the persuasive influence of the prevailing imperial spirit of the day, diminished the reality and viability of the Canadian character or situation. As a result, there is frequently some fuzziness or uncertainty when these components are juxtaposed against their counterparts from the United States or the Old World.

Of the relatively few indigenous Canadian writers near the end of the nineteenth century who addressed themselves to the question of Canada's relationship to her American and Old World connections and legacies, the Brantford-born Sara Jeannette Duncan has deservedly retained the strongest reputation. She possessed a rich talent and an expansive vision that combined with her predilection for the exotic and the unconventional to make her, among other things, a substantial exponent of the exile theme. Though in terms of residency she ceased being a Canadian after her marriage just as her fictional career was getting under way, she retained throughout her life a remarkably fresh and balanced perspective towards her former country and its people. In the broader sense, she was a writer shaped by international rather than exclusively national perspectives, conditioned by at least four societies—Canadian, American, English, and Indian—in which respect, as well as in her artistry, the texture of her prose, and in her informing vision, she quite distinctly anticipates such later writers as Ethel Wilson and Mavis Gallant. It is true that, compared to the characters created by these two writers, Duncan's protagonists seem more like tourists than committed exiles, but from her own situation as an exile familiar with a number of societies, Duncan is able to give her characters a convincing ring, whatever nation they represent and whatever role they play in her novels.

Of the same generation chronologically as Canada's Confederation poets, she was, in part because of Brantford's geographical location, attracted more by American influences than Canadian and, initially at least, more by journalistic examples than by poetic or fictional models. In her twenties, she became a correspondent for the Toronto *Globe,* the Montreal *Star,* and for *The Week,* a pro-United States, pro-annexationist weekly edited by Goldwin Smith, but before these accomplishments, she had already gained a position on the Washington *Post,* a remarkable accomplishment for a woman barely halfway through her twenties. It was in that capacity that she drew an assignment to interview William Dean Howells, her execution of which has been described for us by one of the early reviewers of Duncan's career:

> on her way upstairs to her room in the hotel she passed Mr. Howells' door. Outside the door was a pair of the author's boots. In a flash the journalist perceived what she could write. The day following *The Post* published an interview with Mr. Howells' boots. Evidently the great novelist did justice to the genius of the interviewer, for he sought the acquaintance of the young lady who had written the article.[2]

This anecdote illustrates Duncan's sense of humour and confidence in herself, and helps us, too, to understand the affinity she felt for the benign realism reflected by such contemporary Americans as Howells and James. The best of her novels can profitably be discussed within the perspective of that broad realistic movement, though it would be wrong to push this too far. She never approached the profundity of psychological analysis achieved by James, nor did she address the social issues that Howells and others examined in their works, but in some respects she does emerge as a formidable Canadian counterpart to such writers as Edith Wharton, particularly in her abiding interest in the contrast of international manners and customs. Indeed, the common phrase "custom of the country" that Wharton was to use as the title for her 1913 novel appears in both *The Imperialist* (1904) and *Cousin Cinderella* (1908), though undoubtedly Duncan had long been aware of its ironic possibilities through her familiarity with such novels as James's *Daisy Miller.*

Duncan became an exile out of domestic necessity—or at least out of domestic custom—when she married Charles Everard Cotes, an Englishman who was curator of the Indian Museum of Calcutta. Well before her marriage, however, she exhibited a spirit (detectable in the Howells anecdote) that at the very least spelled out non-conformity, if not rebellion, that suggested some of the components of the exile mentality—restlessness, curiosity, adventuresomeness, and impatience with established custom. Her incipient Bohemianism was early and frequently indulged: along with several Americans, including the jaunty poet Joaquin Miller, she undertook an expedition out of New Orleans to rediscover Ponce de Leon's Fountain of Youth in Florida; she made a number of excursions in British Honduras; and she crossed Canada on the newly completed Canadian Pacific Railway, taking the dramatic Kicking Horse Pass segment, much like the intrepid heroines of *A Social Departure*, on the cowcatcher of the locomotive. It was on this round-the-world trip, incidentally, that she met her future husband in Calcutta; he visited her subsequently in Brantford, and they were married in 1889, after which time she returned to Canada for fairly frequent, but short-term, visits.

Duncan was a prolific writer, but of her twenty or so books, only a half dozen are relevant to the exile theme as it is manifested in various New World-Old World juxtapositions; of these, only two are thoroughly concerned with Canadian character, customs, and issues, though two or three others contain passing references to things Canadian. It is interesting to note that the two novels concerned most exclusively with Canadian matter appeared relatively late during the most productive phase of her career, which began tapering off around 1910, some dozen years before her death. Yet both *The Imperialist* and *Cousin Cinderella* retain an immediacy which belies Duncan's long absence from Canada, a perspicacity undoubtedly kept sharp by such intervening novels as *An American Girl in London* (1891) and its sequel *A Voyage of Consolation* (1898), both of which are centrally concerned with the international contrast of manners.

Her first book is, in the literal sense, the most international of all her works, for its settings range over four continents—North America, Asia, Africa, and Europe. *A Social Departure: How Orthodocia and I Went Round the World by Ourselves* (1890) is, however, more of a sprightly travelogue than an artistically shaped novel, though occasionally heightened fictional elements intrude, and throughout, Duncan's sharp senses pick up the nuances and ironies of social manners, so we ultimately get more than exotic descriptions of changing settings and societies. Only the opening fifty-odd pages are relevant to this study, as well as the last page or so, where some loose narrative strands of the Canadian section are resolved abruptly in the tradition of the sentimental romance. On its literal level, the book unfolds its title implications: it is a chronicle of a voyage westward from Montreal to England via the Orient and Middle East of the narrator and her twenty-two-year-old English friend, Orthodocia Love. It is, however, the social confrontations that these two heroines experience from time to time that generate the most interest and contribute to the book's narrative strain

the framework of Duncan's emerging moral vision and, thus, the components of an organic characterization.

The narrator, never given a name, is the first of many Duncan protagonists to carry the burden of the confusion between the designations "American"
and "Canadian." Though Orthodocia's English relatives refer to her as "that
American young lady," an early remark by the narrator makes it clear that
she is a Canadian. "It is very 'American' for young ladies to travel alone," she
observes, "but not such a common thing in my part of the continent that it
could be acceded to without a certain amount of objection on the part of
their friends and relatives" (*SD*, 5). She also offers Orthodocia a facetious,
though not entirely inaccurate, definition of the railway they are travelling
on, after being asked "What is the 'Seepiar'?":

> The C.P.R. is the most masterly stroke of internal economy a Govern-
> ment ever had the courage to carry out, and the most lunatic enterprise a
> Government was ever foolhardy enough to hazard. It was made for the
> good of Canada, it was made for the greed of contractors. It has insured
> our financial future, it has bankrupted us forever. It is our boon and our
> bane. It is an iron bond of union between our East and our West . . . and
> it is an important strand connecting a lot of disaffected provinces. (*SD*,
> 10)

Only a Canadian, one is tempted to say, could explain these paradoxes and
contradictions, and certainly only a Canadian would live with them. The
narrator's assessment has to this day retained its applicability, and undoubtedly the rest of the world, like Orthodocia, still shakes its puzzled head.

There is on the whole very little direct juxtaposing of Old World and New
World sensibilities in this book; both the narrator and Orthodocia are
presented as balanced but lively protagonists who openly examine whatever
experiences come their way. Duncan directs some gentle satire towards both
worlds, and only in the narrative resolution of the book, where Orthodocia
and Jack elect to live in Vancouver after their marriage rather than in
England, is there a hint of an authorial preference. From time to time,
customs and manners are mildly scoffed at, such as Orthodocia's shocked
response at the C.P.R.'s sleeping car arrangements, a shock quickly dissi-
pated as she discovers the nature of the gentleman who is to occupy the
upper berth: "Then the gentleman came in from the smoking car, and turned
out to be a perfectly inoffensive little English curate, as new to the customs of
the aborigines as Orthodocia, and quite as deeply distressed" (*SD*, 12). We
are also treated to amusing accounts of Canadian manners, as exhibited by
the Canadian Customs officials, by Winnipeg society at a formal ball, and by
small-town prairie folk, but on the whole in these situations, Duncan main-

tains a position of kindly and amused detachment.

She is, however, not unfeeling about human hardship and tragedy, as the episode of Mr. and Mrs. Growthem illustrates, even though some aspects of their story are treated light-heartedly. The Growthems were English settlers, representatives perhaps of what were known as "gentlemen emigrants," who came to the colony with low fortunes but high expectations: a governorship of one of the territories was automatically assumed to be this British gentleman's birthright. But it was not to be, and at times Mrs. Growthem echoes the complaints of Susanna Moodie: "My dear, we didn't get on. It was impossible to get servants, the field labour was very scarce" (*SD*, 20), but of course with no money to return "home," they were compelled to perform these labours themselves, managing to eke out a marginal living, while keeping up as best they could the pretensions of gentility. But it is when Mrs. Growthem recounts the death of their infant daughter that Duncan comes close to the stark realism of such later novelists as Grove and Ross, and where we are forcibly struck by the reality which almost caused the undoing of the Growthems: "We could see the little grave from the kitchen window—for a long time I used to leave a lamp on it, especially when the snow came. After that nothing seemed to matter" (*SD*, 22).

Growthem belongs to that large segment of English society, somewhere between the remittance man and the gentility, that emigrated to the colonies during the nineteenth century to avail themselves of free land and of the possibility of "running the show." Stephen Leacock recalled in his autobiography that in his grandfather's time "there was . . . in England a prevalent myth that farming could be 'learned,' especially by young men who couldn't learn anything else,"[3] and in a very real sense Growthem emerges as a manifestation of that myth. When the narrator meets him, she notices that "he was still a pleasant-looking man, but there were lines on his face that would not have been there if he had not been a banker in London first and a farmer in Assiniboia afterwards" (*SD*, 22)—a comment not all that unlike Leacock's, that his young man "was supposed to remain a gentleman even if he acted like a farmer." In spite of the absence of a governorship, however, the Growthems did achieve a large measure of integration into the New World, but as with the Moodies, Bogle Corbet, and such other Duncan characters as Murchison and Drummond of *The Imperialist,* an "undercurrent of the old allegience" continued to remind them that they would always be exiles in their new land.

But the Canadian West harboured another kind of exile whose plight was socially, if not economically, more desperate than that of the Growthems—the remittance man. In language that again anticipates Leacock as well as Mavis Gallant in her "Varieties of Exile," Duncan offers one of the earlier descriptions in Canadian literature of this special exile unique to the colonies:

The exile was not always a Mrs. Growthem—more often, indeed, a youth who fared badly in examinations for Sandhurst or the "Indian Civil," and had been started, with a hundred pounds or so, to farm in Canada on that large scale and under those indefinite conditions that make farming in Canada a possible occupation for a gentleman. (*SD*, 24-25)

We meet one of these remittance men in the person of a Mr. Carysthwaite, a former member of the English aristocracy, reduced to becoming a lowly recruit in the Mounted Police after failing in a Colorado mining venture. The commanding officer's wife is appalled at the resulting social inconvenience: "He is the third son of an English lord—and we can't invite him to dinner! It's *too* trying!" (*SD*, 39). Carysthwaite may have lost something through his exile to the far West, but he clearly does not share this matron's mortification over his social demotion. His interest, more credibly, is upon Orthodocia, whom he had known earlier in his life, but Duncan resists the occasion to solve this problem by creating any *affaire de coeur* here. Instead, through the ironic voice of her narrator, she establishes the kind of realistic credo that for the most part operates throughout her works:

This is only a faithful chronicle of the ordinary happenings of an ordinary journey of two ordinary people, so I can't gratify you with any romantic episode later connected with Orthodocia and the Mounted Policeman so well qualified yet so ineligible to be asked to dinner, though I should clearly like to. The fact is—and I tremble to think what might become of Orthodocia if I permitted myself any departure from the facts—that we left Corona and one very melancholy John Love late that very night, and the Honourable Carysthwaite did not occur again. (*SD*, 40)

Romantic entanglements of any sort are very much underplayed in this book; with only obscure hints during this Corona episode that something is warming up between Orthodocia and her second cousin Jack Love, the news of their "understanding" in the closing pages seems a bit of a narrative imposition. In succeeding books, too, like *An American Girl in London, A Voyage of Consolation, and Cousin Cinderella,* Duncan resorts to sudden and impulsive resolutions of the various romantic situations, relying perhaps a bit too readily on the conventions of the sentimental romance.

A Social Departure ends, as far as the New World exile theme is concerned, with the heroines taking their leave of Vancouver en route to Japan. Their voyage across Canada has been both realistic (though like many eastern chroniclers of the Canadian West, Duncan confuses the Rocky Mountains and the Selkirks on occasion) and metaphorical, and indeed, is not unlike that undertaken by a later exile, Ethel Wilson's Topaz Edgeworth. Interestingly, too, the Vancouver that Duncan's heroines visit is, in terms of historical chronology, roughly the same city it was when Topaz arrived in her fiftieth year; and Orthodocia's unorthodox behaviour, reflected in her buying and selling of a residential lot, underscores her spiritual affinity with that later innocent traveller. The narrator, too, makes an observation about Vancouver that anticipates the ecstasy experienced by Wilson's characters upon their arrival: "And it was exhilarating to be in a place where vigorous young vitality is so strong as to get into one's own blood somehow, and give it a new thrill, especially for sober-going Canadians, whose lack of 'go' has always been the scoff of their American cousins" (*SD*, 51).

Duncan is not to touch the Canadian West again—except to send Advena Murchison and Hugh Finlay of the *The Imperialist* to a mission post in Alberta—so it would be misleading to attach too much significance to its resurrective powers as suggested by this somewhat slight first book. It is, nevertheless, a convincing world, as are the other worlds described in the course of the heroines' journey; what characteristically emerges throughout Duncan's fiction is a subdued contrast, directly expressed or implicit, between two or more *reasonable* worlds, for there are really no excesses in her vision. In general, however, the partiality for the New World adumbrated in *A Social Departure* carries through in her other novels concerned with the exile theme, but in a fictional pattern where not infrequently the Canadian character occupies an obscure or shifting position between the American and the English.

Beginning with *An American Girl in London* (1891), Duncan's fictional talents reveal a progressive enrichment over what was manifested in *A Social Departure;* increasingly, she places her protagonists in credible moral situations where, with some conviction, they make conscious choices about themselves and their dilemmas. This is especially true of *The Imperialist* and *Cousin Cinderella,* though the latter is by no means free of the superficial characterization and facile moral solutions that seriously weaken both *An American Girl in London* and *A Voyage of Consolation.* But in all these novels, no one society is manifestly superior, and there are relatively few a priori suppositions or pronouncements that get in the way of a psychologically convincing revelation of character or situation.

An American Girl is addressed directly to an English audience, as the narrator Mamie Wick makes clear in a fictional preface, where she quickly but mildly begins taking this English audience to task:

> I have noticed that you are pleased, over here, to bestow rather more attention upon the American Girl than upon any other kind of American that we produce. You have taken the trouble to form opinions about

her—I have heard quantities of them. Her behaviour and her bringing-up, her idioms, and her "accent"—above all, her "accent"—have made themes for you, and you have been good enough to discuss them—Mr. James, in your midst, correcting and modifying your impressions—with a good deal of animation, for you. (*AG*, 2)

In the opening pages, Mamie self-deprecatingly puts herself in an inferior position to the English, as regards both her present status and her ancestry, though there is of course no mistaking the irony in her confession that "a grand-aunt . . . was burned as a witch in Salem, Mass.—a thing very few families can point back to, even in England" (*AG*, 6). What is juxtaposed throughout the novel in Mamie's various social confrontations are a number of obvious oppositions: New World freedom against Old World regulations: irreverence against decorum; present status against ancestral tradition; impulsive behaviour against propriety, and so on. Mamie's superiority in all these situations is perhaps too glibly dramatized, as compared, for example, to the more complex dilemmas of Mary Trent in *Cousin Cinderella;* measured against such caricatures as Mrs. Portheris, Miss Purkiss, or Lady Bandobust, even the most gauche and unlettered American is bound to win. Against more substantial English individuals, like Lady Torquilon, Miss Peter Corke, or Charles Mafferton, the result is closer to a draw, though Mafferton's potential is effectively choked off by both a grasping opportunistic family and his own inbred caution. His intrinsic worth, however, is suggested by Duncan (as is, incidentally, the innate worth of things American) in a minor episode on board ship, where Mamie detects him reading a novel by Howells:

> I remember I was surprised to find an Englishman so good-natured in his admiration of some of our authors, and so willing to concede an American standard which might be a high one, and yet have nothing to do with Dickens, and so appreciative generally of the conditions which have brought about our ways of thinking and writing. (*AG*, 16)

In *A Social Departure* and *The Imperialist* Duncan portrays exile figures from England deprived of the protection and rules of social class, custom, and tradition and dramatizes the effect that pragmatic expediency consequently has on them. In the three novels set in the Old World, the reverse pattern operates: we see the customs of the country being tested or even assaulted by innocents from the New World, whose moral and ethical vision has been shaped by individual rather than institutional or traditional imperatives. And what would have given the Growthems or Alfred Hesketh confidence in the New World—a rigid and predictable sense of order and decorum—is precisely what unsettles Mamie Wick and the Trents in the Old. Mamie reacts to this atmosphere her first morning in the breakfast room of the Hotel Métropole:

> I felt, for the first time in my life, that I was being made imposing, and I objected to the feeling . . . . [It] was the demeanour of everything that weighed upon me. My very chair lived up to its own standard of decorum; and the table seemed laid upon a pattern of propriety that it would never willingly depart from. There was an all-pervading sense of order in the air. I couldn't make out exactly where it came from, but it was there, and it was fearful. (*AG*, 22)

This reaction is not simply the prejudice of an unsophisticated American confronting a more complex and foreign tradition; it reflects rather Duncan's consistent view that there is something unnatural about a social order that fails to allow for any flexibility in human behaviour. We have already seen how this phenomenon operated in a minor way with Carysthwaite in *A Social Departure,* and it receives an even stronger dramatization in *Those Delightful Americans* (1902), a product of Duncan's more mature artistry. Here, the central figure is a young English woman, Carrie Kemball, who displays the rationality, sense of humour, and balance that have become the hallmarks of the Duncan protagonist, and she turns these attributes upon many facets of American life she observes during an excursion with her somewhat unimaginative husband. Even before departing, she senses the advantages of the democratic, life-enhancing American attitudes over her own English traditions:

> I had a fancy that life in an island, even in the island of England, was apt to be too condensed, that there was not space for the accumulation of centuries to diffuse themselves properly, and that we lived in a kind of moral purée. In America I knew the air would not be so thick; one could see people better. (*DA*, 17-18)

And in a subsequent dinner scene that conveniently emerges as a dramatic counterpoint to Mamie's breakfast scene in London, Carrie sees her anticipation fulfilled: "The occasion of the moment was dinner, but people were not dining solidly, silently, and a little suspiciously, as they do at Bailey's" (*DA*, 109).

The problem here—and generally this is true in most of Duncan's works being considered here, except *The Imperialist*—resides in the fact that these lively characters are rarely given a sufficiently introspective nature to allow us to be vexed or enlightened by their international assessments. Her protagonists are sensible, perceptive, witty, but they are never uncomfortable or intellectually bewildered, and as a result neither are we. We applaud Mamie's victory over Mrs. Portheris and Lady Bandobust and admire her brilliant repartee, but we do not have our opinions threatened by such episodes, nor are we permitted to contemplate any ethical or moral alternatives, as we frequently are, for example, in Mavis Gallant's international confrontations. Only one of Duncan's protagonists, Elfrida Bell of *A Daughter of To-day*, is willing to take the risks attendant upon being in a state of exile; tourists like Mamie Wick, Carrie Kemball, and Mary Trent, though interested in the foreign lands they visit, are also dedicated to the supremacy of their own land. But even with Elfrida, Duncan exhibits a failure of imagination, for she does not permit her to explore the logical extensions of her initial self-exile from the New World. That she suffers the fate that historically many exiles have lamented about, and indeed, in some cases pined for, is as a result, only melodramatic and not aesthetically or emotionally convincing. Her suicide, it is true, does up to a point satisfy narrative demands: her consistent equating of artistic talent with life dictates the appropriateness of the corollary of that equation, and we are left in no doubt throughout the novel that she is sadly bereft of any genuine talent.

On the whole, the international contrasts examined and dramatized in these novels vindicate the appropriateness of the opinion voiced by Senator Wicks in *A Voyage of Consolation* that "it's no more a virtue to be born American than a fault to be born anything else" (*VC*, 34), though the strategic positioning of the two contrasting abstract nouns unmistakably suggests his prejudice in the matter. On balance, the New World triumphs over the Old in most of Duncan's confrontations, though her protagonists are frequently equivocal in their expression of such views: "Our advantages," Mamie muses as she observes the sights of London from the top of her omnibus, "have a way of making your disadvantages more interesting" (*AG*, 29). And like Kipling, Duncan occasionally arranges a confrontation between two strong and spirited people, like that between Mamie and Miss Corke, to encourage us to think, for a moment at least, that in such situations there is really neither east nor west.

To return to *An American Girl,* the high point of Mamie's pilgrimage to the Old World comes with her presentation at the Court of Queen Victoria, a social achievement which, as we learn in *A Voyage of Consolation,* inconsolably vexes Mrs. Portheris, obliged to go through life denied this ultimate recognition. But Duncan does not let Mamie (or the Americans in general) off scot-free on this occasion, for she directs her gentle satire towards the American propensity for antimonarchical sentiments. In spite of Mamie's determination prior to the ceremony that she would remain totally democratic, the actual experience itself engenders a strong vestigial response:

It was all very well to allow one's self a little excitement in preparation; but when it came to the actual event I reminded myself that I had not the slightest intention of being nervous. I called all my democratic principles to my assistance—none of them would come. "Remember, Mamie Wick," said I to myself, "you don't believe in queens." . . . I was launched at last towards that little black figure of Royalty with the Blue Ribbon crossing her breast . . . . *Didn't* you believe in queens, Miss Mamie Wick, at that moment? I'm very much afraid you did . . . . It was over at last. I had kissed the hand of the Queen of Great Britain and Ireland, and—there's no use in trying to believe anything to the contrary—I was proud of it. (*AG*, 306,307)

If this ceremony does not represent a moment of apotheosis for Mamie, as a similar occasion with Queen Mary later did for Wilson's Topaz Edgeworth, it certainly constitutes for her, both psychologically and socially, a resolution of a major contradiction that separates the Old World from the New. It is a situation that Duncan, with her own balanced appreciation of both the monarchical and republican spirits, undoubtedly enjoyed setting up: Mamie is not unlike that hypothetical American visitor to Canada Duncan extols in her 1887 essay, "Our Latent Loyalty," written for Smith's pro-Annexationist *The Week*: "He finds the little court, alien to our social system as it is, transferred from place to place with marvellous adaptability, and whole democratic communities standing on tip-toe to see Viceroyalty drive by."[4]

Mamie emerges in *An American Girl* as a reasonably credible figure, and her triumph over her English adversaries, from the snobbish Mrs. Portheris to the grasping Maffertons, represents in one sense the triumph of New World innocence and common sense over Old World propriety and tradition as manifested in the English social system. If she is not entirely like James's Daisy Miller, "an inscrutable combination of audacity and innocence," she nevertheless shares with that earlier heroine the incapacity to be cowed by the dictates of custom and expectations. Daisy is clearly in a more vulnerable position than Mamie, and is less prepared emotionally and intellectually to look after herself; Mamie of course has the added protection of Lady Torquilon and Peter Corke, who are careful to ensure that her initiation into the intricacies of the English social world is properly guided. The kind of advice that Winterbourne gave to Daisy—"when you deal with natives you must go by the custom of the country"—is in effect heeded by Mamie, even though she is unorthodox in her outward behaviour, while Daisy, to her misfortune, prefers "weak tea" over "excellent advice."

Whether viewed as a sequel to *An American Girl* or as a novel with its own justification, *A Voyage of Consolation* represents something of a falling-off of Duncan's talents. Certainly, the seven-year gap between the two suggests that Duncan was not trying to exploit the popularity of the earlier novel, yet she must have felt obliged to resolve what some readers may have seen as loose ends or moral uncertainties, particularly the mention on the last page of the novel of Mamie's engagement to Arthur Page of Yale. But on the whole there were no important narrative strains in *An American Girl* that required a sequel to resolve; Mamie had successfully escaped the nets set for her by the Mafferton family, Mrs. Portheris, and Lady Bandobust, so we can take only ironically her disclaimer in the final paragraph that she was "taking [her] informed mind back to a comparatively immature civilisation" (*AG*, 321). Both the narrative unfolding and the final outcome of this novel demonstrate clearly the supremacy of the New World values and possibilities over their Old World counterparts.

Perhaps the reader's major reservation about the earlier novel centres on the character of Charles Mafferton, who gains our admiration initially by his sincere concern for the safety and welfare of Mamie. A Jamesian kind of figure in his sensitivity and deportment, Mafferton seems to offer at the outset a promising protagonist for Duncan to use in exploring dramatically the Old World-New World possibilities, but as the novel proceeds, he is relegated more and more into the background. Even so, however, he seems to have more fibre to him than does the Arthur Page we meet in the opening pages of *A Voyage of Consolation*, and Mamie's decision at the end of this novel to marry him must be seen ultimately as a failure of nerve or imagination on the part of Duncan. Mafferton's family, it is true, is insufferable, and reason enough for Mamie to discard him, but that hardly salvages Page; Mamie's unorthodoxy throughout both these novels dictates that she should probably have remained a free spirit. In a way, Mafferton emerges as an early version of *The Imperialist's* Alfred Hesketh: reasonably decent but incredibly dense in his understanding of people and situations, once removed from his own self-centred English world. "Even in Rome," Mamie chides him in *A Voyage of Consolation* "London is 'town' to you, isn't it? What a curious thing insular tradition is" (*VC*, 162).

The central concern of this novel is the attitudes of Americans, as represented by Mamie and her parents, towards the culture of the Old World, this time continental Europe rather than England. Though Mamie is again the narrator, the emphasis is on Senator and Mrs. Wick, who represent in a sense the wholesome and democratic spirit of the New World. But there are other Americans as well, not so favourably depicted: the mercenary Malt family on the prowl for *any* English count for their insufferable teen-age daughter, the snobbish and fastidious Misses Bingham of New York (who vacated a Canadian-filled coach because the Canadians "were probably not foreign enough"), and the loud, garish Hinkson of Iowa, an American booster-type who aggressively insults all who dare call into question the notion of American superiority. It is this latter individual whom Duncan uses to dramatize the American-Canadian distinction, her first attempt at such juxtaposition since *A Social Departure,* with the Canadians here winning by default, as it were, since it is virtually impossible to lose against the voluble Hinkson.

In this episode, a group of Canadians is led by one Mr. Pabbley from Simcoe, Ontario, who finds it necessary (as, we recall, Lorne Murchison does in *The Imperialist*) to explain to Hinkson that he is an American, "but not the United States kind," which touches off a mild international debate. Predictably, the boastful Hinkson goads Pabbley into a spirited but rational statement of national loyalty:

"Mister," said Mr. Pabbley, "I flatter myself that Canadians are a good deal like United States folks already, and I don't mind congratulating both our nations on the resemblance. But I'm bound to add that, while I would wish to imitate the American people in many ways still further, I wouldn't be like you personally, no, not under any circumstances nor in any respect." (*VC*, 69)

The scene comes to a somewhat ludicrous resolution when the Canadians to a man ("I guess we aren't any of us annexationists") refuse to pose with the Americans for a tourist photograph, because Hinkson has decked his person with a large Stars and Stripes handkerchief. That none of the Canadians carries a Union Jack is perhaps one indication of the distinction between Americans and Canadians, but Duncan is clearly urging us not to become too exercised over this issue. If anything, given that Pabbley is the spokesman for the Canadian viewpoint, Duncan seems to argue in favour of some form of continentalism, stopping far short of annexation, with Canadians retaining their own individuality.

Against the English, Duncan is less equivocal, though with Mrs. Portheris and Mafferton again representing this group, she really does not have much choice. The Wicks meet them accidentally atop the Eiffel Tower, and at the moment of recognition it is Mamie who takes the initiative, rationalizing that "the woman who hesitates is lost, even though she be a British matron of massive prejudices and a figure to match" (*VC*, 87). Confronted by this sudden and most heterogeneous gathering, Mrs. Portheris is clearly out of her element: "I confess I am not in the habit of meeting my connections promiscuously abroad," she protests (*VC*, 88), and without the social machinery that protected her in *An American Girl* she is effectively rendered helpless. Ironically, it is a remark about her physical bulk by the kind and well-intentioned Mrs. Wick that evokes Mrs. Portheris' most violent outburst about the difference between American and British manners:

"That is the latest, the very latest Americanism which I have observed in your conversation, Augusta. In your native land it may be admissible, but please understand that I cannot permit it to be applied to me personally. To English ears it is offensive—very offensive. It is also quite improper for you to assume any familiarity with my figure. As you say *I* may be aware of its corpulence, but nobody else—er—can possibly know anything about it." (*VC*, 201)

This novel lacks the structural and thematic tightness of its predecessor, and for the most part it relies on coincidence and clumsily arranged melodramatic scenes (such as Mrs. Portheris, Dicky Dod, and Mamie getting lost in the Catacombs of Rome) to sustain our interest. As in most of her early novels, except in *A Daughter of To-day*, the international characters Duncan presents are tourists rather than committed or suffering exiles. It is Duncan herself who is the exile from all the societies she describes, though she is a contented one, and thus can depict Canadians, Americans, and Britons alike from the perspective of an experienced and kindly observer.

This same vision carries over into *Those Delightful Americans* (1902), which in a sense is both corollary and a vindication of the implications of *A Voyage of Consolation*, for here the worth of American character and attributes is verified on home ground. Here it is a reverse pilgrimage: the English narrator Carrie Kemball and her husband Kaye undertake a voyage to the United States, with the charitable and intelligent Carrie recording her impressions. She and Mamie clearly emerge as transatlantic counterparts of each other, and undoubtedly much of Duncan herself went into the creation of these two sensitive characters. It is only Carrie among the Old World figures in this novel who emerges equal in moral and ethical stature to the strong Americans we meet; like Mamie, Elfrida Bell, and Mary Trent, she possesses something of the mental equipment of the exile figure—curiosity, intellectual awareness, impatience with custom and tradition. "The greatest pleasure in life, it seems to me," she muses at one point, "is doing things differently; why we go on and on the way we do in England is more than I can conceive" (*DA*, 263-64).

Much of the novel is given over to musings of this sort, wherein Carrie gives us a number of variations on such Old World-New World contrasts as propriety versus openness, tradition versus pragmatism, or the class system versus democracy. The novel fails on the whole to dramatize such situations sufficiently, but occasionally, as in the sustained exchange between Verona Daly and Carrie, some telling points are scored about the other's society and customs. "I don't think it matters in England whether your ancestors were very respectable," Verona chides, "so long as they were important enough" (*DA*, 201-22), to which Carrie counters: "After all I don't suppose it much matters, once you become an American, what you were in any previous state" (*DA*, 203). Consistent with Duncan's views throughout her fiction, both these observations make sense, logically as well as experientially, and they reflect the kind of balanced and reasonable Duncan vision alluded to earlier. But such sharp moments are all too rare, and on the whole this novel adds little to Duncan's international views as proclaimed in her earlier novels. It is interesting, incidentally, that this scene of light-hearted bantering conveys essentially the same point that Grove's Phil Branden makes when he states that "in Europe the poor man is tolerated if he can look upon a great past; in America if he looks to a future."[5]

Duncan's major Canadian novels, *The Imperialist* (1904) and *Cousin Cinderella* (1908), in one respect reflect what had become a sociological fact in Canada, the disappearance to a large extent of the manifestations of the garrison mentality that had characterized many works from *Emily Montague* on. But doubtless, it is more accurate to say that, as an individual, Duncan had simply ignored the theoretical existence of a garrison mentality: *she* had no problems with her identity, or with her significance in the world she grew up in, and on the whole her fictional Canadians more than held their own against any colonially-minded types they encountered. We saw signs of this confidence in *A Social Departure* and in the Pabbley-Hinkson confrontation in *A Voyage of Consolation*, but it achieves a full fictional expression in the two Canadian novels frequently regarded as among her best.

With the dissipation of garrison attitudes and the attendant consolidation of a confidence about the Canadian reality, the exile theme in these two mature works is played out in cultural contexts where we are able to assess characters and opinions with a great deal of conviction. As in Henry James and Edith Wharton, both the Old World and the New have the opportunity of being the shaping influence, though as is true throughout her work, Duncan generally opts for the New, a tendency made quite explicit in these two novels. It is in this respect that Duncan's vision diverges most strongly from that of James, where characteristically it is New World innocence that emerges as the deficient quantity. James disturbs us far more fundamentally than does Duncan: while his New World characters like Christopher Newman, Madame de Mauves, or Isabel Archer achieve moral triumphs of sorts, they do so at a heavy cost. In the face of Old World chicanery, they manage to retain a form of innocence, but they really have no impact upon the forces of the Old World. Duncan works this theme differently, as do such other exile writers as Lowry, Moore, and Gallant, and I suspect that one reason for this is that Canadian innocence is neither so obvious nor so pure in derivation as the American version. Innocence, it can be argued, is the American's birthright, deriving from both an individual and a constitutional inheritance of the ideals of perfection and incorruptibility, whereas Canadian innocence seems less sacred, more resilient, more of a compromised quantity.

Whatever the national or psychological causes behind these distinctions, the twentieth-century Canadian innocent, whether at home or abroad, seems on the whole (an exception is Mordecai Richler's André Bennett of *The Acrobats*) better equipped to accommodate himself to the world of experience than his American counterpart. Canadian fiction abounds in exile figures who quite routinely make compromises with their newly acquired versions of reality: not only such Duncan characters as Lorne Murchison and Mary Trent, but a whole catalogue of Gallant protagonists, Richler's Norman Price, Levine's Joseph Grand, Blaise's Paul Keeler, Engel's Sarah Porlock, to name only a few. Whether their dramas unfold in Europe or in Canada, or in both, these individuals ultimately emerge from their immersions in cultural conflicts as wiser, and not always as sadder, people: a common result is both wisdom and contentment, and the loss of innocence itself stands significantly as an enriching experience.

These observations are pertinent to both *The Imperialist* and *Cousin Cinderella,* particularly the former, where there is a more complex testing of Old and New World possibilities. Duncan's journalistic and fictional interests coincide in this novel, with its topical derivation from the prevailing British imperial policy of the day, and its dramatic component arising out of Duncan's interest in cultural conflicts and her international perspective on things Canadian. Though there is no longer much residual interest in the political reality of an imperial policy, the psychological reality of the imperialist Lorne Murchison and of the people surrounding him remains relevant. It is a measure of Duncan's irony and her aesthetic talents that in this unfolding of her fictional plot, the central character receives less sympathetic treatment than some of the more peripheral characters, and by novel's end he is in a position of complete isolation from the realities of his world. The more minor figures can conveniently be paired into couples, as the realities of courtship dictate: Advena Murchison and the Reverend Hugh Finlay, Dora Milburn and Alfred Hesketh, the Reverend Drummond and Christie Cameron, in each of which relationships there is a New World-Old World opposition, a pattern that allows Duncan to examine conflicting attitudes and moralities in a convincing fashion.

As these comments intimate, *The Imperialist* is clearly much more than a novel of exile; indeed, it probably makes more sense to analyze it as a novel of manners, a political novel, or as a sentimental novel of romance and marriage. But Duncan at its writing had been in exile in the Old World— voluntary and happy as that state might have been—for some fifteen years, and as such she could bring to bear upon her characters a perspective and a pattern of values that had, in part at least, been created by that decade and a half of exile. And for the first time in her fiction—again with the exception of

A Daughter of To-day—she presents us with characters about whom we have strong feelings and compassion, and whose credibility is never in doubt.

The relationship that most convincingly exploits the New World-Old World oppositions is that between Advena Murchison and Hugh Finlay, the Scottish minister, whose first words anticipate his eventual integration into his new country: "Ah, well, it's something to be in a country where the sun still goes down with a thought of the primeval" (*I,* 70). A light-hearted bantering ensues between them over the effect of sunsets, a kind of moral preliminary to the main bout, as it were, but this initial meeting near sunset of an April day emerges dramatically as a precursor of a new life for both of them. Finlay seems intuitively to be at home in the New World, and his observation that "the world is wrapped in destiny, and but revolves to roll it out" (*I,* 71) is very much a reflection of Duncan's vision expressed earlier by Carrie in *Those Delightful Americans* in her words to Verona: "You are the world's new serial, coming out chapter by chapter. We are an old story, published in full ages ago" (*DA,* 200).

Advena, however, is the active agent, the pursuer, in this relationship, and though she pursues Finlay without much passion, she has working for her the qualities of common sense and persistence. Finlay's dilemma is rooted in the fixed code of his Scottish background, for he feels a moral obligation to marry Miss Cameron, to whom he was previously bespoken by some rigid Scottish custom. What in effect unfolds therefore in this drama is the triumph of a New World pragmatism over an Old World Calvinistic determinism. Taking a leaf from Howells, Duncan provides a quantitative moral solution to this dilemma, just as Howells did in *The Rise of Silas Lapham:* better to have one person miserable and two happy than to obey stale custom and have all three miserable. But in keeping with the opportunities of the New World, Miss Cameron, too, is rendered happy, for she is taken up by the Reverend Drummond, Finlay's superior even while he was rationalizing and procrastinating over his dilemma. Hugh's untested moral principles predictably break down in his new world of pragmatic experience—*and* under pressure of Advena's charm and common sense—and at last sight they are off to a mission post in Alberta to fulfil themselves. Quite clearly, Duncan is still close to the worlds of Frances Brooke or Jane Austen here, in her exploitation of the marriage theme, but what is of chief interest in this relationship is the process of conversion which is indicative of a genuine change in an individual's awareness of both himself and his world.

Initially at least, Advena's brother Lorne is far less realistic about his world than she is, though their town of Elgin in effect views him as its most promising young citizen. It is one of the fine ironic strokes of this novel that Lorne, who at the outset is totally ecstatic about things British, eventually loses his fiancée Dora Milburn to the Englishman Alfred Hesketh, whom he met while a member of a Canadian trade deputation to England. It is therefore appropriate that it is to Dora that he utters his rhapsody about what England signifies for him:

> "But I'll see England, Dora; I'll feel England, eat and drink and sleep and live in England, for a little while. Isn't the very name great? I'll be a better man for going, till I die. We're all right out here, but we're young and thin and weedy." (*I*, 98)

The uncritical nature of this outburst illustrates that Lorne, like Graham Trent of *Cousin Cinderella*, is in love with the *idea* of England rather than its reality, and like the Trents he, too, becomes somewhat disillusioned once he experiences England. Lorne is of course the imperialist of the title, and his coming to maturity at the outset of the novel is signalled by a number of accomplishments that Elgin seems eager to hand over to him: defence lawyer in a celebrated court case, secretary to a trade delegation, Liberal candidate in a by-election. Duncan deftly draws the parallel between these social manifestations of Lorne's maturity and his political attachment to British imperialism, and then subtly reverses the pattern: Elgin's increasing suspicion of imperialism is accompanied by Lorne's increasing isolation from his friends and family, and as Duncan reminds us in the last sentences of the novel, "for Lorne and for his country, we lose the thread of destiny" (*I*, 268).

It is while Lorne is in England that experience begins to modify his vision of his world and of himself. His impressions of England had derived in part from historical conditioning, from the legacy of colonialism in Canada which reinforced the idea that things English were superior to things North American. Like Mamie Wick and Graham Trent, Lorne thus becomes ecstatic about monuments, shrines, and buildings—visible manifestations of the greatness of England's past—but his disillusionment unconsciously begins to set in when he as a Canadian is rendered insignificant or even non-existent in the eyes of the English. I alluded earlier to his annoyance about being compelled to explain to the Britishers the distinction between an American and a Canadian, but the fundamental unimportance of the Canadian trade delegation emerges in the comments Duncan uses to describe the host country's reception, organized by Wallingham:

> There were other "colleagues" whose attendance he would have liked to compel; but one of them, deep in the country, was devoting his week-ends to his new French motor, and the other to the proofs of a book upon Neglected Periods of Mahommedan History, and both were at the breaking strain with overwork. (*I*, 113)

It is therefore perhaps not surprising that the Canadian delegation is soon ready to return. "They were glad, every one of them, to turn their faces to the West again. The unready conception of things, the political concentration upon parish affairs, the cumbrous social machinery, oppressed them with its dull anachronism in a marching world" (*I,* 125). This passage reflects Duncan's penetrating perception of the nature of an established social and political order, represented by the Old World; it is a notion of England that was later subscribed to, though articulated quite differently, by such exile writers as Wyndham Lewis in his *Self Condemned* and Malcolm Lowry in "Through the Panama."

Only in *Cousin Cinderella* is Duncan as pro-Canadian and anti-English as she is in *The Imperialist,* a sentiment which emerges quite strongly not only in her depiction of Alfred Hesketh, but quite appropriately, in her initial description of the Milburn family, linked eventually to Hesketh through his engagement to Dora Milburn. Dora is a flighty and inconstant character, given over to mannerisms and affectations, traits quite in keeping with the family that produced her:

> Mrs. Milburn and her sister . . . seemed to have inherited the strongest ideas . . . about keeping themselves *to* themselves. A strain of this kind is sometimes constant, even so far from the fountainhead, with its pleasing proof that such views were once the most general and the most sacred defence of middle-class firesides, and that Thackeray had, after all, a good deal to excuse him. Crossing the Atlantic they doubtless suffered some dilution; but all that was possible to conserve them under very adverse conditions Mrs. Milburn and Miss Filkin made it their duty to do . . . . It was recognized that there was "something about" Mrs. Milburn . . . that you did not come upon that thinness of nostril, and slope of shoulder, and set of elbow at every corner . . . . In this respect Dora Milburn, the only child, was said to be her mother's own daughter. The shoulders, at all events, testified to it; and the young lady had been taught to speak, like Mrs. Milburn, with what was known as an "English accent." (*I,* 48-9)

That Dora rejects Lorne in favour of Alfred Hesketh is therefore not surprising, and the reader wholeheartedly applauds Lorne's escape; with Hesketh and the Milburns to propagate what is left of the imperial theme, its future relevance is cast in some doubt. It is Stella, Lorne's younger sister, who has the last word on Hesketh: "[He] may pass in an English crowd, but over here he's just an ignorant young man" (*I,* 176), an assessment which proves resoundingly true when he speaks at Lorne's political meeting, and manages to offend every person in the hall by his condescending prattle about colonies and colonials. Forced by the taunts of the crowd to cut short his speech, he appropriately takes his seat in a schoolroom chair which, Duncan pointedly reminds us, "had been used once before that day to isolate conspicuous stupidity" (*I*, 195).

Though Duncan in this depiction of Hesketh is uncharacteristically sarcastic, she does not throughout this novel oversimplify the Old World-New World contrasts. Hesketh may be the novel's silliest individual, but Dora from the New World runs him a close second, and another Old World figure, Hugh Finlay, is surely the rational and balanced spokesman for Duncan on many occasions. Ultimately, however, Duncan opts for the New World here, as she has consistently done throughout her fiction, and Finlay's remarks to Advena reflect her abiding opinion of what this world means: "I have come here into a new world, of interests unknown and scope unguessed before . . . . One finds a physical freedom in which one's very soul seems to expand; one hears the happiest calls of fancy. And the most wonderful, most delighted thing of all is to discover that one is oneself . . ." (*I*, 140).

Cousin Cinderella, with its subtitle, "A Canadian Girl in London," seems at first glance to constitute a parallel to Duncan's earlier *American Girl,* but the resemblance ends with the title. Compared to Mary and Graham Trent, Mamie Wick seems in retrospect little more than a cardboard character, and in this later novel Duncan presents a number of solidly realized English individuals against whom we can genuinely measure the Trents. Issues and characters here are not artificially defined and juxtaposed as they frequently were in the earlier novel, and in many respects, *Cousin Cinderella* marks a new maturity in Duncan. As Thomas Tausky correctly points out, though the novel on one level seems to be merely a comedy of manners, it is "in fact . . . a shrewd and penetrating study of the psychology of cultural alienation."[6] It is unique among Duncan's novels of exile in that it is the only one where we are able to examine credible Canadian characters exclusively in an Old World cultural setting, and where we are therefore able to assess with some authority Duncan's attitudes towards her former homeland and its values.

We are helped in this task by Duncan's selection in Mary Trent of a sensitive and intelligent narrator, one of the most balanced and mature of all of Duncan's protagonists. Unlike Mamie Wick, she is not at the centre of the action, but rather on its edges, from which position she can focus on a number of characters who constitute the novel's central core—her brother Graham, the American Evelyn Dicey, and a number of English families, but particularly Lady Doleford, her son Peter and daughter Barbara Pavisay. We thus can observe the action and mannerisms of three national types, and on the whole in this Jamesian kind of novel, no one can be written off as excessively silly or gauche. Duncan's choice of a Canadian narrator undoubtedly reflects her own preference among these three national groups, and the drama of the novel substantially supports this perspective, though the final act in this drama, the engagement of Mary and Lord Doleford, ensures that an element of equivocality remains. She had earlier confided that Pavis Court would not be enough to seduce her into remaining in England, so we must assume that, like Jack and Orthodocia in *A Social Departure,* they will opt for Canada after marriage; Graham, on the other hand, was consistently attracted by English accomplishments, antiques, and buildings, and his engagement to Barbara was really an attachment to Pavis Court, and thus, on purely human grounds, required to be broken off.

Throughout the narrative, a number of English-Canadian oppositions emerge, and generally in these situations, the English (and the American Evelyn Dicey) tend to look somewhat silly. Canada is simply not regarded as having a reality of its own: it is still spoken of in terms of Upper and Lower Canada, its parliament is erroneously placed in Quebec, and when Lord Lippington is appointed Governor-General after much behind-the-scenes manipulation by his ambitious wife, they are predictably told, "It will be simply exile, of course, for you both" (*CC*, 297). Like Lorne Murchison of *The Imperialist* or the Pabbley group in *A Voyage of Consolation,* Graham is obliged on occasion to explain that he is not an American, and his explanation to Miss Game, whose flat they are to rent, stands perhaps as Duncan's own code in this matter:

> "We are not Americans, we are Canadians," replied Graham quite calmly, as if it were of no importance. "I would have been proud to be an American if it had happened that way; but as it didn't happen to happen I am prouder to be what I am." (*CC*, 20)

Miss Game's bewildered look, "as if she didn't see the necessity for pride in either case," constitutes a predictable response to the situation, but it is of the same derivation as Lady Doleford's question, "can one be at home out of England?" or Lady Lippington's gushy condescension about how Canada has "the greatest fascination" for her.

Graham's and Mary's responses in these situations reflect a maturity about the Canadian reality and identity, a consciousness of Canada's intrinsic worth that fictionally Duncan was among the first to exploit, and certainly the first to do with such artistry. There is a consistent moral dimension to Duncan's perspectives on her Old World-New World juxtapositions, and, in her later novels particularly, she rarely resorts to trickery to achieve her ends. Unlike Hinkson in *A Voyage of Consolation,* Mary does not believe that an enthusiasm for the Old World diminishes her respect for the New; to her, London is vastly superior in almost all respects to her home town of Minnebiac, but the London as represented by the dishonest and conniving

rental agent is morally inferior, and the England that will offer its Pavis
Courts to the highest marriage bidder is ultimately not worth defending.
Mary has a high regard for "the custom of the country," a regard that has not
always been reciprocated by those going in the opposite direction; that
Mary's trust in this particular case is eventually betrayed by the agent (and
perhaps by Miss Game) does not lessen its intrinsic merit. Both Mary and
Graham too, possess a sense of humour that allows them to turn the unfelici-
tous remarks of Britishers and Americans against those who utter them.
When Evelyn Dicey, for example, wonders why Graham and Mary are not
flattered by being called Americans, Graham replies, "we are, but our
modesty shrinks from any category but our own" (*CC*, 81).

Evelyn Dicey is not, however, the caricatured American that Hinkson
was, but like Henrietta Stackpole of James's *Portrait of a Lady,* she earns
both the admiration and the misgivings of her creator. In this novel she fulfils
a number of roles which depict her as the very antithesis of the American
innocent abroad: she initiates the Trents into social roles and situations they
would never experience in such touristy places as the Poets' Corner or the
National Gallery; she resolves, with a vigorous sense of expediency and
manipulation, the decaying Pavis Court situation; and she forthrightly and
somewhat sarcastically simplifies the differences between the American and
the Canadian. Though her ignorance of Canada is matched by that of the
Britishers, she is forgivable because of her lack of condescension, and her
explanation to the Trents of Canada's subservient position in Britain in
contrast to America's renders her specific ignorances irrelevant:

> "I expect Canadians are something new over here . . . . Americans
> were new once, and frequented Bloomsbury boarding-houses and brought
> introductions from Emerson and Thoreau, and wrote their experiences
> afterwards in the magazines. Now you are . . . . The fact is you haven't
> become foreigners yet—you still belong to them, so of course they think
> you're of no importance. Become foreigners, get Mr. Ambassador Bryce
> to come over and write you a Declaration of Independence, start a
> President, and take no further notice of them. They'll adore you." (*CC*,
> 76,77)

Duncan seems to use Evelyn, too, to demonstrate that when it comes to
manipulation and self-interest, the Americans and the English have very
little to teach each other. The narrator's comments that Evelyn speaks of
England "exactly as if she had shares in it " not only alludes to her family's
ownership of large chunks of the world, but of course anticipates her
eventual possession of Pavis Court. She is matched in this propensity by a
number of English women in this novel, as Mrs. Jarvis' shameless solicitation
to Mary quite adequately illustrates:

"You must have noticed that American men are very seldom absorbed in this country. American women, of course, go down like anything—we can't swallow them fast enough; but the men, somehow—no. But with your nice brother it's different. Colonial he certainly is, but only to the extent of a few mannerisms, which he would soon lose. Try to think of him as a country gentleman in England, and he's quite in the picture, isn't he? You and he together . . . might do a great deal for Canada in this country." (*CC*, 128)

In this respect, though he is both a product and a perpetrator of the English proclivity to control things, Lord Doleford is also a rational and sensitive analyst of this tendency. His relationship with Mary is less precipitous than is his sister's with Graham, but that it is the lasting one reflects their basic compatibility and respect for each other quite separate from such issues as domination and subservience. Doleford admits quite readily that he chose India over Canada because Canadians "run their own show," and he agrees with Mary's contention that there is more to life than this:

"I know. I suspect it's the mistake we make, we English, that we must always be in the management, wherever we go. The Colonies teach us better, but we're slow at seeing things. And there's always India to keep up the idea." (*CC*, 140)

England for him represents a kind of "penal servitude," a fact which, allied to Mary's view of Pavis Court, reinforces the idea that they will opt for Canada; like Hugh Finlay of *The Imperialist,* he undoubtedly is flexible and adaptive enough to accept the New World without necessarily having to "run the show"—and Mary is sufficiently like Advena to ensure that.

As with Lorne Murchison's in *The Imperialist,* Graham's and Mary's attitudes towards England range from an uncritical celebration to varying degrees of disillusionment. Graham is the more mercurial in this respect, and through Mary's narration, we can trace his transition from an exuberance born out of England's spectacles and history to a weariness deriving from his psychological responses to her people, whether as individuals or as a class. Graham's outburst late in the novel is in part a reaction against his breakup with Barbara, and in part his attempt to rationalize his own basic democratic attitude towards the excessive mannerisms of the class system. But it is Mary who, upon observing Graham walking with Lord Lippington's group on the dockside prior to embarkation, puts things into perspective:

I noticed what a difference sat upon Graham—something in his step and his shoulders and the outlook he expressed upon life—from the Lippingtons'

friends who were native to the island . . . who seemed already, as they
walked together, to have assumed the insular yoke. He, Graham, was
more free than they, more free of a thousand things—traditions and
conventions and responsibilities, privileges and commandments, interests and bores, advantages and disadvantages and fearful indispensable
sign-manuals. That was the great thing that was published in him
. . . , and surely it was something as precious in its way . . . as any
opportunity or any possession, something which gave even Pavis Court
one aspect of a mess of pottage. (*CC*, 309-10)

Mary's observation can quite reasonably be taken to reflect Duncan's own
attitudes, for they are consistent with her views as expressed in the half
dozen or so novels I have been discussing here. Some twenty years out of her
native Canada, Duncan was at this point at the height of her aritstic development,
and it is clear that her period of exile had produced not nostalgia or
bitterness, but a balanced and benevolent attitude towards the many societies she had experienced, and not least of all Canada. Throughout her
career, Canada remained for her, not something artificially elevated or rare,
and not something to be dismissed or ridiculed, but an intrinsic world of
experience, and rendered, I think, a little bit special through birth, residency,
and shaping influence.

4

The New World Triumphant

We saw in an earlier chapter that a recurring motif in the exile literature produced during Canada's formative years was that of the New World as an actual or a potential paradise. Given that most of this literature was non-fiction, that it reflected literal rather than imagined experiences, it is not surprising that what it revealed was a flawed Eden, one which was rendered memorable, but hardly perfect, by all the hardships and realities that "roughing it" really involved. This junction of the ideal and the experiential continues to inform much of the literature of the twentieth century, and it provides a consistent dramatic pattern in the fiction of such writers as Grove, Niven, Salverson, and Wilson. Though these writers on the whole celebrate the triumph of the New World over the Old, their fictional protagonists are not always at ease in their new situations, reflecting quite frequently the ambivalence and uncertainties of the more disturbed or unhappy exile figures.

   Not all these writers are exiles in the sense that I defined this term in my opening chapter: Laura Salverson was born in Winnipeg to Icelandic immigrants who had only recently arrived, and Ethel Wilson, born in South Africa to English parents, arrived in Canada at the age of ten, hardly time to be shaped or influenced by the Old World. But as with greatness, some writers have exile thrust upon them by conditions which lie beyond their control, by parental accident, and by parental conditioning. Such writers become witnesses to the history of a culture which shaped their parents or their guardians, more than they express a sense of personal alienation, though this element is not necessarily missing. They are exiles, therefore, in the sense that they have been nurtured in two opposing cultures, and though they are not infrequently comfortable in both, they also experience particular conflicts that arise from both. But rarely is there the note of bitterness or anguish in these writers that characterizes many of those who in their maturity were, for personal or artistic reasons, compelled to become exiles; Grove stands apart from the other three writers in this respect, for his celebration of the New World was, as we will see, a particularly painful experience in some respects.

We sometimes, too, apply retroactively the label of exile to writers who in actuality were perhaps only part of the great historical migration to the western world, as indeed Susanna Moodie herself was. To lament about being alienated from society is a romantic concept, and in some instances there might well be a tendency to overemphasize this psychological factor at the expense of historical imperatives; the stronger the fiction is, I suspect, the more valid it is to do this, though one must not rewrite history in the process. Laura Salverson's parents *did* leave Iceland for Canada because of an actual event, the great 1876 eruption of the Hekla volcano, but that Salverson could imaginatively reconstruct that episode as a dramatic prologue to her 1923 novel, *The Viking Heart*, helps to confirm her artistry and to see her protagonists as credible exiles in a new land.

On the whole the writers I am concerned with here tend to depict various New World paradises as potential rather than actual Edens—regions that rational and pragmatic man can modify and improve, avoiding the economic, social, and political forces of determinism that characterized their lives in the Old World. Of the works to be discussed, only Ethel Wilson's *The Innocent Traveller* projects an image of an untainted Eden, certainly one that does not need cultivating, as it were, though even here there are muted hints—the Benbow Island episode and the machinations of Yow—of a darker or a more uncertain world lying alongside the innocent one. These writers are closer in spirit to those of the nineteenth century than to that other twentieth-century celebrator of the New World, Malcolm Lowry, whose compulsive search for an Eden, as we will see in a subsequent chapter, was predicated on the premise that only an unspoiled wilderness, rather than a cultivated one, is worth attaining. For him, progress leads to dispossession; for the writers I am concerned with here, it leads to possession and consolidation. Their exile protagonists are like their nineteenth-century non-fiction fore-bears in that their voyage to the New World is in large part one of economic necessity, but of course it is easier in fiction, and more justifiable, to see this quest in other than literal terms: as a quest for identity, for self-discovery, or to discover a mythology that can replace the one that shaped their formative years.

Frederick Niven was born in exile, in Valparaiso, Chile, of Scottish parents, and spent a great deal of his life travelling back and forth between Scotland and the New World. In the strictest sense he was more of a celebrator of the frontier—the frontier of countries throughout the Western Hemisphere—than a writer imbued with a profound sense of exile. By far the most prolific of these writers—he wrote well over thirty novels and countless pieces of non-fiction—he is also the most uneven, for a disproportionate number of his novels are little more than romantic pot-boilers. In many respects something of a literary vagabond, Niven was equally at home in the fashionable salons of England and in the railway and lumber camps of British Columbia, and his early fiction reflects superficially the cultural and social realities of these diverse worlds. The novels which constitute his western trilogy— *The Flying Years* (1935), *Mine Inheritance* (1940), and *The Transplanted* (1944)—are in a sense more interesting for their documentary value than for their artistry, but *The Flying Years* in particular reflects a tension that derived in large part from Niven's attempts to resolve his lifelong Scottish-Canadian conflicts and loyalties.

In this novel, exile is a product of economic and social compulsion: the harsh eviction laws of Scotland drive the Munro family from their farm at Loch Brendan, and they emigrate to the Red River Settlement of western Canada, where the original Scottish settlers had arrived some four decades earlier. Behind this immediate necessity, however, other Old World forces operate—the legacy of '45, the conspiracies of the ruling classes and the clergy, the harsh rule of the British masters—so in many respects their exile is a blessing. But what they give up is painful and immeasurable, manifested most poignantly in the sudden drowning of young Robin Munro, an event that makes it impossible for the elder Munros ever to discard their commitment to Scotland. These circumstances produce aesthetically a tension that is to recur throughout the novel, articulated initially by Daniel Munro:

"Scotland," said Munro, and again, "Scotland. Just a few sad songs and old ballads! That's all. I see it getting worse every year. God knows what the end will be. And yet—and yet—we'll take Scotland with us: a kingdom of the mind."[1]

This ambivalent sentiment remains strong in the younger Angus Munro, the novel's chief protagonist, but increasingly as his life in the New World advances he can subscribe more unreservedly to his father's other attitude, blurted out as their steamer takes them away: "To hell with Scotland!" (15)

That this curse has both a personal and a social justification does not make their departure easier, and Mrs. Munro in particular is haunted by it until her death, which occurs shortly after they reach their new land. The family members reflect all the standard responses to exile—uncertainty, bravado, isolation, fear—but the mother's action, willing herself *not* to live, is the exile's ultimate recourse:

"She will tak' nae nourishment," the Scots physician's voice came huskily. "If she could but have taken into her blood some nourishment . . . " His voice dropped, and in a tone of sad complaint he ended, "but she will not assimilate." (24)

Both the physiological and the psychological connotations of "assimilate" apply to Mrs. Munro, and she attains that release which exiles throughout the ages have pined for in their lamentations of anguish and self-pity. The death of both the elder Munros is a large step in the cancellation of the Old World legacies, but though the younger Angus does "assimilate" himself fairly thoroughly into the New World, he never completely forsakes that earlier legacy.

As in *Emily Montague* and *Roughing It,* the initial description of the New World in *The Flying Years* is couched in paradisal imagery:

> The odours of the new land, before they had sighted it, came out to meet them through a white mist over the sea, odours of robustiously scented forests. The steamer crawled on, calling and calling with her siren till the vapour was dazzlingly infiltrated with sunlight and then, by the sunlight, dissipated away — and there were rocky promontories glittering a welcome. (16)

Appropriately, this opening scene of the second chapter suggests a kind of cosmic rebirth, which stands juxtaposed against the image of a dying world at the close of the previous chapter: "It was as if Nature held breath, as if the spinning of the world ceased a moment" — a death marked by "the sound of bagpipes . . . in the slow measure of a coronach" (16). This recurring Old World-New World, death-rebirth, polarity is emphasized by a number of narrative episodes and characters, and not surprisingly, given the Calvinist roots of Niven's world, by timely biblical injunctions. The Munros' arrival in Red River is celebrated by a modest feast laid on by the Frasers, and it is appropriate that the Scripture reading is from Revelations, the most apocalyptic book of the New Testament: *"Shall hunger no more, neither thirst any more"* (20) a prophecy that contrasts the plenitude of the New World with the impoverishment of the Old.

Angus, to whom these words "meant the new land," rises fully replenished from this feast, and in the literal sense he never does hunger again, but his psychological assimilation is not so easily attained. He does, it is true, experience initially a vast release in the New World, brought on in part by his parents' deaths, and in part by his discovery of the limitlessness of the West, of the Rocky Mountains, physical manifestations of his visions from *Revelations.* He is beset by a welter of confusion and anticipation, by a spiritual awareness that "something happened to him beyond his power to express; something happened, wordless, like music" (34). In one sense, this natural world that Angus discovers transcends or cancels out all history, including the legends and legacies of Scotland, and thus it emerges as a scene of creation juxtaposed against the episode of dissolution that marked the beginning of

Angus's exile. But the hermit in *Emily Montague* notwithstanding, even an exile cannot live long alone, and Angus's liaison with the Cree girl Minota marks a further stage in his assimilation, though it also launches him into a world that he cannot really understand, and that he ultimately helps to destroy.

His "marriage" to Minota represents symbolically a total immersion into the New World, a world that existed before the Europeans arrived and as he realizes, it is clearly "another step away from Loch Brendan" (47). He learns the language of the Indians (something, we will recall, that Colonel Rivers was unwilling to do), a necessary step in the total integration of the exile, but he is to find that this cuts two ways. The elemental rhythms of the Cree, the legends and superstitions that Minota teaches him, all transport him back to the Old Testament chants and Hebrew myths of his Scottish youth, and increasingly he finds himself looking both ways. Significantly, his "marriage" to Minota is not a total commitment in the traditional religious sense, but merely a ceremonial signing in a book; it is the kind of marriage that both can opt out of, as indeed happens. Angus returns to Scotland, Minota to her own people, but the price she pays is high: she gives birth to Angus's son, and shortly afterwards dies during an epidemic of measles, a white man's disease. Angus therefore unwittingly conveys both life and death upon her, and though he ultimately discovers and pays tribute to his son, his betrayal of Minota haunts him for the rest of his life.

Minota's death of course allows Niven to resolve this novel in the pattern of romantic fiction: Angus is now free to marry Fiona Fraser, "one of his own kind," and to establish himself as an influential member of the ruling class of his new land. His paternalism towards the Indians is rendered a bit more acceptable through his continuing concern for his son and grandson, but he stops far short of a total integration with these indigenous people. Niven's choice of words occasionally betrays his ultimate inability to alter his belief in white superiority—Mrs. Hodges, for example, is described as "an English *lady*," as opposed to Minota, "an Indian *woman*" (my italics), and in spite of Mrs. Hodges' silly nature, it would go too far to credit Niven with a sense of irony in this particular case. There is no question but that Angus is enriched by his marriage to Minota and his subsequent relationship with other Indians, and in that regard he achieves psychologically a strong measure of integration. It is his own private accomplishment, never revealed to Fiona or their son, and only in his old age, long after their deaths, does he confide his secret to his lifelong friend, Sam Douglas. In a sense, this confession expiates his guilt over his betrayal of Minota, though he has already paid an ironic price: his own son by Fiona is killed in World War I, while his grandson by Minota survives.

Just prior to that war, Angus makes the exile's obligatory return trip to his native land, accompanied by his wife and son, to visit the Loch Brendan farm from which he had been evicted a half century earlier. Ordered off by the local gamekeeper, he refuses to leave, and thus is now able to frustrate the same forces that caused his exile in the first place: "Angus was suddenly proud of an emotion that possessed him. His Scotland was perhaps chiefly a kingdom of the mind, but he had learnt something in that other country, his country of exile and adoption . . . and he was glad" (238). His polite defiance of the gamekeeper's commands constitutes a variation of his father's earlier "To hell with Scotland" imprecation, and his acknowledgment that "his country of exile and adoption" now has priority in the shaping of his responses bespeaks a clear moral triumph of the New World over the Old.

Like Frederick Niven, Laura Goodman Salverson was the inheritor of a historical and cultural legacy that never really left her, though like him, too, she viewed the New World in overwhelmingly positive terms. Born in Winnipeg to Icelandic parents who had emigrated three years earlier, she grew up nurtured by the sagas and legends of that Scandinavian culture, and in many respects her most important novel, *The Viking Heart* (1923), constitutes her attempt to create her own Icelandic Saga in the New World. That she does not completely succeed is a failure in artistic execution rather than overall conception: all too frequently, especially when dealing with second-generation Icelanders, she takes refuge in the clichés of historical romance, and fails to exploit convincingly the perturbations of the immigrant or exile mind. Perhaps her main contribution to the literature of exile in Canada is her depiction of immigrants who successfully embrace two worlds: they retain their original language and culture, yet they partake fully of those of the New World, and this sounds a new note in Canadian literature.

There is an interesting parallel between *The Viking Heart* and *The Flying Years*, aside from the fact that they are largely episodic in structure, with the inevitable sacrifice of characterization in the process. More significantly, in terms of how Salverson and Niven view exile in its human implications, they both use individual deaths within families as a device to frame their novels, though not surprisingly, given the romantic textures of these works, the deaths in question are somewhat heroic in nature, stylized and happening off stage, as it were. In *The Flying Years*, we recall, young Robin Munro perished in the stormy fjord off Loch Brendan on the eve of the Munros' eviction, while the second generation son Daniel died for Canada on the French battlefields of World War I. In *The Viking Heart,* Carl Halsson dies in the volcanic eruption that precipitates the Icelanders' exile to the New World, and forty years later young Thor Lindal dies in the same war. In this way, the authors dramatize the duality that the exile characteristically experiences, but that they depict the second-generation sons electing to die *for* a country, rather than being the victims of a malicious fate, suggests a moral superiority inherent in the New World.

In the strictest sense, Salverson's protagonists are exiles twice removed, for historically Iceland was itself settled by exiles from Scandinavia proper, driven out, much like Niven's Scottish exiles, by harsh social and economic conditions. Ironically, then, Iceland was at one time regarded as a paradise of sorts, an unknown world in which to start a new life, and one of the strengths of Salverson's novel is the manner in which she depicts realistically and symbolically the destruction of this paradise. The actual event was the great Hekla volcanic eruption of 1876, but behind this dramatic compulsion there are sufficient hints that social and personal forces were at work upon the potential exile. Ironically, it is the most restless of the Halsson family, the most eager to make a move, who is killed in the eruption trying to save his sheepdog, and thus he emerges as a heroic and tangible reminder of what was good in the Old World. Salverson's description here clearly links Carl with the exiles and heroes of the Viking sagas:

Carl's eyes were alight with the dreams of distant places. The old restlessness of the ancient Norsemen—a longing for the new and the strange—a desire which has never wholly left their descendants, was awake in his young veins.[2]

In its social components, however, Salverson's Old World, like Ethel Wilson's in *The Innocent Traveller*, is benign and well-ordered, unlike Niven's Scotland, which tends to be narrow, Calvinistic, and lacking in charity. The father's readings from the Old Testament psalms suggest, however, that the divine order is not without its threats, with words like "merciful" and "gracious" and "plenteous" being counterbalanced by more ominous ones: "anger" and "chide" and "sins" and "iniquities." Indeed, God's anger is manifested in the subsequent volcanic eruption, bringing about the destruction of this world while the New World is for the Halsson family not much more than rumour or speculation. "Einar pulled at the oars as only those who are bred to the water can. Behind him was a belching furnace, ruined hopes, and death. Ahead lay the open sea and life" (21). That they go to a place named Gimli may be a matter of historical fact, but "Gimli" has a mythological dimension as well, for it is "the new heaven and the new earth in the faith of the Norsemen" (40). It is a place, therefore, where the ideal and the real can be simultaneously achieved, though Salverson is realist enough here to recognize that this "low swampy place" is "named rather prematurely Gimli" (40). Still, it is not the rocks and fires of Iceland, and on the whole the Darwinian image of a world evolving from a swamp is not at all inappropriate.

But paradise for these Icelandic exiles is like the paradise Susanna Moodie experienced at Grosse Isle: it is almost immediately transformed into a kind of hell by separation, by pestilence, by death. The five original members of the Halsson family are soon reduced to one, and the rest of *The Viking Heart* becomes a chronicle of what happens to Borga, of how in effect she sustains virtually intact the Icelandic community in her new land. Unlike a novel like John Marlyn's *Under the Ribs of Death,* for example, whose Hungarian protagonist assimilates totally by anglicizing his name and becoming indistinguishable from the indigenous Canadians, Salverson's novel celebrates the possibility of cultural duality, and the importance of not forsaking one's heritage.

Appropriately, then, the novel proper, after the long prologue, "They That Go Before," begins with the birth of Borga's son Thor, and ends with his death, which coincides with the birth of Thor II to her daughter Elizabeth. Much romantic claptrap attends all this, like Byronic epigraphs, raging storms, sailings into the sunset, and the like, for of course Thor is much more than Borga's son: he is both in name and spirit the earthly representative of Norse mythology with a mandate to preside over the establishment of a Norse Kingdom in the New World. The attributes of a Viking heart that he possesses—strength, courage, loyalty, faithfulness—must ultimately be put to a final test, and therefore his death in the mud of Passchendaele emerges as an obligatory epic device rather than an aesthetically satisfying requirement of realistic fiction. Because Salverson projects an optimistic rather than a tragic vision of life in this novel, it would be a distortion to interpret Thor's death, and those of his forebears at Gimli, as the price the exile pays for attempted assimilation—an interpretation not out of place in a novel like Moore's *An Answer from Limbo* or Lewis's *Self Condemned.* The New World triumphs in *The Viking Heart,* as it does in *The Flying Years,* because it does shape people like Thor and Dan Munro, not perhaps a wholly popular notion today, but unquestionably one that found a measure of support between the wars.

What Salverson attempted to do fictionally in *The Viking Heart* she does in many respects more convincingly in her autobiography, *Confessions of an Immigrant's Daughter* (1939), for here the actual events of her life convey a vision, and a sense of reality frequently missing in the earlier work. There is an epic sweep here, as there is in Moodie's *Roughing It* or in Grove's two *Search* books, and in all cases the image produced of the individual exile searching for a home and an identity in the formlessness of the New World is a memorable one. Chapter titles in Salverson's book spell out the odyssey of the exile—"The First Horizon," "Introduction to Exile," "First Taste of the New World," "The World Enlarges," "I Settle in My Own Country"—a device not unlike that which Grove had used over a decade earlier in *A Search for America.* Salverson quickly zeroes in, however, on the human implications of exile for her parents, recalling that her mother's fears on this voyage seemed to have both marital and cosmic derivations:

"Now this I will not endure," she had said, with hard, quiet finality. Other things, too, she had said, which the child could not understand, but now she realized that this race through the night was an effort to get away from the things her mother would not endure. And somehow she knew it was not just the wolves her mother heard in this awful clamour, but the savage tongues of this dark land, itself the voice of the wilderness for which her mother had no heart and against which she fought with a cold determined resolution.[3]

The elder Mrs. Munro, we recall from *The Flying Years,* willed herself to die upon reaching the New World, but here Mrs. Gudman (as the name was originally spelled) experiences gradually the ameliorating power of this world. "It was a miracle," the youthful Laura records, recalling an act of kindness by a local doctor, "that melted some of mamma's bitterness against what had always been little better than humiliating exile" (43). Juxtaposed against what they encounter at the outset in the New World—and it is not all pleasant—is a lengthy account of their Icelandic ancestors and their world, an account that is a mixture of fact and legend; significantly, the mother increasingly takes refuge (as many exiles do) in the safety of far-off legend rather than remember the realities of her immediate past. Laura's father, on the other hand, emerges as a kind of eager adventurer, a perpetual traveller, not unlike the Lowry protagonist forever in search of some unevictable paradise. Both ultimately are rendered stronger in the New World, and Salverson proudly implies that this survival quality is very much linked to that exhibited by the original Icelandic exiles: "As Norsemen, they had so loved liberty that rather than accede to the demands of a king whose policy of beneficent dictatorship offended their ancient rights, they chose exile on a barren island at the world's end" (96).

Salverson herself seems to have inherited a bit of the exile spirit from her father, for very early in life she found herself "dimly aware that strange, alien powers existed beyond [her] little bowl" (62). This characteristic she later enlarges to embrace what she considers the qualities of the "true Icelander": a downplaying of materialism, a celebration of the intellect, a concern for the abstract and the spiritual, and making one of her first judgments about the shortcomings of the New World, implies that these are largely missing in Canada. "No doubt these pleasant conceits will be wiped out of us in this enlightened country, Canada," she muses, "where everything from a baby's bonnet to a literary masterpiece is conscientiously gauged by dollars and cents" (149). Sarcasm is of course a fairly standard response to a new land indulged in by the exile, as the fiction of Lewis, Lowry, and Moore reflects to

varying degrees. In Salverson it is less characteristic—she was not of course
an exile in the same sense as the others—but it underlies a few of the
observations she makes about Canada in her autobiography. On the eve of
one of their many moves, this time to the United States, she conveys an
attitude towards Canada which probably reflects her father's mercurial
temperament, and which also is not all that flattering to the English:

> Canada wasn't much of a country anyhow. So far as she had been able to
> make out, not even the English thought of it in favourable light. It was
> nothing but the hapless hunting ground for misbegotten upstarts who
> dreamt of easy fortunes with which to dazzle other fools back home.
> (219)

Confessions of an Immigrant's Daughter is not of course entirely about
the nature of an exile mind, for it explores tentatively but sensitively such
emerging issues as the place of women in the scheme of things; not for
nothing did Salverson dedicate her second novel, *When Sparrows Fall*
(1925), to Nellie McClung. In the latter portions of *Confessions* she links her
own development as a novelist to this issue, also recalling her epiphany-like
revelations about the meaning of words and the meaning of her name, as for
the first time in her life, she wrote her name and address on a library card:

> They stared up at me from the face of the card, and seemed to say: Now
> you have really come into being. This is yourself, this string of wobbly
> ovals. This is your passport into the world of men. (298)

Early in her writing career she knew clearly what she wanted to accomplish:
"to write a story which would define the price any foreign group must pay for
its place in the national life of the country of its adoption" (509), and out of
this credo came *The Viking Heart*. Years later she met other Canadian
writers, including Nellie McClung, which occasion she used in retrospect to
contrast Canada unfavourably with Iceland:

> It was a pleasant evening, and I was purring with contentment that a
> woman both celebrated and handsome was free of all vanity and pretence.
> Yet I was a little disappointed that nothing was said of books, as such. I
> had, without being conscious of it, I suppose, a purely European attitude.
> I should have liked the guest of honour to hold forth in fine Bjornson
> style on some aspect of politics, or discourse upon points of literature
> after the famed Anatole France pattern. Certainly I could not imagine
> any group of Icelandic intellectuals behaving so mildly! (502-3)

Like her contemporary, Frederick Philip Grove, Salverson was occasionally guilty of striking a pose, and perhaps even of name-dropping (there is little evidence in her own work, for example, of Bjornson's grim realism). Nevertheless, her concern about Canada's deficient literary scene at the time was valid, even though she herself did not over the long run contribute to it as much as *The Viking Heart* gave early promise that she might.

Her criticism of Canada went well beyond the state of the arts: upon her return from the United States to resume her residency in Winnipeg, she noted how contemptuous Canadians as a whole are about their country, and she found their "deprecating manner" in sharp contrast to the attitudes in the United States, "a country that believed in its own destiny, and took pride in American endeavour" (450). Salverson is not alone in unfavourably contrasting Canadians with Americans: as we saw in the preceding chapter, this note echoes through much of Sara Duncan's work, and Mavis Gallant in her short story, "In Youth Is Pleasure," depicts the youthful Linnet Muir experiencing virtually the same response as Salverson when she returns from New York to reside in Montreal. Clearly, these are not all defensive stances on the part of an insecure exile, but rather they seem to imply something significant about the nature of the Canadian psyche itself. Like Grove, Salverson thought that Canadian society could be immeasurably enriched by an appropriate blending of Old World culture, and this is the ideal that is dramatized in both *The Viking Heart* and *Confessions of an Immigrant's Daughter:* the New World does triumph over the Old, but only if it incorporates, with appropriate modifications, what is worth preserving from the Old.

This kind of dual loyalty is in large part shared by another of Salverson's contemporaries (in age rather than career) who, like her, was shaped, as far as direct experience is concerned, almost entirely by the New World. Born to English parents in Port Elizabeth, South Africa, Ethel Wilson was orphaned by the age of nine and sent to Vancouver to be raised by her maternal grandmother and various aunts, themselves fairly recent arrivals from England. Educated in both British Columbia and England, she pursued a teaching career in her adopted province for well over a decade, and in 1921 married a prominent physician with whom over the next three decades or so she travelled extensively throughout Canada and the world. Though she wrote a series of juvenile tales and sketches for the Vancouver *Province* in 1919, it was much later that she embarked upon a permanent writing career, publishing her first short story at the age of forty-seven and her first novel at fifty-seven. Four other novels and a collection of short stories appeared over the next decade and a half, and her last pieces, two short stories and an essay, were published in 1964.

This brief summation suggests a mind slowly and carefully nurtured, one that seems to belong more to the settled values of an earlier time than to the turbulence of the nuclear age. But the artistic and moral vision she reflects in much of her fiction reveals a writer well in tune with the ambiguous realities of the post-World War II period; furthermore, she demonstrates superbly that the most traditional novelist in terms of style and technique can very precisely exploit and order the contradictions of experience, often held to be the exclusive province of our more experimental writers. It is true that on another level Wilson emerges as one of the most consistent of Canada's regional realists, for almost all her short stories and all her novels reflect the strong attachment she has to British Columbia, a response that she admits has very clearly shaped her artistic credo:

> I see my Canadianness, for example, in that my locale in a sustained piece of writing (that is, in a book) has to be British Columbia. There are other places in the world that I know and love, but none that I know, and feel, and love in the same way. But I did not choose it. It chose. It is very strong.[4]

Throughout her fiction, but most consistently in *Hetty Dorval* (1947), *Swamp Angel* (1954), and *Love and Salt Water* (1956), she celebrates the physical facts of British Columbia—its rivers and lakes, its mountains, its coastal inlets—frequently transforming these realities into their metaphorical or symbolic dimensions. And where the Old World does take over momentarily in these novels, or more substantially, in two or three of her short stories and in *The Innocent Traveller* (1949), it is characteristically juxtaposed against some beneficence or possibility inherent in the New.

As with Salverson, Wilson's admiration for the Old World was largely a product of family inculcation or transmitted belief rather than of extended personal participation in that world, though undoubtedly her extensive travelling contributed to her international perspective. Sometimes, as in the short story, "Haply the Soul of My Grandmother," the world that is discovered is an unsettling one, for there Mrs. Forrester, ever "susceptible to the power of Place," finds the tombs and temples of the Nile valley frightening in their ancientness and darkness. Juxtaposed in her mind against British Columbia, or the prairies, or such familiar parts of the Old World as Devon, London, or Greece, this country, she reflects, "made her uneasy. It was too old and strange."[5] But it is a fear that emanates from much more than the immediate physical reality of what she discovers in Egypt; rather, it derives, as so much does in Wilson, from a hint of the irrational or inexplicable, and it poses a threat to human relationships and stability:

> It's odd . . . that I am Canadian and am fair, and have my roots in that part of England which was ravaged and settled by blond Norsemen; and

[my husband] is Canadian and is dark, and before generations of being Canadian he was Irish, and before generations of being Irish—did the dark Phoenicians come?—and he finds no strangeness here and I do. (26)

In another story, " We Have to Sit Opposite," this sense of alienation is manifested in a kind of absurd paranoia, and again it is Mrs. Forrester who confronts a seemingly inflexible and irrational force. This time, on board a Salzburg to Munich train, it is the logic of a Germanic mind, to which she responds initially with frustration and fear, but which, she decides on a sudden impulse, she can confound through her own absurd interpretation of reality. What ensues constitutes in a sense merely a version of the New World tall tale, with its obligatory ingredients of bears and Canada's arctic climate, but it serves its purpose. The pragmatism and imaginativeness of the New World, in the persons of Mrs. Forrester and Mrs. Montrose, triumph over the inflexibility and suspicion of the Old, but for a moment we are confronted with a vision of what this kind of Germanic logic can lead to:

She pondered on the collective mentality that occupied the seat near to them . . . and its results which now filled the atmosphere of the carriage so unpleasantly. She had met this mentality before, but had not been closely confined with it, as now. What of a world in which this mentality might ever become dominant? Then one would be confined with it without appeal or relief. (59)

Such visions of a disturbing or threatening world are not all that uncommon in Wilson, for of her five novels it is only in *The Innocent Traveller* that these hints are comfortably subordinated to a prevailing optimism. In its portrayal of the effects of exile, too, this novel stands apart from virtually all the twentieth-century novels being examined in this book; its affinity is more with the fiction of Sara Jeannette Duncan or with Catharine Parr Traill's *Backwoods of Canada,* works that generally reflect a favourable attitude towards the New World, though it is clear that this generalization does not hold consistently for either Wilson or Duncan. In both cases, beneath their surface optimism, beneath the simplicity of their polished prose styles, appear occasional glimpses of a world that is not entirely ordered, of experiences that are potentially disruptive, though these disturbing elements, it is true, are rarely pursued to any length in these writers.

On the levels of realism and history, *The Innocent Traveller* constitutes a chronicle of migrations, of the dispersal of British families to various outposts of the Empire, and to this extent offers a fictional verification of the kind of situation that in part governed the Moodies and the Traills. But as a novel with a life and justification of its own, it transforms this surface reality into the components governing the psychological and moral growth of one of the migrating individuals. And as we follow Topaz Edgeworth through her century-long life, we become witness, too, to the emergence of a part of the New World that literally was not in existence at the start of her life. One of Wilson's major achievements in this novel is the unobtrusive way she juxtaposes a solid world of Victorian certainties, a seemingly permanent Old World, against an anticipated New World in which Topaz will spend precisely half her long life, and where she will eventually die. The implication of the novel's title is not unlike that suggested by Lowry's *The Voyage that Never Ends,* reflecting as it does the exile in a state of perpetual movement and growth, though Topaz is not part of the multiple protagonist we find in the separate episodes of Lowry's works. She does take on layers of experience that progressively transform and modify her, but as the title also implies, she never loses that childlike curiosity about the world that characterizes her first appearance on the novel's opening page.

Wilson chooses an appropriate approach and technique to convey the inseparability of innocence and experience as far as Topaz is concerned; hers is a qualitative kind, akin to a Blakean innocence that is never eroded by exposure to the world, whereas Frankie Burnaby's in *Hetty Dorval,* for example, is quantitative in nature, progressively reduced by the encroachments of experience. What is involved in *The Innocent Traveller* is first of all an expansion of space, from the circumscribed area beneath the Edgeworth dining table in the town of Ware in Staffordshire, to the new nation of Canada, and by implication the whole New World just coming into being, or at least into the consciousness of the people of the Old World. Second, there is an accompanying or parallel expansion of time, from a specific moment where the occasion is clear, and human relationships precisely defined, to a diffused segment of time where events and relationships are telescoped and lacking in proportionate significance. Topaz's entire life can within these perspectives be viewed as her subconscious obsession to effect a harmony between time and place, between event and herself, between herself and the world she happens for the moment to occupy. "All the journeys of Topaz," we are told, "whether great or small, were packed with adventure and reminiscence. The world blossomed daily into incident; and so the years passed too quickly."[6]

Topaz's first journey is, significantly, one in a counter-clockwise direction, as she moves from one pair of feet to another beneath the dining table. There she had been sent for refusing to observe the prevailing order that governed the ritual of dining in the Edgeworth home, particularly when so illustrious a guest as Matthew Arnold is present. Thus from the outset of her life she displays the characteristics that are to mark her as a perpetual rebel or exile, and virtually every incident from this point on that directly involves her can be viewed in terms of a conflict between decorum and impropriety. Interestingly, too, her initial response to the other travellers of her world (and she gives us a rundown of their voyages as she proceeds around the table) is with respect to their feet; reality for Wilson, as for Hopkins, implies the necessity of "having trod" upon the firmament, and Topaz at her mother's funeral is described as "the youngest walker of the family."

Above the table, all is apparent order. Indeed, one is tempted to say divine order, for with Joseph at one end and Mary at the other, and Mr. Arnold, the apostle of "sweetness and light," giving the sermon, so to speak, the Edgeworth world seems to be a blessed world in every respect. But though the benign spirit generated by this New Testament-like tableau continues to inform the worlds that Topaz inhabits, there are signs that what is being presided over is the end of an order: Arnold's advanced views on education, the proleptic announcements of various deaths, including Mrs. Edgeworth's, references to marriages and children and migrations—all these factors antici-pate the changes that are to strike this family and the kind of world it represents. Formally, the opening scene is remarkable in its evocation of the novel's recurring themes—the roles of innocence and education, the inter-play of past, present, and future, and the tension between a fixed order and the forces that can disrupt it. And though in the literal sense Wilson is correct when she states that "above the table the future hung implicit, almost palpable, around the family" (7), the real future of the family is Topaz, now asleep beneath the table, and who has already given us the future of all the members of the family. And of course in reality the family does quickly disperse and disintegrate, for fathers suddenly become grandfathers and then great-grandfathers, and aunts, great-aunts, and nieces become increas-ingly difficult to sort out. All these consequences of time and place are given a quiet harmony and inevitability through Wilson's incremental patterning and structuring of this novel.

Topaz alone appears to emerge unchanged by the unfolding of events, for upon attaining her majority at the age of fifty, she is described as "only a girl grown old." In a very real sense, she remains a passionate pilgrim all her life, for whatever part of the world she is in, or whether she views it via maps or more directly, she acts as a catalytic agent to transform it into a place of infinite wonder and possibility. She defines herself by what she experiences at the moment, not by a role that others think she should assume, nor by what she possesses. "She travelled light,' Wilson tells us, borrowing an image from Forster's Mr. Fielding. "A native toughness enabled her to carry her few strong loyalties without inconvenience to herself, but for the rest, the joy of living was daily renewed in her and was seldom checked by things, people, or events" (103). It is this largeness of spirit, this hunger for life's possibilities, this refusal to be restricted by time and place, that transform her exile from Ware into an experience of anticipation rather than one of regret. Her enthusiasm for her new country never palls, and is shared by those who accompany her. "I'm so glad I came to this country I can't tell you!" exclaims her niece Rachel. "Why didn't we come before? It's my kind of country and I never want to go home again" (113).

There are sufficient hints throughout the first part of this novel about the nature of the Old and the New Worlds to indicate where Wilson's preference ultimately lies. Though the world ruled over by people like Joseph Edgeworth is ordered and comfortable for its immediate inhabitants, it is nevertheless a world "to which . . . Mr. Charles Dickens and others had begun to call their attention" (40), and at ninety, Joseph has long been bypassed by the Dickensian reality that everywhere informs the Victorian world:

> Great-Grandfather Edgeworth was a kind and just employer, but he accepted without question what he saw, and he saw a world at last become static. His imagination . . . did not pierce the squalor of the Poor so near at hand in the grim town. The Poor took their familiar deplorable place in squalor, and it would have seemed a novel and disturbing idea to Great-Grandfather Edgeworth that the Poor should reasonably aspire to eat well, drink well, live well, and die well. Not wrong of course, but chimerical. Each age, like our own, has its large blind spots. The social conscience was stirring but not awake. Great-Grandfather Edgeworth was a product of the ages which preceded the young Victoria. Here he was, sleeping in the garden, ninety years old, an upright old man in a world which he really thought was upright. (74)

Juxtaposed against this is a New World, a "yet unnamed place far away where some day Topaz Edgeworth would live and die" (36-37), but long before that, at Mrs. Edgeworth's funeral, Wilson alludes to the flexibility and adaptability of the New World inhabitant when facing the shifting realities of the modern world. Here Wilson assumes the roles of both Topaz and the omniscient narrator, and directly enlists the support of the reader:

> If Father had ever faltered in his faith, how deep would have been the crack, the fissure, the ultimate chasm into which he would have fallen. You and I, who pick our way unsurely amongst the appalling wreckage of our time, patching the crack here, avoiding the split there, anticipating the unsure footing, rejoicing in a bit of solid ground and going ahead until we again trip and fall on our noses—we can take our troubles much more easily than Father could have done. (9-10)

It is true, of course, that in *The Innocent Traveller* the troubles that the
exiles to the New World do eventually encounter are hardly shattering,
compared, for example, to what happens in a novel like *The Equations of
Love*. But Annie, Rachel, and Topaz all cope flexibly with the new situations
they face almost from the moment they board their ship, with only Annie,
"now several times the Grandmother," experiencing anything approaching
the traumatic.

It is appropriate that the chapter which constitutes the transition between
the Old World and the New, "The Journey," is by far the longest in the novel,
underscoring as it does both the literal and the symbolic dimensions of the
step being taken. The literal journey for these three women, though unquestionably a long one, is nevertheless a much easier one than was the case for
the Munros in *The Flying Years* or the Halssons in *The Viking Heart*,
travelling as they are in relative comfort to a home already prepared for them
in Vancouver. Thus, in their particular situation, the lament of "leaving
behind them all the familiar safe things" is only a faint echo of what such a
loss has normally meant for exiles, and it is quickly superseded by the
realization that in the New World "life extended immeasurably and
intoxicatingly," a revelation that fills Topaz with particular joy when at last
they reach their destination:

> British Columbia stretched before her, exciting her with its mountains,
> its forests, the Pacific Ocean, the new little frontier town, and all the new
> people. Here was no time limit, no fortnight's holiday. Here she had
> come to live; and, drawing long breaths of opulent air, she began to run
> about, and dance for joy, exclaiming, all through the open country. (122)

This response to the world is of course in keeping with the irrepressible
nature she has exhibited from the very beginning, when she told Matthew
Arnold that their new toilet goes "woosh, woosh!" or when on the continental tour with her brother John she "exclaimed all day every day in Paris," or,
when on the train crossing Canada, she impulsively visits the gentlemen's
smoking car. "We've come to a free country, haven't we?" she rationalizes to
her sister and niece. "Now that you've come to Canada, you know, you'll
have to be less conventional, you know" (109). There is no lamentation or
self-pity in these three exiles as they cross their new land: too much is
exciting and visually beautiful, there is frequent occasion for jesting about
Canadian place names, or being gulled by fanciful tales of the West. Only
occasionally does a dark note disturb this harmony, a recurring device
Wilson uses throughout her fiction to remind us, as she does in *Love and Salt
Water*, that wherever we are in the world "most things are dangerous.
Nothing is safe." On a brief stop in Regina, Topaz wonders aloud to an

elderly gentleman why people do not flock to the prairie's open spaces, and receives a grim reply:

> "Jever spend the winter on a prurrie farm, outer sight of any human bean? . . . . Well, I spent twenny-five of them. There's women can't stand it. Asylums full of farmers' wives can't stand it. Drives 'em crazy. The prurrie don't always look like this." (117)

This scene, not unlike one that Sara Jeannette Duncan portrayed in *A Social Departure,* is one of three or four in this novel that Wilson uses to remind us that though the New World is on the whole paradisal, it is not without its darker side.

But in keeping with her somewhat shallow nature, Topaz is not deeply moved by this grim tale, only momentarily horrified, and then, "rearranging her feelings," turns to look at some Indians. For Annie, on the other hand, the entire voyage has far more profound implications, and though she reflects throughout her long life a kind of spiritual gentleness and charity towards all things, she does wonder if she is too old "to be able to assimilate great change" (111). We have already seen, however, in an incident on board ship involving the American actor Otis Skinner, that she is capable of change, though the experience is an unsettling one. Wilson here dramatizes quietly but convincingly how one's garrison view of reality can begin to disintegrate:

> The Grandmother went quietly to her cabin after the service, spiritually refreshed but a little shaken too. A crack had appeared in one of her tiny strong bastions. Some stones had fallen out and a fresh air was blowing in. Through the aperture Grannie saw a disturbing view that she had not seen before. Her so-sure condemnation of the Stage was now not so sure. (95)

And characteristically, over the years Annie is to translate this modified view of the stage into a charitable view of Americans in general and of the entire American nation. The garrison view of the New World, as we first encountered it in *Emily Montague,* has retained a stubborn presence in exile literature in Canada, but Wilson shares with relatively few others, notably Lowry and Moore, the vision to see it superseded by one deriving from the indigenous reality of the New World.

Quite clearly, the three Edgeworth women did not go into exile strictly out of the kind of necessity that drove Susanna Moodie and Bogle Corbet to Upper Canada, or the Munros and the Halssons to the Red River Settlement.

Their reasons are ultimately unknowable, Wilson suggests, and she concludes her chronicle of their pilgrimage by drawing an analogy with migrating birds that applies as much to Topaz's death as to her original impulse to exile:

[They leave] their habitat at a season when food was ample and the climate salubrious, leaving as it were against their will . . . The birds are uncertain, restless; they are forced to go. One last bird remains alone, restless, nervous, undecided, wishing to go, awaiting something. After pitiful agitation the bird at last rises and follows the flight with confidence. (274)

But, she ironically concludes, "there are certain things about which one can only form a theory"—and that is perhaps as far as one can go in trying to fathom the nature of this inveterate and innocent traveller. The triumph here, strictly speaking, is not so much of the New World, as it is a continuing one of an irrepressible and innocent nature, alive to the possibilities of any world.

On the whole, the three writers discussed so far in this chapter uphold the supremacy of the New World, though in all three the residual influence of the Old constitutes a fairly strong component of their fiction. They probably reflect a vision, therefore, that is somewhat in advance of the attitudes and inclinations of many of the immigrants who came to Canada during the years covered by the novels in question. This point Wilfrid Eggleston enlarged upon a quarter of century ago in his influential book, *The Frontier and Canadian Letters:*

[The European settlers] were determined to re-create on North American soil a civilization similar to that which they had left behind in Europe, with, of course, some of the old weaknesses and evils expunged, and more noble qualities substituted in their stead. Those who thought about it might well have conceded that the environment of North America would dictate some modifications of European customs and habits. But the spirit and philosophy of the new North American society was to be European, certainly not Indian, or anything else.[7]

This observation is particularly relevant in a discussion of the fourth of the exile writers to be considered in this chapter, Frederick Philip Grove, a paradoxical figure in that he is at once the most European and the most Canadian of the four.

Until fairly recently, of course, Grove's life presented more of a puzzle than did most of his fiction, but with the publication of Douglas Spettigue's *FPG: The European Years* in 1973 and Desmond Pacey's edition of *The*

Letters of Frederick Philip Grove in 1976, much which had been in the realm
of exotic speculation was reduced to prosaic fact. But now, obviously,
readers must pay attention to two novelists instead of one: the Felix Paul
Greve who wrote novels in German at the turn of the century and who faked
a suicide in 1909 to escape disastrous personal circumstances, and the
Frederick Philip Grove who surfaced in Winnipeg near the end of 1912 and
began his Canadian writing career in the early 1920's. An exile probably
cannot do better than this, for he not only changed his skies but also his very
identity and background, and for the rest of his life in the New World he had
to resolve his various self-generated legends: that he was of Swedish-Scottish
stock, that he was a world traveller, that he was an intimate of turn-of-the-
century *littérateurs* in Germany and France, that he participated in the
opening of the Canadian West in the 1890's, that his manuscripts lay piled up
on his desk from 1892 on, and that though he was educated in the halls of
Europe he really belonged to the soil, and to the Canadian soil at that.

All these legends helped to consolidate the notion that Grove was a man
to be reckoned with, and they evoked a number of epithets, some coined by
himself, that invariably accompanied any assessment made of him: "prairie
realist," "a solitary giant," "spokesman for North American Society," "a
Canadian of Canadians." "spokesman of a race," "Lear of the prairies."
From this mystique Grove emerged as some kind of misunderstood genius or
unsung prophet, patiently waiting for his adopted countrymen to heed his
messages about the state of the world. "To have greatly tried and to have
failed," he lamented in 1929, "to have greatly wished and to be denied; to
have longed for purity and to be sullied; to have greatly craved for life and to
receive death: all that is the common lot of greatness upon earth."[8]

This is the lament not only of a misunderstood genius but of a defensive
and insecure exile, for that is what Grove remained to the end of his life. His
affinity was always to a remote ideal of culture, and it was undoubtedly
tempting for him, with the considerable intellectual and linguistic competence he had acquired during the "Greve" portion of his life, to equate
himself with this ideal, and at the same time to denigrate the cultural stature
of his newly adopted society. This tendency, according to Spettigue, was also
common in Grove's other self: Greve's failure to break into the literary
circles dominated by such writers as Stefan George and André Gide he
apparently never attributed to his own mediocrity, but rather to the ungrate-
fulness or insensitivity of his compatriots. Grove's immediate dilemma upon
surfacing with a new identity in Winnipeg in 1912 must therefore have been
how to reconcile his required assumption of a Canadian identity with his
deeply ingrained conviction about the supremacy of a European culture. In
oversimplified terms, both *A Search for America* (1927) and *In Search of
Myself* (1946) constitute his attempts to resolve this dilemma, though it is

one of the final ironies of his life that the revelations of Spettigue, Pacey, and Margaret Stobie have in large part reversed the fiction-autobiography sequence that these two books were originally seen to reflect.

A Search for America is now widely regarded as more autobiographical than fictional, filling in the details of the three-year transition between the disappearance of Felix Paul Greve and the appearance of Frederick Philip Grove, a gap that neither Spettigue nor Stobie addressed in their books. Whatever its derivation and form, my concern is to examine both it and its sequel as revelations of the exile mind, in which perspective, as we have already seen, autobiography and fiction frequently overlap. The two books are complementary rather than repetitious, for though they cover some of the same territory, the former is almost exclusively concerned with the exile's North American wanderings. while the latter documents both the prior European phase of his life, and what transpires after this wanderer becomes repatriated to Canada at the end of his American odyssey. "Wanderer" is of course a term with a precise relevance here: the very first book that Greve / Grove published was, as Spettigue points out, prophetically entitled *The Wanderings,*[9] and in *In Search of Myself,* Grove recalls a minor incident that was clearly related to "[his] earliest distinct and undoubted memory of [his] life as a wanderer over the face of Europe."

As mentioned earlier in connection with Salverson's *Confessions,* Grove carefully structures *A Search for America* to evoke the tangible stages of an exile's immersion into his new land. But he goes further than this, for he seemingly wants both to convey a highly subjective account of Philip Branden's odyssey, and to formalize and universalize this experience. To accomplish this, he sets off section headings that are metaphorical or mythical—"The Descent," "The Relapse," "The Depths," "The Level"—against consistently personalized chapter titles: no fewer than twenty-four of the twenty-six separate chapters begin with the pronoun "I," and of the other two, it is missing only in one, appropriately entitled "The Issue Is Obscured." There is a further symmetry in this deliberate structuring: the numerical total of chapters— seven in each of the first three sections, and five in the fourth—is balanced chronologically by the twenty-six months that elapse between Philip's arrival in Montreal and his eventual re-entry into Canada at Winnipeg. It is interesting to speculate on why there is such a contrast between the precise ordering of experience in this book and the loose structuring of *In Search of Myself,* where the chronological divisions—"Childhood," "Youth," "Manhood," "And After"—seem almost carelessly applied. Perhaps the explanation resides in the degree of tangibility of the exile's experiences in each case, with the uncertain structuring of the later book reflecting ultimately its high proportion of invented detail.

The subjective nature of Branden's quest becomes quickly evident as the narrative opens, and almost at random one can find a passage that demonstrates how consistently Grove observes the centrality of the first person reflected by the table of contents:

> Here I was in a different world. Here I stood entirely on my own feet. Whatever I might have to go through, if finally I arrived somewhere, if I achieved something, no matter how little, it would be my own achievement; I must be I.[10]

There is a combination here, as there is in the musings of so many Grove characters, of bravado and anguish, deriving in Branden's case, in part at least, from the circumstances that led to his exile in the first place. Essentially, though he admits at the outset that he has "the wandering instinct," he elects emigration because of a social snub, brought on by his father's sudden bankruptcy. Though he rationalizes that he no longer "cared to rub elbows with nobility," he was clearly hurt by this sudden change in his social standing, and a measure of his desolation is reflected by the fact that he allowed chance to dictate his next move: "to ask for the next boat which [he] stood any chance of catching . . . no matter where she might be bound" (11).

Unlike the exiles in *The Innocent Traveller,* who carried few of their Old World prejudices to the New, Branden comes veritably loaded down, and he is to find it a painful process to discard them. His aristocratic tendencies, his sense of cultural superiority, his condescending attitudes towards the colonials, his polished manner and formality—all these are immediately challenged by the casualness, the informality, the democratic spirit he encounters in the New World. It is only in retrospect, years later, that he can see what an incongruous figure he must have appeared to North Americans the day he stepped ashore in Montreal, and he feels it is small wonder that he suffered the inevitable "wounded susceptibilities and mental jolts," though his Old World conditioning enabled him "never to betray an emotion, to keep his mask intact" (15). Yet he remains consistent in his overall positive view towards the New World, both for moral reasons, in that he is grateful for the opportunity to start a new life, and for missionary reasons, so to speak, "viewing as I did the colonials as probably sorely in need of [culture] influence" (13). Though he is to sink socially much lower by the time his odyssey is over, he retains this sense of superiority to the end, and within this perspective, his decision to become a teacher in Manitoba provides him the opportunity to formalize this inclination.

The pattern established by the four separate books of this novel reflects, as in Lowry, the view that the route to moral and ethical clarity involves a descent into the chaos and depths that lie beneath the surface appearance of society, and the epigraphs from Stevenson, Carlyle, and Thoreau lend a kind of scriptural authority to this argument. Questions of morality, of the needs and wants of society, of the relationship between individual and social man—considerations such as these attend Branden as he wanders across the continent. On its literal plane, his odyssey generates a reasonable narrative and sociological interest, and his disclaimer—that his search is not meant as "a huge indictment of the Americas"—has essentially the same reverse effect as Mark Twain's memorable ones in *Huckleberry Finn*. His plight as an exile is rendered convincing as he secures his first job in the New World, as is his realization of what the process of integration involves:

> I had stepped from what I could not help regarding as a well-ordered, comfortable environment into what had upon me the effect of an utter chaos . . . . I felt that not only had I to learn a great many things, the social connections of a world entirely different from the world I knew . . . but I also had laboriously to tear down or at least to sub- merge what I had built up before—my tastes, inclinations, interests. (39)

In the course of his journey, Branden encounters lying and cheating, graft and corruption, even among those he considers loyal friends, and in a sense the gambling hoax and bookselling episodes he experiences in New York are merely formalizations of these traits; indeed, he sees as one of the great strengths of America "the power to assimilate no matter what, even graft" (100). He is human and fragile enough at times, however, to be severely disturbed by what he discovers, and occasionally he finds it difficult to ignore his deeply ingrained view of himself as an intrinsically superior being, though he concedes that "to entrench oneself behind the feeling of superior- ity is invariably a sign that one has become the underdog" (133). After one of his more upsetting experiences, being dismissed abruptly by a New York restaurant captain, he takes refuge in sounding off against American civiliza- tion as being "crude, raw [and] unfinished in the extreme," and then inter- prets himself, ironically, in precisely the way that the indigenous New World inhabitant has not infrequently viewed the newcomer from Europe:

> I was, suddenly, the representative in a foreign country of an older, of a superior civilization. I forgot that I had come among these "colonials" and "Yankees" to ask them for a living. I felt as if I were conferring a favour upon them by condescending to accept an adequate remunera- tion for my mere presence upon their shores. (134)

It is when his search takes him out of New York, a city that he calls "a mere bridgehead of Europe in the Western hemisphere" that he begins to

discover the real America. Like such earlier exiles as Colonel Rivers, Susanna
Moodie, and Daniel Munro, he experiences a kind of revelation, feeling "as
those first explorers must have felt when they began to realize that behind
that fringe of coast . . . lay a vast continent, a world unknown" (145).
Discarding all his possessions and books, except *The New Testament* and
The Odyssey, he undertakes the exile's obligatory retreat to the wilderness,
looking in effect for the values espoused by Lincoln to offset those incul-
cated by such Old World educators as Matthew Arnold (whose "Essays in
Criticism" he relegates to the fireplace—an action not unlike that of Wyndham
Lewis's René Harding, who hurls George Eliot's *Middlemarch* into the
Atlantic). While still in New York, he had taken occasional excursions into
the countryside, and for the first time in his life had moved away from a
literary relationship to Nature into a direct one and had become aware that
"processes were at work which were to remould [him], which were to make
[him] into something new, something different from what [he] had been,
something less artificial" (136). This process completes itself during "The
Depths" section of the novel, where in total isolation he is forced to rely on
his own native talents to survive the storms and floods of a primal world, an
experience that confirms the irrelevance of Arnold: "A deep-rooted suspicion of all that is called learning, progress, culture pervaded all my thinking.
I was no longer so sure of my superiority over those who had not received my
'education' " (260).

It is one of Grove's strengths as a novelist here that he renders credible
Branden's confusion over how to resolve satisfactorily his many Old World-
New World contradictions. Even Thoreau could not stay forever at Walden
Pond, and Branden, too, quickly reassumes human and social responsibili-
ties as his wilderness world is transformed into a world of man. He saves the
life of the sole inhabitant he encounters in his tempest-driven world, a silent,
Bartlebyian kind of recluse whose sole words "I reckon" acknowledge
Branden's decision to move on. Then, as his world quickly populates itself,
Branden is himself ministered unto by various people, some who provide
food and shelter, some jobs, and some who save his life. This world in some
respects is no more ideal than the one he left in Toronto or New York, for
there is still suspicion and cheating and cruelty. But Branden himself has
examined its basic texture at first hand, and finds himself convinced that the
American ideal is vastly superior to the European: the spontaneous good-
ness of the human heart, as opposed to a forced obedience to the dictates of
the theory of original sin. And of course Branden, too, has changed, as he
acknowledges:

> When I came from Europe, I came as an individual; when I settled down
> in America, at the end of my wanderings, I was a social man. My view of

life . . . had been, in Europe, historical, [while], it had become, in America, ethical. (382)

In two respects, therefore, Philip Branden seems to have moved into a modified state of exile: he is no longer the rebel, standing in isolation against the world, and he has fairly thoroughly assimilated himself into the fabric of North American society, a development that unequivocally spells out the triumph of the New World over the Old. But the novel does not end at this point: perhaps Grove already had his sequel to this novel in mind, for he has Branden "repatriated" to Canada, to the same city that Grove himself surfaced in in 1912. This may solve the symmetry of this novel, since Branden's search for America began in Canada, but it seems to me to constitute artistically a weak conclusion. It might better have formed an organic component of *In Search of Myself,* whose memoir-like qualities allow for a more flexible moving about of the exile protagonist from place to place.

In this autobiography, which clearly cannot today be taken at the face value it enjoyed when it was published in 1946, Grove's own observations render much less certain the New World triumph that Philip Branden announced at the end of *A Search for America.* It is true, of course, that the two books address different concerns, for Branden is merely an *undirected* exile, an ordinary individual engaged in exploring the physical and social realities of a world that is new to him, while Grove is an exile with a precise mission: to be a writer in this New World. Thus, where this world spells out limitless possibilities for existential man, it is a sadly deficient world for the artist figure, denying him the fulfilment that is possible in the Old World. In spite of its title, therefore, Grove's autobiography is not so much a search as it is a complaint, or a revelation of a priori opinions, and for that reason lacks some of the narrative and dramatic tension of the earlier book.

The "Childhood" and "Youth" sections of *In Search of Myself* document the shaping of an exile mind, a mind that quickly outgrows its world, that is impatient with the mediocrity of individuals and institutions, that must continually be nourished by new experiences. "Within the university," Grove laments at one point, "I did not find that enlargement of my horizons which I was looking for. Naturally, then, I soon sought it outside the university."[11] The spirit of Wanderlust takes over, and he is off to Athens, to Paris, to Biskra, back to Paris, "to Rome next year," and so on, with only America, South Africa, and Australia left off his itinerary for the moment. "When I spoke of them," he concedes, "it was only natural that my utterance should be coloured by what was expected of me; I spoke of them with contempt" (163). This *ennuyé* inevitably becomes disillusioned with whatever part of the world he finds himself in, and he cannot make up his mind whether he is a citizen of the world, of Europe, or merely of Rome, where he studied archeology. "I felt divided," he recalls, not surprisingly. "Apart from my underlying ambition to be a writer, I owed the world as it was a debt" (166). In this situation, it is small wonder that the New World appeared to offer a way out, even though, like Philip Branden, he is compelled to lower his sights drastically: he earns his living, "not as a professor of archeology or comparative philology but as a waiter in a cheap eating house on Yonge Street, Toronto" (177).

Grove's personal circumstances undoubtedly contribute to the confusion and contradictions he offers about his own exile in the final two sections of this book. That he feels "an exile from [his] youth and its promise" (236) is not of course surprising, for that is the common lot of all of us, but in a sense both his new country and Europe are seen as obstructions to his artistry, though admittedly the following rationale may reflect Grove's clumsy prose style more than it does an exile's confusion:

> In Europe, I knew at last, I could no longer live for any length of time. I did *not* feel an exile from any definite country. I was no longer a "good" European, let Europe take care of her own troubles; I was rapidly becoming extra-European, partly perhaps on account of my failure to take a sixth trip to Europe. Europe, to me, had suddenly ceased to exist. (236)

This ambivalence carries over into his views about Canada, a country he prefers to the United States because it seems less alien to him as a European; he confesses to experiencing almost a tangible reflection of this realization as he crosses the border—an interesting contradiction to the observation made by Laura Salverson. On one occasion, Canada is described as "a new Siberia," yet on another, it emerges as the same potential paradise that Colonel Rivers anticipated with his Emily: "While to others life here in this desolation might seem exile, to me it held forth the promise of paradise. If I could live here as a married man, I could combine the two great satisfactions for which I craved: I could plant an island of domestic life in the wilderness; and I could write again" (301). But his abiding dilemma is one common to all exiles, and has its derivation in something that transcends geographical displacement:

> I felt an exile. I was an exile. I did not live among people of my own kind; among people who, metaphorically, spoke my language; among people who respected my fierce sensibilities; among people who shared a single one of my interests. (235)

Grove's working title for his autobiography was *My Life as a Writer in Canada*, and within this perspective, this lament helps to explain why he ultimately found this a difficult process. But it is essentially the same in spirit as his earlier European complaints: he is a man too far ahead of his time. If that is true, if he always was an exile out of place and out of time, then his explanation of the artistic process has some validity: "Art has its being, not in the activity of the artist . . . but in the mental and emotional reaction of him to whom it is addressed" (357). And within this perspective, *In Search of Myself* seems to constitute a draw between the Old World and the New.

In light of Grove's need to keep his real identity a secret, it is not surprising to discover how infrequently he used his Old World experiences in any of his works other than the two *Search* books. Only in *Settlers of the Marsh* (1925) and an earlier, discarded opening chapter of that book entitled "The First Day of an Immigrant"[12] is a European the central protagonist, but it is a Swedish immigrant rather than one from Grove's native Germany. Unlike Philip Branden, however, Niels Lindstedt does not undergo the dilemmas of resolving conflicts that derive from the contradictions between the Old and New Worlds: his major psychological problem is a sexual and moral one, which in effect renders him impotent in both worlds. It is, furthermore, a problem that in both worlds he would have to solve within a Swedish society, for in Manitoba it is within the community made up of his fellow Swedish immigrants, the Lunds, the Amundsens, the Nelsons, that his moral dilemma is exposed and eventually resolved, and thus, not even his native language is a problem, as is often the case with exiles. In the literal sense, Niels is an immigrant rather than an exile, for once he realizes his dream—to build a house, marry the right woman, raise children—in short, becomes a permanent settler, he will have none of the residual spiritual or intellectual problems that beset the conventional exile.

Indeed, our first impression of Lindstedt, whether in "The First Day of an Immigrant" or in *Settlers of the Marsh*, reminds us more of Abe Spalding in *Fruits of the Earth* than of Philip Branden. He is a man dedicated simply to the physical task that lies immediately before him, whether it is the breaking of land, the unloading of wheat stooks, or the digging of a well. In Niels's case, it is true, this in part is a response to the deterministic nature of his Swedish world, where his own parents had died in futile, ceaseless labour: "In Sweden it had seemed to him as if his and everybody's fate had been fixed from all eternity. He could not win out because he had to overcome, not only his own poverty, but that of all his ancestors to boot." [13] He is saved from this fate, he believes, "by some trick in his ancestry" (50) that compelled him, much like Salverson's Icelandic protagonists, to undertake a new existence across the seas, for to all these immigrants, Canada was "the land of the million farmsteads to be had for the asking" (51).

The resolution of Niels's dilemma, therefore, is not a matter of intellectually or experientially testing New World moral values against those of the
Old World, as was largely the case with Philip Branden. His major problem
was that of innocence, not only sexual, but of the nature of people in general,
and it was Clara Vogel, rather than any unique New World situation, that
helped him resolve that; undoubtedly her equivalent back in Blekinge,
Sweden, could have performed much the same function. Grove's solution
represents an interesting reversal of the Jamesian concept of innocence and
experience, for here it is the New World character who transforms the
innocent European into a wiser and sadder being. Niels often rationalizes
that he has acquired a new vision—"the mere fact that he was uprooted and
transplanted had given him a second sight, had awakened powers of vision
and sympathy in him which were far beyond his education and upbringing"
(85)—but we see again and again that he has acquired neither the vision nor
the experience to handle either the sexless Ellen or the sexual Clara, and he
increasingly isolates himself from the realities of his New World. It is only
after destroying what represents extreme perversions of his own sexual
fears—the macabre, promiscuous Clara and the gelding Jock—that he is
able psychologically and experientially to acquire a realistic and positive
vision, and thus to fulfil his original dream of becoming a successful settler in
his new land.

Within the pattern of the different kinds of exile I discussed in my opening
chapter, Lindstedt clearly moves from the state of being an immigrant to one
where he becomes a fully assimilated member of his new society. To dramatize Niels's transformation, Grove occasionally exploits such standard devices
of exile literature as the juxtaposing of paradisal and anti-paradisal elements,
isolating the protagonist, or setting up specific Old World-New World
contradictions, but Niels is not sufficiently introspective or perceptive about
his own dilemma to make these as effective as they might be. Unlike Philip
Branden in *A Search for America* or Grove himself in *In Search of Myself,*
Lindstedt is left at the end of his journey with no residual problems to solve,
and far more than those two *Search* books, *Settlers of the Marsh* clearly
reflects the triumph of the New World over the Old.

5

Tourists and Expatriates

As I indicated earlier, reverse pilgrimages from the New World to the Old have not been nearly so frequent or regular on the part of Canadian writers as has been true for their American counterparts, with only Sara Jeannette Duncan in the late nineteenth century emulating the numerous examples from south of the border. This disparity continues well into the twentieth century, for the phenomenon of the American lost generation pilgrimage of the 1920's has no equivalent in Canadian literature, and even after World War II expatriation represented an individual rather than a group response.

The reasons for Canada's lag lie not so much in the population discrepancy between the two nations—after all, it does not take that many writers to constitute a group—as in the attitudes the respective writers hold towards themselves, their country, and the world at large. Canada in the early decades of this century was still a land moving towards fulfilment in social, economic, and constitutional senses, and her major writers at the time, like Connor, Montgomery, McClung, and Stead, were largely preoccupied with her physical and sociological realities, or with received moral certainties, leaving little scope for self-criticism or questioning of the prevailing aesthetic and intellectual values.

American writers, on the other hand, as Malcolm Cowley makes clear in *Exile's Return*, had moved well beyond the literal realities of their country, and in their subsequent questioning of American values found themselves increasingly alienated from what they saw as the residue of Victorian morality and hypocrisy. Expatriation for them, therefore, was seen not only as a liberating process, but almost as an obligatory undertaking, required of anyone who was not blind to the shortcomings of their own nation. "I have never learned to regard myself as a 'member of society'," they quoted from George Gissing. "For me there have always been two entities—myself and the world—and the normal relation between the two has been hostile,"[1] and it was not long before this second-hand sentiment became an article of belief, which could be obeyed only by leaving America'and going to Europe.

It is important, too, to consider the relative effects that World War I had upon the two countries: the United States, with its late entry into that conflict and its relatively small loss of life, undoubtedly had a different attitude towards Europe than did Canada, whose total commitment from the beginning and enormous casualties produced a traumatic and sobering effect across the country. For Canadians, therefore, post-war Europe remained as a grim reminder of the catastrophe they had suffered rather than, as for the Americans, an exciting arena in which they could indulge in a carefree and bohemian life-style. And in fact a goodly number of Americans who found themselves in the war in one capacity or another constituted the nucleus of Cowley's lost generation group, a situation that has no parallel in the case of Canadian wartime participants.

Of the two Canadian expatriates of the 1920's who ultimately established respectable reputations in Canadian letters, only John Glassco reflected the spirit of those times, and I will shortly return to him. The other writer, Morley Callaghan, was essentially more of a tourist than a genuine expatriate, not only because of the brevity of his visit (the summer of 1929), but also because his attitudes towards that world suggest a mind very much rooted in his North American values. Leon Edel's description of him as "very young, very robust, *very* Toronto, and thus foreign to the insouciant hedonism of the young Montrealers,"[2] though a long-after-the-fact recollection, is on the whole verified by Callaghan's vision and opinions as expressed in *That Summer in Paris,* a book faithful to the facts of what happened in that brief summer, but not to the spirit of the times, as reflected in the books by Cowley and Glassco. Not surprisingly, Callaghan's brief expatriate experience failed to reveal new ways of looking at his world, or to suggest new aesthetic directions for him; rather, it confirmed him in the realistic stance he had already competently demonstrated in his *Strange Fugitive* and *A Native Argosy,* where the social realities of North America constituted his concern.

In part, the relative lifelessness of Callaghan's memoirs derives from the time lag between the events and his recording of them, a gap that did not obtain for either Cowley or Glassco; this delay was undoubtedly a factor, too, in the selective nature of his recollections, which by and large show him emerging triumphant and superior from his various "tangled friendships" of the day. The nature of his general and legal education, too, and his conventional formative years, all trained him to become part of society rather than to rebel against it, and as a result, his pilgrimage to Paris seems devoid of any profound intellectual excitement and curiosity, and one is hard pressed to imagine him subscribing to Gissing's credo. "I was intensely North American," he recalls. "Physically, and with some other part of me, the ball-playing, political, debating, lovemaking, family part of me, I was wonderfully at home in my native city," and though he concedes that the intellectual part of him "was utterly, but splendidly and happily, alien,"[3] it is clear that on the whole he remained unmoved by the new literary and intellectual developments, whether at home or abroad. And indeed, when he does ultimately anticipate a visit to Paris, it is not so much for the legendary possibilities of that city as it is for his own self-aggrandizement:

> It did not seem to be comical that I was not thinking of France as the place where I might go to cultivate my mind, become aware of the currents of French literature, see Gide, talk to Cocteau, sneer at the naughty boys, Breton and Aragon, expose myself to the marvelously quick French intelligence. No, I thought of Paris as some kind of magical milieu where there would be a vast number of nameless perceptive men who would appreciate my own stories. (*SP*, 46)

When Callaghan does enter Paris, it is not as a discoverer of a new world, possessed by the euphoria that Glassco had experienced upon his arrival, but rather as a well-prepared tourist who had studied the requisite maps and guides before leaving home. And he very much remains a tourist, in the city but not of it, and certainly not disturbed or exercised intellectually by it. "Paris was around us and how could it be alien in our minds and hearts even if no Frenchman ever spoke to us?" (*SP*, 87), he muses, as he looks about eagerly for glimpses of such literary figures as Joyce, Pound, and Fitzgerald. Time and time again, Callaghan's response to Paris is a learned one, not a felt one; always he is the observer of this world rather than a participant in it, as though he is fighting against the possibility of his becoming intellectually and spiritually an exile. At times, the moral attitudes he maintains against his Parisian experiences border on perversity:

> I told [Loretto] that if I were to stay on in France I should now be soaking up French culture. I should want to be with French writers. If I didn't want the French culture, then I was there in exile. Could the dream I had had for years of being in Paris been only a necessary fantasy? A place to fly to, a place that could give me some satisfactory view of myself? (*SP*, 229)

That he was not an exile, spiritually or intellectually, is of course not to his discredit, and his realization that "all of us in Montparnasse . . . were Peer Gynts who knew in our hearts we would soon have to go home" (*SP*, 225), reflects an honesty that not all expatriates were prepared to acknowledge. And in a sense, his personal resolution of his "tangled" relationships with such lost generation writers as Fitzgerald and Hemingway dramatizes the larger resolution he achieved, that of surrendering his own brief attraction to the expatriate experience to his larger conviction that his writing career could be more properly realized at home.

The one story about expatriates that Callaghan did write during his summer in Paris reflects the kind of cynicism and even bitterness that occasionally characterizes his memoirs. "Now that April's Here," originally published in *This Quarter* in the fall of 1929, depicts the experiences of two Americans from the Mid-west, Charles Milford and Johnny Hill, widely held to be modelled on the Montreal expatriates Graeme Taylor and John Glassco. Like Malcolm Cowley's colleagues who quoted from George Gissing's *The Private Papers of Henry Ryecroft,* these youths were "convinced that the American continent had nothing to offer them,"[4] and indeed, it was another book of a similar spirit, George Moore's *Confessions of a Young Man,* that "had been mainly responsible for their visit to Paris" (52). Like a number of characters in such later writers as Norman Levine and Mavis Gallant, Milford and Hill assumed the superficial poses of the instant expatriate: they each bought a large black hat before leaving America, they avoided places like the Louvre so as not to be mistaken for tourists, and they sat regularly at tables on the terraces of various cafes, "waiting for something to happen to them" (52).

Undoubtedly, as is generally held, this story constitutes a somewhat insensitive attack by Callaghan on his fellow expatriates, whose sexual habits among other things he tended to sneer at, and taken on this level, one can understand Glassco's own rebuttal of Callaghan in his *Memoirs of Montparnasse.* But none of the expatriates in this story escape Callaghan's censure: Fanny Lee, "who had been an entertainer at Zelli's until she lost her shape," latched on to the two boys, "anxious to have them follow her from one bar to another, hoping they would pay for her drinks" (51,52); Stan Mason, "an ingenuous heavy drinker . . . [sat] at the same bars every night, explaining the depth of his sophistication to the same people" (53); Milton Simpson, "a prosperous, bright and effeminate young American business-man who was living in Paris because he felt vaguely that the best approach to life was through all the arts together" (54); and "an elderly English gentleman, who had suggested, after talking to them all one morning, he would pay well to see the boys make a 'tableau' for him" (57). Quite clearly, this was a world where Callaghan was not comfortable, but he transforms his moral dislike and detachment into a sharp, aesthetic irony, initially reflected in the story's title, with its echo of another expatriate's homesickness. The April that the boys had been eagerly awaiting since their arrival in Paris in the previous fall in effect destroys the dreams they had of permanent exile in Paris: its cold, wet weather contradicts everything they had ever heard about Paris in April, and a girl they had met on the Riviera during the winter comes to live with them, eventually destroying their relationship as she elects to return to America with Johnny.

Charlie thus finally attains, now that April is here, at least the appearance of the isolated expatriate, for our last glimpse is of him "sitting alone at his table in the cool evening," wearing his overcoat and the black hat he had bought in America, "the first time," Callaghan ironically points out, "he had worn the hat in France" (61). He looks quite different from what he did with Johnny the previous fall when, in their inseparability and boyishness they had earned a kind of touristy recognition as "the two boys," in spite of their deliberate attempts to cultivate the appearance of genuine expatriates. This story is, among other things, Callaghan's cynical statement directed towards those who manifested only the superficial mannerisms of exile and expatriation, and in that respect, at any rate, represents a sincere dramatization of his own position.

Some six years younger than Callaghan, John Glassco was much more precocious in his grasp of the new intellectual and aesthetic movements of his day, and much more spontaneous and eager in the acquisition of new and varied experiences. In his many personal acts—his rebellion against his family, his dropping out of university, his escape to Europe via a cargo boat—he dramatizes the distinction between the tourist and the expatriate, between one who is totally committed to new experiences and one who merely dabbles at the edges. "He is our one writer in Canadian literature," Leon Edel asserts, "who has completely escaped self-consciousness,"[5] an escape which among other things allowed him to write his *Memoirs of Montparnasse* both as a record of youthful hedonism and as an expression, paradoxically, of exile and contentment simultaneously attained. Though published in 1970, it was written in Glassco's youth, part of it in 1928, when he was still in the midst of his Parisian experiences, and the remainder in 1932-33, when he was a patient in Montreal's Royal Victorian Hospital awaiting an operation which he was not sure he was going to survive. Interestingly, therefore, the urgencies of both life and death came together to dictate the substance and validity of this book, which perhaps explains Edel's retrospective impression that it possesses "the fascination of a long-buried artifact suddenly turned up by a spade."[6]

Glassco's account of his expatriate experience follows in broad outline the pattern that Malcolm Cowley observed about his individuals in *Exile's Return*: initial dissatisfaction with the moral and intellectual atmosphere in North America; the urge to go to Europe, "where people know how to live"; total immersion of self into the hedonistic life of continental Europe; ultimate return, as sadder and wiser individuals, to a homeland which has also changed. Unlike Cowley's exiles, however, Glassco is much less self-conscious about his roots or his Canadianism than they are about their American heritage, perhaps because he was a decade or so younger, and he could therefore give himself to the possibilities of the present moment with more abandon and less conscience, a feeling he obviously experienced as he arrived in Paris:

> The next day we crossed the channel and arrived in Paris around six o'clock in the evening. It was dark, damp, and snowing slightly, and I suppose the city did not look its best from the train windows, but I had only to think that I was now in the city of Baudelaire, Utrillo and Apollinaire to be swept by a joy so strong it verged on nausea. (*MM* 13)

Europe had of course long exercised this kind of effect upon its visitors: a hundred years before Glassco's visit, Washington Irving had been moved to a similar state of ecstasy upon his arrival in Rome, conceding that "to describe the emotions of the mind and the crowd of ideas that arise on entering this 'mistress of the world' is impossible,"[7]

At times, Glassco seems prepared to renounce Canada permanently, though near the end of his *Memoirs*, even before he became ill, there were hints that the party was over, that expatriation as a way of life was already becoming an anachronism: the shadows of the coming depression and of the totalitarian onslaughts were beginning to trouble even such an unbridled hedonist as Glassco. If we can transform his memoirs for a moment into fiction, his literal contracting of tuberculosis can be seen in symbolic terms, not unlike the case of Hans Castorp in Mann's *The Magic Mountain,* representing the sickness and the predicaments of the times. And in a sense Glassco acknowledges the fictional dimensions of Buffy as he looks back on his experiences from the end of the 1960's: "This young man is no longer myself: I hardly recognize him . . . and in my memory he is less like someone I have been than a character in a novel I have read" (*MM*, xiii).

Glassco's confession at the outset that he "already existed in a climate of restlessness, scorn, frequent ecstasy and occasional despair" (*MM,*1) not only echoes the standard lament of romantic, alienated youth, but also foreshadows the inconsistent and vacillating nature that his own brief exile is to assume. Though despising everything about the Montreal business world, he nevertheless eagerly accepts the money his father makes from that world; his literary ambitions, manifested first in a desire to become a surrealist poet, are transformed into mere personal indulgence, alternating between a pretence at writing and a narcissistic recording of his own hedonistic experiences; his appetite for intellectual stimulation regularly gives way to his stronger appetite for the pleasures of the flesh; and his youthful, seemingly insatiable desire for all sensuous experiences is cut off, at the point of his highest ecstasy, by the grim realities of venereal disease and tuberculosis. In short, he returns from his exile in much the same mental state as he was when he embarked upon it, though in a more precarious physical state; his total immersion into the possibilities of the Old World merely confirmed the hedonistic nature of his impulses in the first place.

Glassco remains as an isolated figure in the phenomenon of exile litera-ture in Canada: he has no intellectual or spiritual affinity with Sara Duncan (though her Elfrida Bell reflects some of his impulses), nor did he, because of the delayed publication of his *Memoirs*, have any influence on the decision of the post-World War II expatriates to go abroad, though there are of course occasional similarities between aspects of his vision and those reflected in Richler and Levine. Perhaps a major value of his work lies in the fact that it reveals a latent hedonism and spontaneity in the Canadian character that had not been articulated by writers before his time, and which, in Callaghan's recollections, for example, is either consistently denied or manifested in a touristy, leering way. Though the consequences of Glassco's own life may dictate otherwise, there is nevertheless an attractive argument in his "wine and roses" summation of his philosophy that the Presbyterianism of North America does not readily concede:

for I am persuaded half of man's miseries result from an insufficiency of leisure, gormandise and sexual gratification during the years from seven-teen to twenty. This is what makes so many people tyrannical, bitter, foolish, grasping and ill-natured once they have come to years of discre-tion and understand they have wasted their irreplaceable years in the pursuit of education, security, reputation, or advancement. (*MM*, 147)

Clearly, the first part of this statement, with its philosophy of self-gratification, has a particular appeal to the young, but Glassco conveniently survived to verify his latter point as well. And in large part, it is its implicit condemnation of the prevailing North American attitudes and values that emerges as one of the rationales that lay behind the expatriation of a number of writers after World War II, notably Mavis Gallant, Mordecai Richler, and Norman Levine, though for Gallant, as we will see in the next chapter, a complex of reasons operated. Levine's explanation of why he "was running away from Canada" seems to sum up the feeling of the day:

A lot of people had come to London from different parts of Britain and the Commonwealth. Writers and painters congregated in certain pubs. And there was still a hangover of the war in the loosened class barriers, the romanticism, the idealism. Wanting to be a painter or a writer was equated with wanting the good life.[8]

Of course, both Levine and Richler were running away from their Jewish heritage as well as from Canada, and it is undoubtedly this sense of being doubly an exile that accounts for some of the uncertainties and inconsistencies in their fiction. In many respects they were closer in spirit to Britain's Angry Young Men than they were to Canadians like Glassco and Duncan, both of whom embraced their worlds with varying degrees of passion, whereas later expatriates tended to reject them.

During his first two decades as a writer, Mordecai Richler chose Europe over Canada, and characteristically his fiction centres on the problem of the artistic exile from North America adrift in the political fermentations of the Old World. But Europe constituted a mixed quantity for Richler, for he seldom saw issues in clearly polarized terms; the individual who gains his most sympathetic treatment is the one who has survived various forms of totalitarianism, an individual who could be either the perpetrator of violence or its victim. A standard pattern in Richler is the juxtaposing of these totalitarian representatives against insipid or uncommitted North Americans, individuals who frequently suffer from not having participated in the events of history. Or they find, like Jake Hersh in *St. Urbain's Horseman*, either that the orgy has moved elsewhere or that they cannot participate in it even if it has not; Glassco *could*, but then his world was primarily benignly hedonistic rather than malevolent. In every sense a modern writer, Richler views the world almost exclusively in terms of chaos and uncertainty, conditions that only in a peripheral sense occupied writers like Duncan, Callaghan, and Glassco.

In both *The Acrobats* (1954) and *A Choice of Enemies* (1957), Richler develops his theme of exile in essentially similar patterns by setting up confrontations between characters who are men without countries or men who have temporarily abandoned their countries—expatriates from Canada and the United States, Jews from the ghettos of Europe, assorted Communists, Nazis, and Fascists still upholding causes from the Spanish Civil War and World War II. In both novels the central figure is a Canadian, and though there is not the juxtaposition of values and cultures we find in many other writers, there is a conflict of sensibilities and attitudes, with André Bennett and Norman Price achieving recognizable moral triumphs. In *The Acrobats,* measured against Barney and Jessie Larkin, Bennett simply cannot lose, so gauche are the Americans; and though the Nazi Colonel Kraus impregnates André's girl and eventually kills André, the Canadian emerges as moral victor in the eyes of such survivors as Toni and Chaim. His naïveté about himself and his world stands in sharp contrast to the worldliness and corruption of his European companions, and we sense the futility of the moral definition he offers of himself: "I believe in being good and understanding and being a brother to other men and painting, because it is the only thing I can do half well and perhaps finally it will explain to me what I am looking for."[9] Appropriately, André does not die in a struggle between Communist and Fascist, for that conflict had already been fought, but in one between the committed and uncommitted, and his own commitment to a kind of abstraction simply is not good enough in that world of pragmatic realities.

The sharp contrast in moods between this novel and Glassco's *Memoirs* reflects of course the way the world had altered between the two wars; the characters here on the whole reflect the sense of despair and futility that characterized the post-World War II period, with little sense of the excitement and anticipation that sustained the expatriates of the twenties. When Cowley's exiles exclaimed, "Let's go to Europe. They know how to live there," one is struck by the literal possibilities in that cry, but when André tells the Larkins, "I came here to study life in its entirety. One day I hope to write a book about it" (*A*, 11), the note of cynicism is unmistakable, and as the naïve Canadian immersing himself in Europe for the sake of cultural enrichment, he simply does not come off. And in a sense his mission is doomed anyway, for the Old World itself has learned to turn a cynical, not to say rapacious, eye upon the tourists and expatriates, which is perhaps what Norman Levine had in mind when, after explaining why he had come to Europe, he said, "What I didn't know, at the time, was that I had come in on the end of something that was in the process of breaking up."[10]

The Old World representatives in *The Acrobats* on the whole win Richler's compassion more than those from the New World, undoubtedly because of the genuine nature of their plight. They come together from time to time in Valencia's Mocambo Club, run by Chaim, the homeless Jew who has wandered all over Europe and America, and now is a kind of father figure to all the other homeless exiles. He has compassion for them all, even for the Fascist Colonel Kraus and his sister: clearly, in Richler's vision, it is the plight of running and hiding and surviving, rather than the ideology, that defines the substance of man. Thus it is aesthetically fitting that it is André, the least corrupt of all the individuals in this novel, and the only one who had never literally participated in Europe's holocausts, who is killed by Kraus, who represents the opposite end of that moral and experiential spectrum. That Toni bears Kraus's child, too, constitutes a kind of ironic balancing of the moral books, for in his Montreal days André had impregnated a Jewish girl, who subsequently died from the abortion he arranged: he shares, therefore, a small portion of the overwhelming guilt that attaches to Kraus for the Nazi role in the holocaust, even though he acted out of love and not, like Kraus, out of hate.

Of the Old World exiles, only Chaim and Toni are without an ideology, and it is their willingness to compromise in order to survive that spells out their moral superiority in a world where absolutes no longer apply. It is significant that it is only the ideological exiles who reject André, for they are united in not understanding the nature of love, which they confuse with zeal for a cause. Manuel, as a result, has nothing but contempt for the Andrés of his world: "Why do you come to Spain at all? Does it amuse you? Do you think our women make good whores? Do you think it is droll to be a young idler while better men than you die in prison?" (*A*, 78). The irony is that André is the only one of the New World figures who does not deserve these questions, which should more properly be addressed to Barney Larkin. Guillermo is closer in spirit to André, but they ultimately must go their separate ways as well, for the gap between commitment to a cause and André's undirected love is too great: "Dammit, Guillermo! Will you get it through your head that I am nothing. Not an anarchist. Not a Communist. Not a fascist. Nothing" (*A*, 83).

The Acrobats clearly involves more a conflict of ideologies than a conflict of cultures, with André, a kind of New World political innocent, ultimately unable to survive an Old World characterized by unworkable absolutes. The little that Richler offers us about the American or the Canadian character in the Old World leans too far towards caricature to be convincing, though the more profound dimension of Larkin's exile—his attempt to forsake his Jewish heritage—is more sensitively handled than his crude American tourist image. André's seething, inner tirade against Canadian culture is in part a product of his despair and insecurity, which comes to a head at the party at Chaim's Mocambo Club, where he begins to grasp the truth about his exile: "The Canadian artists! Mediocrity draped in the maple leaf! Sonnets by the aging virgin grand-daughters of Tory tradesmen evoking the memories of rather un-Presbyterian passions, slick paintings by sophisticates with a shrewd eye turned toward New York" (*A*, 89). This anti-Canadian note echoes frequently throughout Richler's fiction and non-fiction alike, and is not to be substantially altered until the appearance of *St. Urbain's Horseman* in the early 1970's.

Published three years after *The Acrobats, A Choice of Enemies* is set in London rather than Spain, but the exile theme here, in spite of Richler's extensive residence in England, involves only superficially a cultural juxtaposition, for again politics and conflicting ideologies constitute most of the novel's tensions. The Canadian protagonist, Norman Price, expelled from an American university in a McCarthy-type purge, is a script writer in London, associated with various expatriates, political refugees, Jews, and other dispossessed members of the international community. And as in *The Acrobats,* the protagonist's dilemma is played out against the chaos and cynicism of the European sphere, with his moral values triumphing in an abstract sense over the intrigues of the Old World, where the operating principle is one of power rather than of morality.

Within the framework of this novel's ideological conflicts, England serves as a neutral arena where the forces of the Old and New World meet—the survivors of the totalitarian regimes of continental Europe and the victims of the McCarthy purges in North America. In this respect, the Toronto editor, Thomas Hale, is correct when, advising Norman to return to Canada, he states that "England's not a battlefield any more, but a playground for sentimental, visiting Canadians like myself" (*CE*, 9), though as "a fierce champion of periphery causes" Hale is hardly the man to understand the nature of Norman's dilemma. Norman, however, has a less romantic view of Canada than Hale:

> Whenever Norman thought of his country he did not, as Americans were supposed to do, recall with a whack of joy the wildest rivers and fastest trains, fields of corn, skyscrapers, and the rest of it. There were all these things in his country. There were magical names in abundance. A town call Trois-Rivières; a mountain pass named Kicking Horse; Saskatchewan—a province. But there was no equivalent of the American dream to boost or knock. The Canadian dream, if there was such a puff, was how do I get out? (*CE*, 10-11)

Getting out was not only Norman's problem; as the novel's opening chapter reveals, it is also Ernst's, and the juxtaposing of the scene of his escape from East Germany against the languid exchange between Hale and Norman dramatizes the distinction that is to run throughout this novel, between various degrees of commitment and the mere tourist. For Ernst, a survivor of both the Nazis and the Communists, this flight from the East is the beginning of a series of furtive voyages that will ultimately bring him and Norman together, for their alter ego roles in respect of one another constitute an important aesthetic component of this novel. And interestingly, their coming together, dictated initially by Ernst's killing of Norman's brother in Munich, is ultimately realized through their mutual claims on Sally MacPherson, one of the least committed of any of the North American expatriates in England. Like Barney Larkin of *The Acrobats*, Sally is on one of Richler's gauche New World tourists, eager to experience sensations held to be unattainable in Canada. "Don't you see that I could do this just as well at home," she rebuffs Norman. "Go to bed with a man, I mean. This is Europe. I want things to happen to me here that could never happen to me at home" (*CE*, 44). That her wish is fulfilled in a tragically different way than she had in mind is, strictly speaking, not necessary for a resolution of the New World-Old World incompatibilities dramatized in this novel, but it does underscore her fundamental inability to understand the kind of world she has permitted to exploit her.

Ernst and the Jewish landlord, Karp, the two individuals most shaped by totalitarian strife, represent the ideological and pragmatic opposites of Sally, for they assume whatever beliefs that will for the moment sustain them, and have no hesitation in using people and situations to their own ends. And though they are outsiders as far as the expatriate colony of Americans and Canadians is concerned, they can easily manipulate these uncertain liberals and fellow travellers, and by novel's end Ernst at any rate has it made, for he has outwitted all his adversaries in Europe and assumed a new identity and stature in Canada. It is there, ironically, where he watches a television debate on *Controversy* on the question, "do you think Canadian artists must leave the country in order to develop?": "Yes," answers Miss Lucy Morgan— perhaps one of Richler's virgin poetesses from *The Acrobats*, because in England the people read poetry, while Canada is culture-starved and provincial; "No," thunders Charlie Lawson, former expatriate television and film writer, because "Canadian artists cease to have value to their own country once they become expatriates" (*CE*, 239)—a prognosis that is crashingly true in his case. Ernst, having met all these types in England, will clearly have his opinion on this question.

The sympathy that Richler extended towards Kraus and Chaim in *The Acrobats* is paralleled here in his development of Ernst, not only as a credible character in his own right, but as a significant agent in the working out of Norman's dilemma. His intrusion into Norman's conscience begins well before the members of the expatriate colony are even aware of his existence: some of the birthday money Norman sent to Nicky is given to Ernst, thereby helping to ensure his survival; the phone call announcing Nicky's murder interrupts Norman's seduction of Sally, thus keeping her on hold, as it were, until Ernst arrives; and finally, Ernst's moving into Karp's rooms allows him physically to begin replacing Norman. As a result of these successful manipulations, he is able, by the time he meets the expatriates at Winkleman's second party, to turn them against each other and particularly against Norman, at the same time ensuring his own continued safety. Ironically, it is Winkleman who tells Norman that "in this world you've got to make a choice of enemies or you just can't live" (*CE*, 126), for that is precisely what Ernst has been doing all along, and for which he is severely castigated by Winkelman's group.

Norman's dilemma derives not only from his being a political exile from the New World, but also from his being tied to a past when it was still possible to choose one's enemies: his father had been killed in the Spanish Civil War, and he himself had been a fighter pilot in World War II. Appropriate to the the uncertain world he now finds himself in, his "red badge" from that war is a kind of functional amnesia that comes upon him when events overwhelm him, as when he learns that Ernst had killed his brother. Since there is no issue or cause that seems equal in worthiness to those which preceded his amnesia, he cannot make a firm commitment to anything, and thus his amnesia provides an escape into a world where no stand is necessary. But even in his normal state of mind he realizes how he and his fellow expatriates had helped contribute to their own vitiation:

> Proud they were. They had come to conquer. Instead they were being picked off one by one by the cold, drink, and indifference. They abjured taking part in the communal life. They mocked the local customs from the school tie to queueing, and were for the most part free of them by dint of their square, classless accents. Unlike their forbears, they were punk imperialists. They didn't marry and settle down among the natives. They had brought their own women and electric shavers with them. They had through the years evolved from communists to fellow-travellers to tourists. (*CE*, 156)

That Norman decides to marry the English girl, Vivian, could suggest that he wishes, by "marry[ing] and settl[ing] down among the natives," to counteract the spiritual and intellectual decline he alludes to in this passage. Such a resolution, however, is unsatisfactory, since Vivian represents too sudden an intrusion, and too uncertain a quantity: she hardly represents a "spiritual superiority" that Norman reflects on at one point, and their marriage is scarcely a day old before their incompatibility begins to be apparent. Another implication of his marrying her is that his amnesiac state is to assume more reality in his life than his more conscious state, but such a resolution goes contrary to the whole import of the novel, where the direction is towards a pragmatic handling of the world's shifting realities.

Richler's attitude towards the Canadian expatriates in these two early novels is on the whole less sympathetic than it is to become in such later works as *St. Urbain's Horseman* (1971) and *Joshua Then and Now* (1980). That his two most naïve and innocent Canadians perish in the Old World and his most selfish and manipulative European triumphs in the New, is one measure of Richler's ironic and ambivalent stance on this question. He himself at the time was an expatriate artist, not unlike André in his views on the world, but because he fled Canada in part to escape individuals like Thomas Hale or Charlie Lawson, it was undoubtedly difficult for him to avoid both a form of narcissism and a temptation to caricature. Over the next two decades, however, he changed substantially in his attitude towards Canada, and this modification becomes most strikingly apparent in his compassionate characterization of Jake Hersh, the expatriate Canadian film and television director in *St. Urbain's Horseman*. The novel is rich and complex, involving much more than the unfolding of an exile theme, for

Jake's problems—and his qualified resolution of them—derive from many factors besides being cut off from his homeland; of all of Richler's characters, he is the one most painfully aware of being adrift historically and temporally, and much of his outrageous behaviour can be seen as his attempts to experience vicariously what is no longer realistically available to him.

The cloak of protective cynicism that Richler wore in his earlier novels is shed here, and he takes on much more the attitudes of the expatriate genuinely alive to the realities of the Old World, with the result that this novel reflects a sense of life missing in the other two. Richler conceded, in a 1968 essay, that it had been important for him in the early 1950's to strike a sophisticated pose, to deny the surge of excitement that was every bit as intense as Glassco's in the 1920's:

> we were not so much non-conformists as subject to our own peculiar conformities or, if you like, anti-bourgeois inversions. And so, if you were going to read a fat Irwin Shaw, a lousy best-seller, you were safest concealing it under a Marquis de Sade jacket. What I personally found most trying was the necessity to choke enthusiasm, never to reveal elation, when the truth was I was out of mind with joy to be living in Paris, actually living in Paris, France. [11]

His forsaking of that stance coincided with his gradually altering responses to the New World, for over the years his standard view of Canada as "thousands of miles of wheat, indifference, and self-apology" underwent a radical modification until, like Jake, "he felt increasingly claimed by it," experiencing, as he sailed down the St. Lawrence back to England, "a sense of loss, even deprivation, and melancholy" (*H*, 5,6).

The ambivalence that Canadians over the years have held towards England, an attitude that surfaced for example, in a number of Sara Jeannette Duncan's novels, is convincingly rendered in *St. Urbain's Horseman*. Like Duncan's Lorne Murchison, Jake, while living in Canada, "had been able to revere London and its offerings with impunity," but after living there, "slowly, inexorably, he was being forced to pay the price of the colonial come to the capital" (*H*, 301). The price, ironically, is one that involves his disillusionment, not about himself, but about the much-vaunted cultural superiority of London: "He would have been happiest had the capital's standards not been so readily attainable and that it were still possible for him to have icons" (*H*, 302). Earlier, he and his friend Luke, "reared to believe in the cultural thinness of their own blood," had just missed the ironic realization of their unique situation among the assorted expatriates in London, a situation that in effect seems to have no solution:

Adrift in a cosmopolitan sea of conflicting mythologies, only they had
none. Moving among discontented commonwealth types in London,
they were inclined to envy them their real grievances. South Africans
and Rhodesians, *bona fide* refugees from tyranny, who had come to raise
a humanitarian banner in exile; Australians, who could allude to fore-
bears transported in convict ships; the West Indians, armed with the
most obscene outrage of all, the memory of their grandfathers sold in
marketplaces. What they failed to grasp was the ironic truth in Sir
Wilfred [sic] Laurier's boast that the twentieth century would belong to
Canada. For amid so many exiles from nineteenth-century tyranny, heirs
to injustices that could actually be set right politically, thereby lending
themselves to constructive angers, only the Canadians, surprisingly,
were true children of their times. Only they had packed their bags and
left home to escape the hell of boredom. And find it everywhere. (*H*,
195-96)

Within this perspective, Jake's situation as an expatriate from Canada
poses no residual problems for him, since he no longer regards himself as an
inferior colonial in one of the cultural centres of the world. His ongoing and
much larger dilemma is with his Jewish legacy, as dramatized in his ambivalent relationships both with his cousin Joey Hersh, the Horseman of this
novel, and with Harry (Hershel) Stein, who emerges as both the archetypal
Jewish victim of the world at large and as a grotesque perpetrator of his own
social exile. Richler's description of Harry's war-time expulsion from London in the language of the holocaust emphasizes that this banishment was in
effect part of a much larger exodus: "ten-year-old Harry, scruffy and sty-
ridden, was uprooted from his Stepney council school, tagged, issued a gas
mask, and shoveled into a train crammed with squealing mums and
babes . . . to be finally disgorged on a station platform in the outer wilds of
Buckinghamshire" (*H*, 21-22). Jake's guilt over Harry's situation, reinforced
in part by what in contrast was his own secure life in Montreal's Jewish
ghetto, is counterbalanced by the fascination he feels for the nihilistic
approach Harry has to life, which contradicts the fundamental morality of
Jake's code, and it is therefore appropriate that their ambivalence is dramatized in their joint sexual involvement with the German *au pair* girl.

Jake's relationship with his cousin Joey is similarly ambivalent, for against
his symbolic reputation as the Avenger on Horseback, searching the world
for the notorious murderer of Jews stands his ordinary human self, in some
respects of which he is scarcely more acceptable than Stein. Both of these
figures transform easily from realistic figures to symbolic figures to gro-
tesques who, as George Woodcock points out, "are dominated by some
obsession or eccentricity of thought that makes them ridiculous or despicable,

but [who] are partly redeemed by inconsistency, by a flaw in the making that allows their mitigating humanity to emerge."[12] That Joey is reported dead at the same time that Harry receives a long prison sentence frees Jake formally and legally from these two aspects of himself, but the lack of finality about their fate dictates that in a larger sense he will never be free of this legacy. Exile in this respect, Richler clearly implies, is a permanent condition for contemporary man, and particularly for individuals like Jake who inherit double legacies, and for whom the changing nature of the world makes them, as he muses at one point, "always the wrong age. Ever observers, never participants" (*H*, 87).

It is this sense of universal malaise and ennui that characterizes the work of another important Canadian expatriate of the time, Norman Levine, who has also, like Richler, frequently expressed a compulsion to escape both his Canadian and his Jewish heritage. This impulse, he feels, is a healthy thing for Canadian literature: "One of the conditions I discovered," he confessed to the editor of *Saturday Night*, "was that to be a writer I had to be an exile. I think that in every generation there ought to be one or two writers who are living outside Canada, away from the literary infighting, being very much Canadian writers but writing from a more detached viewpoint."[13] That his own fiction does not always fulfil the implications inherent in this statement to the extent, for example, that Mavis Gallant's does, does not invalidate the important point he makes about the function of exile literature in general. A recurring note in his own fiction is the dilemma of the exiled artist who, more than the one rooted in time and place, experiences the conflict of being simultaneously a figure of intrigue and expectation, towards whom people gravitate, and a very ordinary figure, whose substance is, as his protagonist in "A Writer's Story" realizes, like footsteps in the sand.

Though Levine has on many occasions expressed a strong dissatisfaction with *The Angled Road* (1952), it has more artistic merits than he concedes, and in fact, even apart from its depiction of the theme of alienation, seems to me to have more substance than his more often acclaimed second novel, *From a Seaside Town* (1970). It is on one level a dramatization of his compulsion to forsake his Canadian heritage that runs concurrent with the process he had already begun to abandon his Jewish legacy: "I found myself pretending I didn't live in Lower Town," he explained in an early interview. "I began to live in a fantasy world: pretending that I wasn't Jewish, giving myself fictitious parents."[14] In his first novel, he made his protagonist non-Jewish, presumably in order to convince himself that he had succeeded in exorcising that part of his background, but much of his later fiction demonstrates that this is not the case.

David Wrixon's rejection of Canada is signalled initially by his mixed attitudes towards his parents, English immigrants to Ottawa's Lower Town, whose reduced fortunes and eccentric life styles evoke in him mixed feelings of anger and compassion. "Both of them looked like two bewildered strangers who have been discovered in a strange land,"[15] he sensitively and accurately assesses them at that crucial stage in his own life when he suddenly becomes aware of the world's imperfections. His wish "to be free from the pettiness and the stuffiness of [his] environment, from the hopeless resignation and tragedy" (*AR*, 46) is given sudden legitimacy with the outbreak of war, even though in an ensuing departure scene, where his new identity is reflected in his RCAF uniform, he experiences momentary harmony between his parents and himself. Indeed, as with Brian Moore's Ginger Coffey, whose past is effectively obliterated when he dons the delivery driver's anonymous uniform, so Wrixon's service uniform guarantees him both a release from the past and a new life, for which only he is responsible. As we will see with Mavis Gallant's remittance man in her "Varieties of Exile," war in a very real sense offers the exile figure the optimum opportunity to make the best of two worlds—the precise one of the past that he wishes to reject, and the undifferentiated and shifting one of the future into which he is being propelled.

But once in England, David finds that the reality of Canada begins to undergo a change, and his difficulty in describing or defining it to his first lover anticipates the problems Levine was to experience some years later in his *Canada Made Me:*

> When she asked me about Canada, I tried to tell her that although I did not know what the country *was,* I was quite certain that it was not what she thought: mounties, maple trees and snow. But even though she listened, I knew that she would continue to think of it in her own terms. For her world depended on the longevity of her images. (*AR*, 77)

Valerie's attitude reflects both her confidence and her insecurity about her world, "a private world filled with the colours she wanted and the things she knew" (*AR*, 76); significantly, it is the displaced and rootless Wrixon who is responsible for her painful disillusionment on this score, but it is not a triumph he savours.

In a manner characteristic of New World expatriates when they first arrive in the Old World, Wrixon tends to downplay or diminish his native land, eager to reject what he sees as his depressingly tangible Canadian legacy. But he follows the pattern, too, as we saw operating with Richler's Jake Hersh or Duncan's Lorne Murchison and Graham Trent, of eventually recognizing that the reality of England does not always conform to the ideas he had held about it, though for some time he continues to take comfort in the physical attractions of his new country:

I liked England. I knew I did not want to go back home again. After
Dorset Street the very pavements were beautiful. I like the houses, the
weather. I liked the people in the streets, their faces, clothes, how they
walk and talk. Above all, I liked the English countryside. (*AR*, 113)

David's role as a flyer, however, allows him both literally and symbolically to
acquire new and inconsistent views of England, a land he begins to see as
"dead," "instinctive," and "mechanical," at times feeling that he is "the one
that was upside down" (*AR*, 113). Simultaneously, in his everyday relationships with the English people, he becomes weary of their decorum and
artificiality, and even finds his second lover, Patricia, somewhat suffocating
in her possessiveness and tendency to manipulate his life. In a period of
recuperation from his flying duties, he elects to remain in isolation, severing
his relationship with her and the England she represents because, as he says
in his final letter to her, "too many strange things are happening . . . . I feel
very much like an unfinished product" (*AR*, 125).

The end of the war leaves him in a state of indecision, for though on the
one hand he "felt divorced from England," he feels alienated as well from
Canada. His decision to go to university to allow, as he says, his "old self to
die, completely," reflects yet another illusion that the Levine protagonist
characteristically experiences, for old selves, no more than old soldiers,
never really die, even though they may proceed to see themselves from
different perspectives. This is a characteristic of Levine's fiction and non-
fiction alike: protagonists, scenes, and dilemmas keep getting recycled with
only minor variations. What Levine cannot ultimately resolve—and to an
extent this is a recurring condition faced by the exile writer—are the obligations he feels towards the various worlds that have shaped him, a dilemma
most strikingly exposed in his remarkable *Canada Made Me* (1958).

Even if this book is not, as he once said, "the only subversive book in
Canadian letters," it is nevertheless an unsettling one, which compels Canadians to reassess some of the realities they have long entertained about their
country. Non-fictional in terms of the literal journey and visits Levine
undertakes, *Canada Made Me* assumes a mythological dimension, with a
structure that is appropriate to the odyssey of the exile figure—not unlike,
for example, Grove's *A Search for America*. The book's twelve chapters
are framed by opening and closing sections entitled respectively "The
Emigrant Ship" and "The Tourist Ship," and giving the entire work an
organic unity is the figure of Levine himself, who at various times reflects all
the stages of exile that are contained in and between the words "emigrant"
and "tourist." What seems to be a haphazard recording of all kinds of
circumstantial detail, of descriptions of city and countryside, of bits of
conversation, adds up to a composite picture of the Canada that has both

shaped and alienated Levine, and of a Canada that constitutes the promise for the emigrant and the memory for the tourist: the country that Levine has chosen to leave is the same country that the emigrants keep choosing.[16]

The opening emigrant ship section allows Levine to use a standard fictional device, that of confining travellers to a fixed space or time and compelling them to tell their tale—a ruse as popular among contemporary novelists as it was for Chaucer or Boccaccio. Shipboard passengers by definition are either emigrants or tourists, in transit between one country and another, and represent, therefore, various degrees of the exile state; such a structural pattern constitutes a fairly regular approach in exile literature, and in this study we see it exploited in works as diverse as Wilson's *The Innocent Traveller,* Lewis's *Self Condemned,* and Lowry's "Through the Panama." Levine employs it here to make some interesting observations on the exile phenomenon. The ship by no means constitutes a unified or socially agreeable world: in many respects it is an arena of hostility, suspicion, and boredom, where we become intensely aware of the abiding despair of the ordinary exile. The emigrants all react differently to the emerging realities that exile implies: one wants to change his name, another to forget completely his past, and all felt "it was better to be separate from the places and the streets and the people who were reminders of the mistakes and the messes one made, and ran away from" (*CMM,* 21)—a reaction that applies not only to the recurring Levine protagonist, but to such other exiles as Grove's Philip Branden and Moore's Fergus Fadden.

There is tragedy and hardship, too, on board ship: an Italian woman suddenly dies, leaving her Hungarian husband and child to resume a shattered life in the New World—a scene reminiscent of the one in Moodie's *Roughing It in the Bush,* where the elderly couple, their only child dead through cholera, face a lonely and bleak future in Canada. And an Irish passenger, revisiting his home streets as the ship calls in briefly at Dublin, is revealed as someone whose exile was dictated by conditions that lay completely beyond his control, and who is now compelled to go through life affecting an identity that is not his own. The waiter's remark to the returning American student about homesickness being a luxury "for those who are romantic and don't want to grow up" (*CMM,* 19) has an ironic application to Levine's situation, for his return to his native land derives from impulses that he does not fully understand, though homesickness is undoubtedly one of the ingredients:

> Though I called Canada home—and by Canada I meant only parts of Ottawa, Montreal and the Laurentians—I felt no particular sense of belonging there. But then neither did I feel I belonged particularly anywhere else. Was that one's inheritance, a rootlessness? Or maybe it

was just curiosity that drives one back to see where one had grown up in?
Or was it something more personal? A kind of personal destructiveness
that one is condemned to carry. Of going back to places that one left
innocent, knowing that now one's equipment has changed. (*CMM*, 22)

In his suggestion that rootlessness is in these days a permanent part of the
human condition, Levine speaks with the voice of the universal exile, aware
of the multiple legacies that constitute both a release and a burden. And as
he points out later, becoming "faithful to a new set of experiences" is
essentially tantamount to acknowledging a form of self-betrayal, which
again, as characters like René Harding or Brendan Tierney exemplify, is one
of the abiding penalties of exile.

The straightforward narrative structure of this book is interrupted briefly
by two epistolary intrusions, consisting of "A letter from Morocco" and "A
letter from Israel," neither of which provides any information regarding the
identity of the correspondents, though there is no question but that they
have the effect of being imaginary letters from Levine to himself. Their
justification resides in their explanation of Levine's reasons for forsaking,
respectively, his Canadian and his Jewish legacies, and, in the first letter, the
setting forth of some of the rationales that lie behind exile in the more
general sense. He maintains a detached and rational attitude in setting forth
his arguments, especially in the first letter, for Canada seemingly produces
little emotional response of any sort in him, and any deficiency that might be
attributed to Canada he promptly claims as his own. Even his most unequivo-
cal reservation—"there is absolutely nothing one can do in Canada, except
go fishing, that one can't do better, or more profitably, or more comfortably,
or more easily, elsewhere" (*CMM*, 44)—seems more in the nature of an
unexamined cliché than an experiential discovery. The arguments he offers
here that militate against exile, such as the basic conservatism of people, and
their addiction to their own language and customs, do not apply to him, who
learns languages easily and is attracted to the exotic. "Since the world is still
reasonably large and reasonably various," he sums up, "it is obvious that a
rootless person like myself . . . will find somewhere that suits his personal
taste better than the place where, through no choice of his own, he was born"
(*CMM*, 44).

Paradoxically, Levine goes into exile in order to escape the country that,
as his journey reveals, was built through the very same process, for everywhere he goes he meets exiles from other lands who for one reason or
another chose Canada as a place to live. Levine reflects an ambivalence
towards these exiles, that in some measure is dictated by the degree to which
they have compromised their origins, a situation revealed, appropriately, as
he reached the ethnic city of Winnipeg:

But it was down Main Street that one felt quickly at home. The huddles of old men outside small restaurants with the foreign newspapers in the windows, who had lived here for thirty, forty, even fifty years and who still remained Ukrainians, Poles, Lithuanians and Germans. They were the Displaced Persons, the failures. Not the D.P.s who have come here since the war or even the more recent immigrants. They have quickly taken on North American values, discarding their background, putting on the thin veneer of conformity, what is demanded of them, in order to be accepted, to be on the way to success. (*CMM*, 95)

Though Levine's attitude here implies a condemnation of the more recent exiles, it is precisely their propensity to deracination that frequently characterizes his own protagonists, a tendency, incidentally, that constitutes a concern of such other exile writers as Laura Salverson, John Marlyn, and Henry Kreisel.

Levine has less sympathy for those temporary exiles from the Old World who merely exploit the New, like the academic who detests Winnipeg, "but where could he get such pay in England?" (*CMM*, 98); he reserves his particular scorn for what he calls the "provincial middle-class English in exile," where he is every bit as biting in his description as Mavis Gallant is with some of her marginal Riviera-based characters:

They were continually running down England, the Socialists, the "bad conditions" they left behind, though they kept in touch with "home", with their friends who had gone to Kenya, Rhodesia, and regularly received *Punch, The Times* Calendar, the *Illustrated London News,* the *Tatler* . . . . In Canada they charmingly accepted hospitality, but as soon as they were back in England amongst their own kind they ran down Canada, the Canadians, and entertained their friends by telling jokes in a Canadian accent. (*CMM*, 173-74)

The English exiles he meets in Victoria, however, reflect none of this ruthlessness, which is limited, he implies, to those living in Ottawa and Montreal. Undoubtedly, this distorted observation reflects the distinction between his own direct involvement with them in the East and what is largely a romantic or literary involvement with them in the West, for he quotes the famous bovine description of Victoria from Emily Carr's *The Book of Small,* which implies that any exiles arriving there are immediately mesmerized by that city's benign determinism: "there she paused, chewing the cud of imported fodder, afraid to crop the pastures of the new world for fear she might lose the good flavour of the old to which she was so deeply loyal. Her jaws went on rolling on and on, long after there was nothing left to chew"

(*CMM*, 174). It is appropriate, incidentally, that he should quote Emily Carr, for like him, she was also an expatriate artist in St. Ives, Cornwall, for a short while.

For Levine, this journey across Canada constitutes both a physical return trip to places that are at once familiar and alien, and a spiritual voyage into the causes and meanings of exile. His response to much of what he encounters is in part shaped by his earlier travels, and frequently it is bitterness, rather than nostalgia or even mere regret, that he experiences, for the places are never as he remembered them. But occasionally, too, what he sees in Canada evokes pleasant Old World scenes and memories, such as Vancouver's Stanley Park engendering his reminiscences about Cornwall, where he had lived a life not unlike the carefree one that John Glassco enjoyed in Paris: "It was all wonderfully absurd. But one felt good. Writing was done; pictures were painted. And one didn't care. One was young. And this was new. And it didn't last" (*CMM*, 150). From this detached perspective in place and time, Levine is able to analyze rationally what being an expatriate in Cornwall really meant:

> On one side it is gay, irresponsible, absurd, and happy. On the other there are depression, quarrels, poverty, and anxiety . . . One had, by choice, turned one's back on a direction that was pulling everywhere else. You kicked against values you refused to inherit. But in the end was it enough? The line separating the retired businessman . . . the divorcees getting older and more desperate, hoping something will turn up, from oneself was very thin. It did not take much to step over and retire oneself and pretend that the gesture of refusing to be involved was in itself a commitment. For this place was a no man's land, let to whoever could pay the rent. (*CMM*, 151)

Exile here in effect meant an artistic dead end, for though there was some appeal in consciously opposing conventional values and directions, it was ultimately difficult to separate the committed from the tourist.

The situation that Levine describes here receives convincing fictional treatment in his second novel, *From a Seaside Town,* as well as in a number of his short stories, notably "The Playground" and "Ringa Ringa Rosie," both collected in *One Way Ticket* (1961). This latter story is a particularly poignant dramatization of the human price that is sometimes paid to justify an exile that seems prolonged by perversity rather than by necessity. The Buchanans have just made their fourteenth move in the five years they have been away from Canada, and George refuses to return until he has a book published. They are now at the end of their resources and possibilities: the typewriter has been pawned, all unnecessary books sold, all further credit withheld. In total isolation, George has contact with his friends only by telephone, none of whom, however, presumably because they have been bitten before, are willing to advance him any money. For the moment, George sustains their two children through the ritual of nursery rhyme games, but Sheila only weeps in her recognition of their hopeless situation.

Dispossession is clearly a recurring characteristic of an exile situation, but with, for example, the typical Lowry protagonist, it seems almost cosmic in derivation, part of the human condition generally; the response to it in that situation is a kind of experiential wisdom that progressively enlarges, and leaves its mark upon both the inhabitant and the world he for the moment inhabits. With the Buchanans, on the other hand, it is destructive and seems to be a consequence of sheer incompetence and day-to-day carelessness, for they possess no moral or philosophical vision to sustain them; though moving had become "an accepted but reluctant part of their lives," they found that whenever they were in a new location, "no serious attempt was made to change the place or impose on it any sense of possession" (*OWT*, 77).

Written about the same time as the previous story, "The Playground" depicts a world that is reminiscent of Fitzgerald's Riviera in his *Tender Is the Night*, for both are worlds that in effect can survive for only so long before their inhabitants' moral credit is expended. Seen largely through the eyes of a Canadian writer, Bill Stringer, Levine's expatriate colony on the Cornish coast moves inevitably through its various phases, from its peak of summer excitement through its autumn days of lethargy and boredom to its winter disintegration, foreshadowed by the growing disputes and infidelities, and confirmed, ironically, by Jimmy Stark's New Year's Eve suicide, he being the only native Cornishman among them. That none of the expatriates attend his funeral dramatizes the separation between the natives and the outsiders, and the realization that ultimately there is nothing of lasting value for them here. When Stringer first arrived in the colony, his immediate impressions were of its physical qualities and now, on his departure after Twelfth Night, it is the same: in this secular world, no visions or epiphanies of a spiritual nature are possible, and he senses the appropriateness of his final vision, of "the sun shin[ing] brilliantly on the discarded Christmas trees floating in the harbour to be swept out to sea" (*OWT*, 75).

The expatriates in this colony come together initially as much out of a general ennui as out of any compulsion dictated by their professed interest in painting or writing, and Stringer's observation to himself, "I didn't worry very much about the book I wasn't writing" (*OWT*, 45), more or less constitutes a working credo for most of the artists gathered here. It is a series of weekly parties that seem to constitute the raison d'être for these assorted expatriates, but they are parties that lack the bohemian ecstasy of Glassco's

Parisian escapades and the political fervour of Winkleman's gatherings in *A Choice of Enemies*. Instead, they are characterized by a kind of irresoluteness: casual or interrupted relationships, desperate flirtations and infidelities, insipid and undirected conversations. "This is really a Chekhov situation," one of the characters remarks. "All we do here is talk. Nothing happens" (*OWT*, 48), an observation that verifies the earlier opinion of a local waitress that the place is "a dump" because "it's so boring" (*OWT*, 13).

As we saw, it is the Canadian Bill Stringer whose arrival and departure frame this story, but it is also his role as a professional writer that filters the impressions we receive of the other characters. Not that he is a productive writer: like Jimmy Stark's wife, Rosalie, who is a collector of painters, Stringer is a collector of names and characters he hopes one day to use in his fiction; for the moment, he has completely lost interest in his current Ginger Coffey-like novel set in Montreal about "an optimistic Irish immigrant trying to survive his first Canadian winter" (*OWT*, 21). Unlike many Levine protagonists, he seems unconcerned about his Canadian roots, being content to drift along in casual relationships with other expatriates, and unlike them, too, he does not feel he has to play a role. Abe Gin, for example, the Winnipeg Jew, wants desperately to cultivate an image of himself as a painter, but he lacks any significant talent; perhaps for that reason, he cannot quite shake his loyalties to his dual legacies, and his drunken refrain as he lies beside a puddle—"Ferryman. Take me across. I want to go home." (*OWT*, 45)—assumes a sudden poignancy in the midst of a world that is on the whole uncaring.

Illusion and pretence characterize a number of other exile stories in Levine's collections, notably "The Dilettantes" from *One Way Ticket*, "I Like Chekhov" and A Canadian Upbringing" from *I Don't Want to Know Anyone Too Well* (1971), and "Class of 1949" and "A Writer's Story" from *Thin Ice* (1979). In many of them, a Canadian protagonist encounters a situation in which reality is difficult to define or to recognize, not necessarily because of any deficiency or residual innocence on the part of the Canadian, but more often because the individuals he encounters shift their ground as they run the risk of being detected for what they are. In "The Dilettantes," for example, the Obodiaks ostensibly are dedicated to helping newly arrived exiles in London find suitable accommodation, but in fact they create their own version of reality with such conviction that their own vicarious involvement in it sustains them from assignment to assignment without diminution. In effect, they exploit situations where there is no chance for rebuttal: editing a journal devoted to an author who has just died; soliciting anonymous acquaintances over the telephone whose responses we never hear; arranging, for a fee, literary parties for exiles to which famous literati presumably are invited, but who never appear. Only when Obodiak is caught

out by an expatriate Canadian dramatist over a putative invitation to Priestley is he momentarily nonplussed, but here it is the Canadian who feels
guilty:

> I felt annoyed with myself. Why did I go and say that? Wouldn't it have
> been better to have ignored it and let him continue his game? Sure, it was
> all pretence. But he had made something out of it. (*OWT*, 156)

As the example of the Canadian dramatist illustrates (he has yet to write a
play), pretence is not the exclusive property of the Obodiaks; exiles in a
sense must always create a new reality out of nothing, and believe in what
they create.

In "A Canadian Upbringing" Levine passes an ironic judgment on the
question of why Canadian writers go abroad, and cleverly manipulates the
reality-illusion pattern. The reality that convinces the narrator, a youthful
Canadian novelist, to go abroad is his discovery of an obscure book, *A
Canadian Upbringing*, by an earlier expatriate, Alexander Marsden, a book
seemingly not unlike Levine's own *Canada Made Me*. But the reality changes
to illusion when he ultimately discovers Marsden living in Cornwall, no
longer a writer, but a maker of toy roundabouts, a craft that, unlike his
writing, has earned him a respectable international reputation. Marsden,
now more critical of England than of Canada, advises the narrator to return
to his homeland while he is still young, attitudes that the latter sees as a form
of betrayal:

> I have not had many heroes lately and as I grow older they get less. But
> Marsden had meant something personal to me. And I felt I had been
> cheated. Of what exactly I didn't know. But the man who wrote *A
> Canadian Upbringing* no longer existed as far as I was concerned.
> (*DWK*, 118)

Whether we see this story as an allegory of Levine's own situation or as a
realistic tale with its own justification, it offers a convincing anti-romantic
comment on the whole question of expatriation.

Levine has had some problems in resolving his own ambivalence towards
Canada and England, and in many respects his stories and novels constitute
dramatizations of his own responses to the question that opens this story:
"When people ask me why did I leave Canada and go over to England, the
answer I give depends on the kind of person who is doing the asking" (*DWK*,
111). The reason that Marsden gave in his book—"not because he wanted to
deny his background but because he feels the need to accept a wider view of
life" (*DWK*, 111)—though it takes an ironic turn in this particular story,

generally applies to most of Levine's protagonists. Not that Canadians always discover "a wider view" of things: in the light-hearted story, "I like Chekhov," the Canadian schoolmaster, caught in a kind of snob warfare that separates the Cambridge-trained masters from those trained in provincial universities, discovers that, because he is "socially unclassifiable," he is accepted by both groups. But in other stories, like "Class of 1949" and "A Writer's Story," the question receives a much more serious examination, for here the reality of one's past plays a crucial part in the protagonist's attempt to come to terms with his current expatriate situation. In "A Writer's Story" the narrator, by deliberately cutting off his past, has come to the realization that he no longer has any fictional material to work with, a deprivation that is emphasized by the steady stream of stories that his Cornwall neighbours tell him about their past. He can only begin to write by leaving, and by making lists of people and scenes and other tangible realities of his own past.

In "Class of 1949" the juxtaposition is between two Canadian expatriates who in a sense are alter egos of one another, for the narrator novelist and his friend Victor share the same past: McGill education, expatriation to London at the same time, first novels completed simultaneously. But when they meet after a long separation, they are leading diametrically opposed lives, for Victor has denied his past, while the novelist has built on his, and is living a routine but artistically productive life. His explanation of Victor's artistic failure may on the one hand be a rationalization for his envy of Victor's current carefree existence, but on the other hand it constitutes a realistic obligation for the writer in exile:

> "I remember when he finished the novel and showed me the typescript. The characters were lifeless. I asked him why didn't he write about people he knew. About his family, about Montreal, his private school. He said he didn't want anything to do with Canada or anything connected with it. I don't know anyone who hates Canada so much. And how can you be a writer if you reject your past? Seeing Victor, I can see the person I was." (*TI*, 22)

That Victor is both a reminder of the past and seemingly an exciting figure to emulate in the present disturbs the novelist and his wife, both of whom, fettered to their Cornwall residence, envy him for the freedom he seems to possess. But his freedom is of course precisely what the novelist sought and attained by leaving Montreal many years earlier, and in that state of freedom chose as an artist to reimpose his fetters to his past. Within that perspective, Victor fades quickly once his visit is over, but undoubtedly he will reappear in the narrator's fiction, for he writes only about people he knows, whose "visit is only the top of an iceberg" (*TI*, 27).

The narrator's wife, Emily, has in a sense already appeared as Emily Grand in Levine's second novel, *From a Seaside Town* (1970), whose question to Joseph reflects the puzzlement that all his protagonists' wives seem to experience: "How come someone as intelligent as you has got himself into this position? Stuck in a cut-off seaside town. How come you let it happen?" (*FST*, 37). To the English-born Emily, the question is a logical one, but to the Canadian travel writer, Joseph Grand, to answer it honestly would be to diminish his present stature, for as with many marginally talented expatriates, as we saw in "The Playground" and "Ringa Ringa Rosie," it is in large part illusion that sustains him from crisis to crisis. Despite her unhappiness, Emily is very much a stable force in his life, but undermining her influence are several rootless, manipulative, or dishonest acquaintances who cater to the disordered side of him. "Part of me wants the conventional," he muses late in the novel, "and some other part wants to be outside society" (*FST*, 162), and this overlapping of personal order and chaos is up to a point reflected in the form of the novel itself, with its digressions, addenda, asides, and most notably, its long story within a story. The effect of all these stylistic devices is to confirm the uncertain nature of the world that Joseph inhabits, with only his home city of Ottawa and his expatriate town of Carnbray giving the illusion of routine and order.

But there are always reminders of other worlds that both disturb and tempt him: in Carnbray the native-born Jimmy Middleton, a solid, dependable marine biologist while at home, but a sexual acrobat abroad, unsettles Joseph with his accounts of his latest escapades; from London come such visitors as the homosexual artist, Charles Crater, and the seductive actress, Anna Likely, with whom Joseph has a brief, precarious affair that almost destroys his marriage. In Canada he is beset by the requirements and demands of his family or by the memories of old acquaintances, and momentarily tempted by the possibilities of a routine academic life where he would be "part of the community." But it is in a scene reminiscent of the *Controversy* debate in *A Choice of Enemies* that Joseph reveals his basic incompatibility with this kind of life: interviewed by an academic critic who wonders why "so many of our writers live out of Canada" and whether Joseph has "come for a renewal of roots," he unerringly anticipates the factitious nature of the interview:

> He was going to write an article about my work for a little magazine. I already knew the pretentious phrases. The way the piece would be slanted. A Canadian in England would become "an expatriate" and linked to the American expatriates of the 1920s. And since I wasn't successful, not yet, I would be someone worth writing about in the little magazine. (*FST*, 146)

From a Seaside Town is by no means completely successful in correlating
its episodic and somewhat disjointed structure with Joseph's own uncertain
vision, but the separate anecdotes do dramatize various aspects of his
dilemmas, and suggest that ultimately they are not resolvable. Charles
Crater, remote in Switzerland now lives only as reproductions in the colour
supplements; his London friend, Albert, obsessed with tracing his Polish
Jewish ancestry, drops out of sight after failing to become assistant editor of
The History of the Twentieth Century; Jimmy Middleton, dead in a car
crash, is given a celebrated home-town burial beside his ancestors; and Anna
Likely descends quickly from stage to pornographic movies to being merely
a picture on a fortune card in a bus station weighing machine. Small wonder
that Joseph ultimately comes to a conclusion that "life seems to be a series of
unconnected brief encounters" (*FST*, 219), a vision, as we will see in the next
chapter, that is not unlike the one reflected on occasion by Mavis Gallant.
Though Joseph's personal fortunes have improved somewhat by novel's end,
Emily's dissatisfaction remains, but she finds some hope in her contempla-
tion of the French crabbers (a recurring image in all of Levine's Cornwall-
based fiction) in the harbour: one of these boats clearly does not belong with
the others, and her thought that one day it will be gone gives her great
comfort.

Norman Levine has for some time now resumed his permanent residence
in Canada, and by geographical definition, therefore, he has ceased to be an
expatriate. One of his earliest writings, however, suggests that the paradoxes
of exile will not easily disappear from his vision, for in his "Letter from
London" he poses the question whether he "would return to parchment
summers and merchant eyes," and provides his own answer:

> Then London and the cocktail parties,
> And the clever young men and the clever young women,
> And the loveliest of fogs made you forget that contentment
> Of grey merchandise spawning in parchment summers.
> An exile you were then,
> As you are now,
> Wanting roots and living on an island.[17]

As we have seen, most of his fiction and non-fiction constitutes his attempts
to resolve the implications of that last line, and some of his work written
since his return to Canada confirms that his exile experiences still very much
shape his aesthetic vision.[18]

6

From the Old World: A Canadian in Paris

Though she is a close contemporary of two of the expatriates discussed in the previous chapter, Mavis Gallant in some respects bears a closer relationship to Sara Jeannette Duncan than she does to either Norman Levine or Mordecai Richler. Born the same year that Duncan died, Gallant is exclusively concerned, however, with a modern world characterized by dislocation and dispossession rather than ordered and predictable worlds of the kind that constituted Duncan's fictional settings. But in terms of their Canadian backgrounds, their long periods of residency abroad, their familiarity with many societies of the New and Old Worlds, their unconscious Canadianism, and their consummate prose artistry, these two writers have much in common, though offering quite distinct perspectives on the whole question of exile.

Duncan's early life and education, as we saw, was conventional and ordered, but Gallant in a sense started out as an exile: at the age of four she was sent off to the first of some seventeen schools that were to provide her formal education. She was on occasion the only Protestant in a Catholic school, and at other times the only bilingual student in monolingual schools whether French or English, and it is therefore easy to see why a frequently recurring exile figure in her work is the child, physically and psychologically cut off from all components of an ordered life.

Both Duncan and Gallant, in their early twenties, turned to journalism and established themselves solidly in that largely male profession before turning permanently to fiction, a stage which in both cases by and large coincided with their departure from Canada. Unlike Duncan, Gallant left Canada not out of domestic necessity, but, after a brief marriage and a six-year stint with the Montreal *Standard*, for reasons that were both psychological and artistic in nature:

I did not, as people mistakenly imagine, "sell a story and throw up my job." My leaving was not an impulsive gesture. I had been thinking of it for over a year. I was twenty-seven when I quit, a few months short of twenty-eight. I saw thirty as a deadline, a trench across one's life.[1]

Her self-exile was thus generated from within and not, as was the case with the 1920s lost generation group or with her own contemporaries, because Europe was somehow seen as the remedy for all North American or Canadian deficiencies. She seemingly approached the Old World, therefore, with few a priori assumptions about it, and the fictional consequence of that attitude has been a rational and extremely complex analysis of the three or four societies that have shaped her that goes far beyond the relatively superficial treatments offered by Duncan.

Duncan was, however, aware that there were peculiar problems facing a Canadian writer, and not long before she herself became a novelist, she described a national and artistic dilemma that in a sense has only been resolved by writers of Gallant's generation:

More than one generation of people who talked of England or Scotland or Ireland as "home," people of refinement, scholarly tastes, and a certain amount of leisure have taken in hand the construction of a Canadian literature. Their ideals were British, their methods were British . . . and they are mostly gathered to their British fathers, leaving the work to descendants, whose present, and not whose past, country is the actual, potential fact in their national life. There is a wide difference, though comparatively few years span it, between a colonial and a Canadian, and we may not unnaturally look for a corresponding difference in their literary productions.[2]

Duncan herself had no doubts about her own identity as a Canadian rather than a colonial, and she would wholeheartedly agree with Gallant's observation made almost a hundred years after her own proclamation: "I suppose that a Canadian is someone who has a logical reason to think he is one. My logical reason is that I have never been anything else, nor has it occurred to me that I might be."[3]

It is in her public pronouncements and interviews rather than overtly in her fiction that Gallant is strongly committed to her Canadian identity, though nowhere is she passionately demonstrative about it. Indeed, she at times chides her erstwhile countrymen for what she perceives as their shortcomings, though she has never been tempted to abandon her citizenship:

I have sometimes felt more at odds in Canada than anywhere else, but I never supposed I was any the less Canadian . . . . I resisted a change of citizenship when it was offered me because I knew the result would be fake: whatever I was called, I would continue to think of myself as Canadian. I believe it is a wholly respectable thing to be. Yet when I say this, it irritates Canadians. They take me to mean conformist, small-minded. I mean the word in its original sense of worthy of respect, the opposite of shameful and disreputable, and I have always made certain that respect was rendered that part of my identity on the few occasions when it has been slighted. (*HT*, xiv)

In her two novels and five collections of stories to date, Gallant has created a cast of international exiles who seldom possess her own certainty, whatever their background, and who are frequently part of what she calls in one story "a raggle-taggle international family," in transit from one temporary residence to another. Even those who remain in their native country, like Rhoda of "The Prodigal Parent" or Jeannie of "My Heart Is Broken," are beset by disturbing notions about their identities and roles, and not infrequently these individuals are at the edge of emotional collapse. Exile in Gallant almost invariably reflects this psychological chaos, and for most of her characters, such conventional solutions to exile as discovering a new paradise or returning to one's homeland are totally irrelevant.

With many exile writers—certainly with most of those I am concerned with in this study—it is at times difficult to distinguish between protagonist and author, for a subjective, even solipsistic, literature not infrequently constitutes their first line of defence. But with Gallant this problem is considerably less pronounced, for she effectively distances herself from her characters and situations in a number of ways: by employing third person narration more regularly than first (two-thirds of her collected stories and both her novels are cast in the third person), by creating a vast range of central characters, from adolescent girls to elderly men and women, and by relying on a carefully controlled sense of irony. It is only in the sequence of Linnet Muir stories that constitute the conclusion of *Home Truths* that there is an obvious parallel between protagonist and author, but even here Gallant offers a timely caution:

[Linnet Muir] is obviously close to me. She isn't *myself*, but a kind of summary of some of the things I once was. In real life I was far more violent and much more impulsive and not nearly so reasonable. Straight autobiography would be boring . . . . The stories are a kind of reality *necessarily* transformed.[4]

Gallant's long residence abroad, too, has compelled her to adopt a detached view towards the many societies that have shaped her; all her fiction, except for the four stories published between 1944 and 1950, has been written during her Old World residency, mainly in France, though she also lived for short periods in London, Spain, and Austria. Interestingly enough, unlike the other countries she has lived in, England has rarely provided the setting for any of her fiction (I can think only of "Two Questions," and even there the main action is in Spain), though it is a place where many of her characters come *from*. Gallant's response to London was not unlike Carol Frazier's of "The Other Paris" to that city: "London in 1950 was not welcoming or open. I found it ugly, heavy, very remote from my idea of it, which had been purely literary."[5] This experience may help to explain the largely negative views of the English which emerge in her fiction, particularly of the numerous marginal types in such Riviera-based stories as "The Remission" or "Acceptance of Their Ways" or, as in the Montreal-based "Varieties of Exile," where the ubiquitous remittance man is her target.

Throughout virtually all her fiction Gallant depicts her various worlds in terms of a universally-sensed malaise about the impermanence and rootlessness that characterize their inhabitants, and in this respect she has emerged as one of the most consistent and powerful analysts of exile among English-language novelists of the modern world. The fact, however, that she began her writing career in the immediate post-war period allowed her to discover all around her dramatic evidence for this cosmic vision, for the manifestations of personal dispossession and social breakdown were everywhere visible in the aftermath of the war. By juxtaposing a residual New World innocence against the disintegrations of various Old World scenes, scenes that can never again fulfil one's traditional expectations, Gallant transmits a particularly original and disturbing vision of her world, a vision that only in the recent Linnet Muir stories has undergone modifications that point to a satisfactory resolution of experience.

In her first collection of stories, however, Gallant offers a vision of exile experience that is on the whole an upsetting one. Some nine of the twelve stories that constitute *The Other Paris* (1956) have as their central concern the uncertainty or bewilderment that New World protagonists experience in the moral and cultural confusion they encounter in the Old; of the three remaining stories, all set in Canada, only the delicately balanced recollection of childhood, "Wing's Chips," conveys a totally positive vision. The title story of the collection reveals Gallant at her best at this stage of her career, its power deriving largely from the way she leads us into understanding the protagonist's ultimate inability to come to terms with a world that in so many unexpected ways continues to defy her conditioned expectations. Though Carol Frazier is at times naïve beyond belief, she is presented with compassion and understanding, and only occasionally does Gallant's ironic stance allow us to feel superior to her. Carol's "other Paris" is of course all around her, had she the willingness to accept what she saw everyday—"shabby girls bundled into raincoats, hurrying along in the rain, or men who needed a haircut"—but New World innocent that she is, she keeps looking for the Paris that exists only in her imagination:

> Where was the Paris she had read about? Where were the elegant and expensive-looking women? Where, above all, were the men, those men with their gay good looks and snatches of merry song, the delight of English lady novelists? (*OP*, 6)

Gallant's ironic and realistic view of Paris stands in sharp contrast to the romantic vision of earlier expatriates, as we saw reflected by the youthful John Glassco in his *Memoirs of Montparnasse,* though that earlier experience reflects its own subjective truth in a most convincing way. Gallant is both more detached and more sophisticated in her perspective on the Old World, qualities that allow her to manipulate her characters with purpose and precision. We find therefore in this story that it is not only the New World innocent who is incisively measured and found deficient but also the Parisian Odile, whose assumed world weariness and conventional cynicism are also shown to constitute barriers to a genuine understanding of one's world and oneself. Neither girl gets off easily under Gallant's penetrating vision, and if we were obliged to measure respective New World-Old World values in terms of these two, we would be hard pressed indeed to arrive at a conclusion. She seems to display more sympathy for Carol than for Odile, or at any rate she analyzes her with more detachment and ironic humour. Her depiction of Carol's engagement to the conventional Howard, a proposal which took place not in "a scene that involved all at once the Seine, moonlight, barrows of violets, acacias in flower," but "at lunch, over a tuna-fish salad" (*OP*, 3) reflects not only the anti-romantic vision that characterizes Gallant's fiction in general, but also the kind of disconcerting satire that she is prone to direct against any individuals, whether exiles or not, who seem perversely blind to the realities of their world.

The power of this story, and its sadness, are generated not so much by the miserable pretensions of Odile and her pathetic family as by the unrealized potential of Carol as reflected by her incipient feelings of compassion, and perhaps even love, towards the dispossessed Felix. In terms of Gallant's overall vision referred to earlier, Felix emerges as a universal exile figure, a man without a past or an identity, without a country, and with a future that is limited to a tenuous day-to-day survival. On an immediate level Felix occupies a similar role in respect of Carol that the laundromat habitué Duncan does for Marian McAlpin in Atwood's *The Edible Woman*—an exotic

though unwashed alternative to the conventional men they both seem
doomed to marry. But as Ronald Hatch hints at in a perceptive essay on
Gallant (though he does not pursue the point at length),[6] Felix is also a kind
of third force in this story, a new "underground element" whose denial of all
traditions and whose pragmatic survival skills give him a stature that neither
of the preconditioned women possesses. Gallant does not develop him
sufficiently to allow us to see him fully as a version of Dostoevsky's underground man or Ellison's invisible man, but he does possess characteristics of
both. Though she rationalizes her escape from him, Carol is disturbed more
by him than by any of her other Parisian experiences, and for her he does in
fact constitute "the other Paris," though she is not prepared to acknowledge
that. Ironically, too, Carol for Felix must also constitute that very "other
Paris" that she kept looking for, represented by "the elegant and expensive-
looking women."

For Gallant, as for virtually all North American writers in the exile
tradition, Paris stands as a matter of course as a kind of objective correlative
in the fictional exercise of juxtaposing the Old World against the New. From
Henry James to Irwin Shaw, from Sara Jeannette Duncan to Mordecai
Richler, French culture, particularly the Parisian, has been seen to possess a
transformative power that would permanently dissolve the moral and artistic
blockages produced by North American parochialism. That it does not
necessarily or consistently do this is of course the stuff of which fiction is
made, as Gallant demonstrates in another story from that first collection,
"One Morning in June," and in a 1963 story collected in both *My Heart Is
Broken* and *Home Truths*—"The Ice Wagon Going Down the Street." In the
earlier story, Barbara and Mike are products of the general post-war uncertainty and malaise about things, sent to the Old World to find something
presumably unattainable in New York. Barbara had been conditioned to
believe "that she was to get something from her year in France, and return to
America brilliant, poised, and educated" (*OP*, 176), while Mike had been
sent abroad "because the words 'art' and 'Paris' were unbreakably joined in
his family's imagination" (*OP*, 178). Strangers to each other until thrown
together by Barbara's no-nonsense, manipulating aunt during a Riviera
vacation, they had both passed an obligatory year or so in Paris, where
Barbara had done the museums and galleries, compiling a "Souvenirs de
France" album, and proud mainly "of the fact that she had shivered in
unheated picture galleries and not spent her time drinking milk shakes in the
American Embassy restaurant" (*OP*, 176). Mike, an art student of limited
talents (not unlike Duncan's Elfrida Bell), "had spent the first three weeks
standing in the wrong queue at the Beaux-Arts" (*OP*, 178), and eventually, on
the lukewarm advice of an art instructor, had come south to paint the open
air Riviera scenes.

There is a nonchalance or casualness about these two youths that derives from a kind of stunned notion about their possibilities rather than from any confidence about themselves though, curiously, they are 'not lacking in confidence: they merely seem unmotivated or undirected, and their exposure to Paris produces no transformation whatsoever. The possibility exists for something more dynamic when they meet, for there is initially a "tremulous movement of friendship between them" (*OP*, 174), but they are ultimately rendered impotent not only by the aunt's "paralyzing" words, but by their own lethargy and by their inability to understand the world they have been compelled to inhabit. At the end they clasp hands, but this does not evoke the strong paradisal hand-in-hand image that defines, for example, Sigurd and Astrid in Lowry's "The Bravest Boat"; rather, it signifies the illusion of a relationship that for the moment sustains Barbara's aunt, if not themselves. Mike is aware of "the tenuous human claim" that, upon their separation, their subsequent correspondence can at best sustain, and like Carol Frazier, he and Barbara will in all likelihood resume safe refuge in the New World, no more to be disturbed by the incomprehensibilities of the Old.

In "The Ice Wagon Going Down the Street" Paris fulfils a somewhat different function, and is not merely a catalytic force that can cause things to happen. Interestingly, where Carol Frazier's fixed impression of Paris was a pre-experiential one, that of Sheilah and Peter (coincidentally, also named Frazier) was post-experiential, though every bit as illusory and impractical as Carol's:

> Peter's wife had loved him in Paris. Whatever she wanted in marriage she found that winter, there. In Geneva, where Peter was a file clerk and they lived in a furnished flat, she pretended they were in Paris and life was still the same. (*HT*, 111)

Typical of Gallant's expatriate families who move around the world, unconcerned about what happens to their children, Sheilah and Peter in a sense date their whole existence from that start in Paris. Everything after that, including their banishment to Geneva, their posting to the Far East, even their return to Ontario, is for them the real exile. "It was a mysterious period of exile," Peter reminisces about his stint in Geneva, "[and] he thought he had been sent to Geneva because of a misdemeanor and had to wait to be released" (*HT*, 111-12). This in fact was what did happen, for Peter had committed an unforgivable social blunder, and like Ovid, was banished to an unfriendly region where he sensed "a closed conspiracy," a region of exile with unfamiliar language and customs. They ritually went through the obligatory process of being "disgraced, forgotten, and rehabilitated," with the resurrection coming, appropriately, at a Mardi Gras costume party given by their social superiors, just as the earlier banishment had been instituted by other social superiors.

As in the other two stories about New World individuals and their response to Paris, we do not find it easy here to assess the relative merits of the contrasted worlds. It was in Paris that the Fraziers learned to be corrupt and manipulative, yet they were denied ultimate success because as Peter recalls to Sheilah once they are back in Canada, "we weren't crooked . . . [and] we weren't even smart" (*HT*, 108). They were dispossessed of their paradise, and Gallant presents this recollection with a mixture of irony and compassion:

> There seemed to be plenty of everything and plenty of time. They were living the dream of a marriage, the fabric uncut, nothing slashed or spoiled. All winter they spent their money, and went to parties, and talked about Peter's future job. It lasted four months. They spent their money, lived in the future, and were never as happy again. (*HT*, 109)

In a sense, the Fraziers are doomed forever to relive those blissful months of their lives, for their expulsion from paradise has made them only sadder, but not wiser, people. Paris remains for them, as the ice wagon of her Saskatchewan town does for the Norwegian-Canadian Agnes Brusen they meet during their exile in Geneva, an indelible memory of childhood, and an experience they are ultimately unable to transcend. Peter and Sheilah will undoubtedly try again to manipulate their way into international recognition, but Gallant makes it clear that she reserves her compassion—and her admiration—for the children of such families, who have to learn very early on the methods of survival:

> Sandra and Jennifer are waiting for Sheilah and Peter to decide. They are waiting to learn where these exotic parents will fly to next. What sort of climate will Sheilah consider? What job will Peter consent to accept? When the parents are ready, the children will make a decision of their own. It is just possible that Sandra and Jennifer will choose to stay with their aunt. (*HT*, 108)

It is clearly the human relationships and human dilemmas shaped by this situation of exile that interest Gallant more than any conscious desire on her part to measure the relative advantages or disadvantages of the societies she is juxtaposing. Nevertheless, whether the setting is Paris or Geneva, Army and NATO bases in occupied Europe, *pensions* on the Riviera, or a tour ship on the Mediterranean, we at the same time do learn much about the kind of world in which the protagonist is compelled to react. The nineteen-year-old army bride in "An Autumn Day" suffers in large part because of her physical and psychological immaturity, but the farmhouse where she lives near Salzburg, with its atmosphere of suspicion and fear, contributes very much to her dilemma. And beyond this microcosmic cross-section of the Old World, both spatially and temporally, lies the whole machinery of European ideological strife with its echoes of the holocaust and the destruction of nations. Small wonder that the time she spent there takes on in retrospect a frightening significance: "those three months stand out in my memory like a special little lifetime, neither girlhood nor marriage. It was a time when I didn't like what I was, but didn't know what I wanted to be" (*OP*, 34).

A classic example of Gallant's fractured characters—mother dead, father remarried, brought up by a married sister—Cissy Rowe finds the other Americans around her no more comforting than the Europeans, and she imagines betrayal on all sides. Like the traditional romantic exile figure, she is profoundly moved to a fit of homesickness by the beauty of song, seemingly a disembodied voice from the farmhouse, though in reality belonging to an American soprano temporarily resting and rehearsing there. Cissy does not recognize any of the songs, though appropriate to the international cast of characters residing in the farmhouse, Miss West sings in Italian, French, English, and German, and it is only when Herr Enrich translates the song "Herbsttag" that she grasps its relevance. "But when he came to the part about it being autumn and not having a house to live in, I suddenly felt that this poem had something to do with me. It was autumn here, and Walt and I hadn't a house, either" (*OP*, 40-41). Deprived of the opportunity to meet Miss West because of the machinations of Herr Enrich, Cissy is at first inconsolable, and then attains a sudden and somewhat bitter maturity about the reality of her life. Nevertheless, the recurring German refrain, *"Wer jetzt kein Haus hat, baut sich keines mehr,"* continues to haunt her: whatever reassurances Walt gives her, she knows that she, like the singer, will never build, because she, too, has no house.

Cissy Rowe is only one of a multitude of displaced people who populate Gallant's fiction, and it is not only in the geographical sense that displacement occurs. Cissy's alienation is as much sexual and psychological as it is geographic, and her attraction to Miss West is in part an incipient adolescent crush on her that enables her to postpone a full sexual relationship with her husband. "It seemed to me that a girl friend was the only real friend you could have" (*OP*, 41), she rationalizes, but of course Miss West's departure forces her to accept a new reality about her marriage, though there is a kind of desperate bravado about her final assertion to Walt that "we'll be all right. Take my word for it. We'll be all right" (*OP*, 53). Again and again in Gallant's fiction, in stories like "My Heart Is Broken" and "The Wedding Ring," or in her two novels, the state of marriage creates for the wife a painful state of exile, the solution to which is frequently fantasy, promiscuity, or a rootlessness, such as that reflected in *Green Water, Green Sky* with its "lost, sallow, frightened Bonnie wandering from city to city in Europe, clutching her daughter by the hand" (*GWGS*, 23).

Gallant's concern for displaced people undoubtedly is partly autobiographical in derivation, but it is important to note that it is not a motif that is dictated by the geographical settings of her fiction. For Gallant, there is nothing inherent in either the Old World or the New that determines the responses her protagonists make to their situation: Cissy in Salzburg or Odile in Paris are no more realistic or productive than, for example, Jeannie of "My Heart Is Broken" is in a construction camp in northern Quebec. And as we saw in "The Other Paris," Felix represents a kind of paradox of displacement: he is at once both homeless and at home wherever he happens to be; continental Europeans in this respect are quite distinct from displaced Englishmen in Gallant's fiction, for the latter, as a character in a 1956 story, "In Italy," observes, have an "extraordinary habit . . . of taking bits of England everywhere they go," a comment, incidentally, not unlike the one made by Mamie Wicks to Charles Mafferton in Duncan's *A Voyage of Consolation.* But all of Gallant's characters, wherever they live, are acutely aware of the unrealized nature of their lives, and not infrequently, like Jean Price of "Its Image on the Mirror," can only "[wake] from dreams of love remembered, a house recovered and lost, a climate imagined, a journey never made" (*MHB*, 155).

In stories like "An Autumn Day," "The Picnic," and "Malcolm and Bea," the dilemmas of the relatively youthful exiles, usually Americans or Canadians associated with military or NATO operations in Europe, are quite short-lived and even trivial in origin, but they are disturbing nevertheless for the individuals concerned. For these people are rootless in a double sense: the nature of their temporary service lives overseas frequently creates marital or social tensions which compound the larger cultural complexities they already find themselves in. Again, it is not that Gallant deliberately sets up superior Old World characters or situations against which New World individuals and ideas are measured and found deficient, for her compassion and sense of irony are characteristically directed towards both worlds. In "The Picnic," for example, a 1952 story collected in both *The Other Paris* and *The End of the World,* while it is true that the American military families, the Marshalls, the Goulds, and the Barings, are gently satirized for their behaviour and for the way they go about organizing a picnic as a "symbol of unity between two nations," it is equally true that Madame Pégurin, in whose house the Marshalls reside, is not exactly an enlightened representative of a superior European vision:

Madame Pégurin had tried, as well as she could, to ignore the presence of the Americans in Virolun, just as, long ago, when she traveled, she had overlooked the natives of whichever country she happened to be in. She had ignored the Italians in Italy and Swiss in Switzerland . . . . For she *would* speak French, and she carried with her, even to market, a book of useful phrases. (*EW*, 37)

The Americans and Madame Pégurin clearly live in separate worlds that cannot easily be bridged: when Mrs. Gould asks her if she has a vacuum cleaner, her response is quick and revealing: "No, I have a servant," and when the cook, Louise, retrieves food the Americans had discarded in the garbage can so that the poor people can have it, "Mrs. Gould, after a moment of horrified silence, burst into tears and quite irrationally called Louise a Communist" (*EW*, 40). But it is the Barings who commit the ultimate social blunder: they not only call upon Madame Pégurin without an invitation, but give her as a Christmas present "a subscription to the *Reader's Digest* in French" (*EW*, 43). Obviously, the Americans are not familiar with "the custom of the country," but Madame Pégurin's inflexible and hostile attitude towards other worlds constitutes another kind of deficiency which underscores how unrealizable a goal the "unity of nations" really is.

In "Malcolm and Bea," a 1968 story collected in *The End of the World,* the confrontation is within the expatriate community associated with NATO and the military in France, with the indigenous French society hardly visible, except for a beleaguered *gardien* who goes into a paroxysmal state every time someone from the occupying families walks upon the forbidden grass. The situation in this story offers, incidentally, an interesting reversal of the garrison structure we saw earlier in *Emily Montague,* where the occupying forces were socially and culturally in the ascendancy; here they are despised, and there is nothing here of the "unity of nations" business we saw in "The Picnic." Gallant uses contrasting scenes of children at play to illustrate the cultural and social gaps that separate the New World from the Old, but again her subtle style and ironic sense make it difficult to decide what side she champions:

Nato is leaving, and by the time school has ended Malcolm and the embattled children will have disappeared. The children, talked of as rough, destructive, loud . . . are identifiable because they play. They play without admonitions and good advice . . . . The new children gradually replacing them do not mix and do not play. [They] attend school on Saturdays, and when they come home they go indoors at once . . . . When they walk, it is in a reasonable manner, keeping to the paths. They seem foreign, but of course they are not: they are French, and Résidence Diane, six miles west of Versailles, is part of France. (*EW*, 106)

But the main conflict in the story is psychological and marital rather than cultural, involving two Canadian families on the eve of their departures to Belgium and Germany, and what we witness is the resolving for the moment of two imminent family breakups. The English-born Malcolm had pulled strings in Canada to receive his NATO posting in the first place, and part of his problem is the Anglophobia that he perceives in Bea. "Who do you hate most, Bea?" he asks on one occasion. "The English, the French, or the Americans?" (*EW*, 107), and essentially he keeps trying to convince himself of her deficiencies as a wife and mother, and of her inferiority to him in general. Bea, however, is one of Gallant's resilient survivors, eminently adaptable and pragmatic in her views on life, and with far more integrity and substance than Malcolm will concede. "All she knows is Malcolm. The father of Roy hardly counted. She slept with him 'only the once,' as she puts it, and hated it," and though the Baums are at the point of breaking up because of Leonard's Danish mistress, Bea will not pass judgment: "Malcolm has seldom heard her gossiping. Gossip implies at least a theory of behavior, and Bea has none" (*EW*, 109). Unlike such expatriated wives as Cissy Rowe and Paula Marshall, Bea lives only in the present; indeed, once she meets Malcolm, she sets out deliberately to ensure that nothing remains in her past that would interfere with her day-to-day survival:

> Before we left she took her cat away to be destroyed. She had already stopped watering the plants, and the birdcages were empty. By the time we were married and she went away to start a new life with me, the household, the life in it, had been killed, or had committed suicide; anyway, it was dead. (*EW*, 114)

Malcolm's moral stature, on the other hand, is as undefined as his past, and the rootlessness that gives Bea her practical resilience serves mainly to justify his vacillating between hate and love, between selfishness and a genuine concern for his family. An expatriate twice over, he openly relies on string-pulling to survive, first to get to Canada, then to his NATO posting, and there are enough hints in the story to suggest that he will always be a marginal survivor, dependent on someone else's influence to sustain him. His essential insignificance is reflected in his state of isolation in Canada, where he thought it would be easy to find both friends and money, and where he allows himself to be picked up in a movie theatre by two girls who turn out to be Bea's younger twin sisters. He thinks they are Indians—"blueberry blondes" he insensitively calls them—but he is saved, as he recalls, by his accent. "My English accent, so loathed, so resented out here, seemed hilarious to Pattie and Claire. I was hardly a generation away from signs reading, 'Men Wanted. No British Need Apply,' but the girls didn't know that" (*EW*, 111). Ironically, it is in part Bea's accent that saves her, too, salvaging as it does the potentially explosive situation that her sisters bring him home to:

> We had walked into a quarrel. When two people are at right angles to each other they can only be quarreling. I saw for the first time Bea's profile, and then heard her voice. The voices of most Canadian girls grated on me; they talked from a space between the teeth and the lips, as if breath had no part in speech. But the voices of all three Griffith girls were low-pitched and warm. (*EW*, 112)

Malcolm's moral vacillating continues throughout his married life, and on many occasions he is overtaken by "the desire to be rid of Bea" (*EW*, 108), the last time near the end of the story, when Verna Baum is trying to apply her amateur psychology to his family. Roy's reaction is in part responsible for Malcolm's breaking this resolve, but more important is his sudden epiphanic understanding of what he and Leonard had been talking about earlier that day, the idea of "going to Pichipoi"—an unknown, imaginary destination invented by Paris Jews to relieve them of their wartime agonies:

> I should have told Leonard, Malcolm thought: The real meaning of Pichipoi is being alone. It means each of us flung separately—Roy, Ruth, Bea—into a room without windows. It can't be done. It can't be permitted, I mean. No jumping off the train. I nearly made it, he said to himself. And then what?
> "No," he said aloud.
> A sigh escaped the child, as if he knew the denial was an affirmation, that it meant "Yes, I am still here, we are all of us together." (*EW*, 119)

There is no assurance this truce will last, and given the combination of Malcolm's and Bea's volatility and the tensions of an expatriate existence, one should not be too optimistic. The resolution is very much in keeping with Gallant's unrelenting realism about the fragility of human relationships, a condition that is exacerbated but hardly caused by social and cultural rootlessness.

Another category of exiles in Gallant's fiction suffers dilemmas that are of quite a different derivation and of a seemingly insoluble nature, for these are exiles out of time as well as out of place. They are characteristically elderly or middle-aged individuals, almost invariably from England, who inhabit decaying *pensions* or rented villas on the Italian and French Rivieras, sustained by memories of lives or places that have ceased to exist. Many of these individuals, like the three widows in "Acceptance of Their Ways" or

Miss Horeham of "The Moabitess," stories collected in *My Heart Is Broken*, have in a sense been by-passed by the progress of the world, and they sustain themselves through regularly repeated rituals of pretense rather than by resolving the dreary actualities of their lives. In the first of these stories, the rituals of class snobbery, of social conflicts, of personal triumphs are played out year after year within the circumscribed world of Vanessa Freeport's *pension*, with the three widows mutually depending on each other to go along with the game, for they desperately need each other. "For Mrs. Freeport couldn't live without Lily, not more than a day. She could not stand Italy without the sound of an English voice in the house. In the hush of the dead season, Mrs. Freeport preferred Lily's ironed-out Bayswater to no English at all" (*MHB*, 4).

By employing a series of shifting perspectives in this story, Gallant achieves a subtle and complex irony, and we move from what seem to be certainties about these three individuals to a whole range of uncertainties. Lily seems to be the most rational of them, but then she suddenly and without any emotion envisages Mrs. Garnett "doubled in two and shoved in a sack" (*MHB*, 7)—which makes us wonder again what part she had in the deaths of her husband and her lady travelling companion. The other two widows, too, exploit the memories of their deceased husbands, but nagging questions remain as to how they really feel. And in a sentence like the following, the reader cannot really be sure who is deceiving whom: "Mrs. Garnett had been coming to Mrs. Freeport's every winter for years, but she left unfinished letters lying about, from which Lily—a great reader—could learn that dear Vanessa was becoming meaner and queerer by the minute. Thinking about Mrs. Freeport as 'dear Vanessa' took flexibility, but Lily had that" (*MHB*, 8). It is obvious that when it comes to deception and dissembling, the three are a match for each other, but Gallant has compassion for them nevertheless: indigent and without connections, they are doomed to remain exiles forever in a social world that is itself in an advanced state of decay.

Miss Horeham's situation in 'The Moabitess" is even more pathetic, for she is a prisoner both of Mme Arnaud's *pension* with its assorted inmates, and of the legacies and memories of her dead father, a man for whom she had sacrificed her own life and who then died, leaving her penniless and debt-ridden. Like the biblical Ruth, she is in an alien land but, alas, there is no Boaz in her life, and she measures her wealth, not in sheaves of barley, but in boxes of worthless trinkets and clippings of by-gone days. Like Mansfield's Miss Brill or Moore's Judith Hearne, Miss Horeham wins our compassion not only because of the pathetic creature she has become, but also because of the fleeting glimpses she offers us of some of her "ancient girlhood dreams" that "she had to dig under the leaves of her memory to find" (*MHB*, 48).

A 1975 story, "The Four Seasons," collected in *From the Fifteenth District*, dramatizes the dilemmas of *pension* exiles at a point in time when all order is about to disintegrate in the face of the Fascist onslaughts in Europe. Britons, Americans, and Jews all play out their final days of peace here, with most of the action being filtered through the consciousness of the thirteen-year-old maid, Carmela, who, like Felix of "The Other Paris," would be quick to learn the game of survival: "Among the powerful and the strange she would be mute and watchful. She would swim like a little fish, and learn to breathe under water" (*FD*, 5). Though she lives in her own country, she is the outsider in this world rather than the exiles from abroad—the Unwins from England and the Marchesa from the United States—for of course the Anglophones bring their own language with them, and like Mme Pégurin of "The Picnic," they ignore the natives as much as they can. In her isolation, therefore, it is appropriate that as she sets out on her wanderings after the dissolution of the villa, her strongest recollection is of another wanderer, the Jewish Dr. Chaffee, being marched away by the Fascists, as he raised his hand and waved to her: "one smile, one gesture, one man's calm blessing" (*FD*, 35). With the Unwins and the Marchesa having returned to their native lands, Dr. Chaffee and Carmela become representatives of the universal exile that World War II produced; in a realistic sense, within the perspective of that holocaust, Chaffee's final benediction constitutes a painfully futile gesture, but in a spiritual sense it remains as a sign of hope, transmitted from one human being to another.

The Unwins represent what was once a reasonably affluent and influential English colony on the Riviera, but they are now in greatly reduced circumstances, dabbling in real estate and running a small private printing press. They are more akin to the *pension* and hotel exiles in such stories as "The Remission" and "The Moslem Wife" than to the elderly remnants of an Edwardian world discussed above, for they are essentially of the commercial classes, escaping high taxes and the threat of Labour in England. Through Carmela's eyes, we are able to observe the nature of this Anglophone colony, and to perceive the mechanisms of its disintegration:

> Carmela understood that the Unwins' relations with the rest of the foreign colony were endlessly complicated. There were two layers of English, like sea shelves. Near the bottom was a shelf of hotel-keepers, dentists, people who dealt in fruit and in wine—not for amusement but for a living. Nearer the light dwelt the American Marchesa, and people like Miss Barnes and her companion, Miss Lewis . . . . Between the two shelves the Unwins floated, bumping against the one or the other as social currents flung them upwards or let them sink. Still lower than any of the English were Russians, Austrians, or Hungarians, rich and poor

alike, whose preoccupation was said to be gaining British passports for their children. (*FD*, 18)

Such social distinctions apparently carry through to the grave: at the funeral of Alec Webb in "The Remission," there is mention made of occasionally turning "one of the Russians out, to make room" (*FD*, 115).

These Riviera self-exiles bear some resemblance to the remittance men who were exiled by their families to the colonies in the nineteenth and early twentieth centuries, in that they very consciously wear their Englishness for all to see, even when the worlds they inhabit dictate the vestigial value of that trait. A real crisis in their lives renders them totally ineffective, reduced to taking refuge in safe opinions, as reflected, for example, in the Unwins' response to the Italian deportation of Jews: "[They] were proud that this had not taken place in their country—at least not since the Middle Ages—but it might not be desirable if all these good people were to go to England now" (*FD*, 26). Some of these exiles retreat increasingly into a parasitic existence, like Roy Cooper of "In the Tunnel" or Walter Henderson of "An Unmarried Man's Summer," sustaining themselves on the generosity of lonely expatriate women. Perhaps no one is more adept at insinuating himself into the lives of others than Eric Wilkinson of "The Remission," whom Gallant depicts with merciless precision:

> If he sounded like a foreigner's Englishman, like a man in a British joke, it was probably because he had said so many British-sounding lines in films set on the Riviera. Eric Wilkinson was the chap with the strong blue eyes and ginger moustache, never younger than thirty-four, never as much as forty, who flashed on for a second, just long enough to show there was an Englishman in the room . . . . Wore a tie that carried a message. What did it stand for? A third-rate school? A disgraced, disbanded regiment? A club raided by the police? No one knew. Perhaps it was the symbol of something new altogether. (*FD*, 95, 96)

The story makes it clear that it is this last hypothesis that is correct, for one of the residents of the colony speculates at Webb's funeral about the real nature of Wilkinson. "Most people looked on Wilkinson as a prewar survival," he muses, "what with his I say's and By Jove's, but he was really an English mutation, a new man, wearing the old protective coloring" (*FD*, 114).

If this is true, then the title word, "remission," involves much more than the physiological phenomenon of Alec Webb's delayed death; it suggests a diminution of a nation's moral fibre, reflected in Alec's initial uprooting of his family merely to avoid "queueing for death on the National Health Service" (*FD*, 75), and in Barbara's taking Eric as her lover while waiting for

Alec to die, and of course in the parasitic Wilkinson himself, whose moral decadence is camouflaged by his readiness to be of service to others, provided he receive something in return. And in the closing scene of the story, at the wake following Alec's funeral, the word reflects another meaning: an existential forgiveness, so to speak, for all transgressions this expatriate colony has committed on behalf of Alec, a remission produced merely by dismissing his reality:

> It then happened that every person in the room, at the same moment, spoke and thought of something other than Alec. This lapse, this inattention, lasting no longer than was needed to say "No, thank you" or "Yes, I see," was enough to create the dark gap marking the end of Alec's span. He ceased to be, and it made absolutely no difference after that whether or not he was forgotten. (*FD*, 116)

Gallant's expatriates on the Riviera do not on the whole fare too well in her moral judgment, for they seem to be either parasites or opportunists, or elderly anachronisms living out their fantasies in decaying *pensions*. Occasionally, however, a stronger type appears, usually young, more frequently female than male, a person who, like Bea Armitage of "Malcolm and Bea," lives more in the present than in the past. This type is best represented in the Riviera stories by the English Netta Asher (Ross) in "The Moslem Wife" and the Canadian Sarah Holmes in "In the Tunnel," both of whom are characterized by a combination of innocent frankness about themselves and a guarded indifference towards the people who try to regulate their lives. Strictly speaking, of course, Netta and Sarah are at completely opposite ends of the exile-tourist spectrum, for Netta was born into the expatriate colony and intends to remain for life, whereas Sarah is little more than a temporary tourist. But both reflect an ambiguity in their relationships with people who are both morally and geographically rootless, an ambiguity that allows them to emerge, not unscarred, but toughened, by their experiences.

Netta stands apart from the other expatriates, in part because she has never lived in England, and lacks some of their polish and sophistication. Both she and her husband, therefore, "worked hard at an Englishness that was innocently inaccurate, rooted mostly in attitudes" (*FD*, 39), and even in her speech she is not quite the real thing, for she "talked the English of expatriate children, as if reading aloud" (*FD*, 52). But she knows her mind and her destiny from an early age; her marriage to her hotelier cousin, Jack Ross, may violate her father's wishes and expectations, but she nevertheless dedicates her entire life to the hotel-keeping world that she inherited from him. It is a world that she single-mindedly preserves, even when it is threatened by Jack's infidelities, by his wartime separation from her, and by the

Italian and German occupations of the Riviera colony. Thus by the time the story ends and she is reunited with her husband, she is well on the way to fulfilling the obligation her father passed on to her when, at the age of eleven, she "watched him signing papers that, she knew, concerned her for life" (*FD*, 36).

An element of ambiguity remains in the story concerning the appellation affectionately bestowed upon Netta by Dr. Blackley, an expatriate physician who repeatedly attempted, without success, to seduce her. "The little Moslem wife," a phrase "collected and passed from mouth to mouth in the idle English colony" (*FD*, 43), mildly disturbs Netta only because it refers to her marriage, but she is not sure whether it refers to her habit of picking up after Jack or to his habit of womanizing. The story suggests it is related to their sexual relationship, for it is in connection with this aspect of her life that she ultimately resolves the term. During Jack's absence, she seduces a young American about to return home, and she explains, appropriately to Dr. Blackley, the significance this experience has for her:

> "I've discovered the limit of what you can feel about people. I've discovered something else," she said abruptly. "It is that sex and love have nothing in common. Only a coincidence, sometimes. You think the coincidence will go on and so you get married. I suppose that is what men are born knowing and women learn by accident." (*FD*, 60-61)

This confession, which fills her with relief and amazement rather than guilt, is in the nature of an existential commitment to herself as architect and judge of her life, with Jack for the moment relegated to a "restricted area" of memory. "In the mirrored bedroom there was only Netta. Her dreams were cleansed of him. The looking glasses still held their blue-and-silver-water shadows, but they lost the habit of giving back the moods and gestures of a Moslem wife" (*FD*, 61).

Unlike Netta, Sarah Holmes is only a summer visitor to the Riviera, having been sent by her father initially to Grenoble, ostensibly to study French culture, but in reality to get her disentangled from an affair with her professor in British Columbia. Like Carol Frazier of "The Other Paris," she brings with her certain preconceptions about France: for her, "the word 'Riviera' had predicted yellow mornings and snowy boats, and crowds filling the streets in the way dancers fill a stage" (*HT*, 73), but the reality she encounters is quite different. *Amoureuse* that she is, she is more obedient to her own compulsions than to her father's injunctions, and after a weekend with a man she meets in Nice, she writes to her father that "instead of French civilization taught in airless classrooms she would study expatriates at first hand" (*HT*, 85). There is a nice irony in this statement of intent, for it has the sociological slant of the thesis she was helping her professor with, "Urban and Regional Studies of the Less Privileged in British Columbia," for in the colony of expatriates she moves into, she herself is very much seen as an underprivileged interloper.

The colony is small, consisting only of Sarah's lover, Roy Cooper, who is now a retired ex-prison official from a former British Asian colony, the owners of the "Tunnel," Tim and Meg Reeve, expatriates only because they abhor Britain's Labour government, and Meg's niece, Lisbet, a psychologist-cum-personnel officer whom Roy flatters to her face, but out of earshot, viciously castigates: "God, what a cow! Planeloads of Lisbets used to come out to Asia looking for Civil Service husbands. Now they fly to Majorca and sleep with the waiters" (*HT*, 91). Roy and Lisbet, however, as we learn later, are much alike, "with fortunes established in piracy. He liked executions; she broke people before they had a chance to break themselves" (*HT*, 98), attitudes that they are eventually to direct towards Sarah. As for the Reeves, they inhabit a kind of world of their own, communicating with each other in a private, childish prattle, and deeply suspicious of any intruder who is not British. "Who was she?" they wondered immediately on meeting Sarah, "a little transatlantic pickup, a student slumming round for a summer?", and disturbed by the "Labour" implications of her studies, suggested that her thesis "contained only one reassuring word, and that was 'British' " (*HT*, 82).

Gallant does not offer a facile juxtaposition here between decadent English expatriates and an innocent Canadian one, for her worlds are too complex to allow for such easy categorizations. In the literal sense, of course, Sarah is precisely what the Reeves think she is, though her capacity both for love and for self-sacrifice transforms her into something more substantial than their flippant assessment suggests. In a very real way she is caught between the two men who try to control her, and because she is "not as innocent as her father still hoped . . . but not as experienced as Roy thought, either" (*HT*, 79), she ultimately must dismiss both of them, and thus she escapes from two tunnels at once. She remains, however, a compulsive *amoureuse*, for she possesses an unexpendable capital of love, and once back in Canada it is not too long before she forms a new liaison. This time, however, she is the instigator, and interestingly enough it is again with an exile, an American who has been forced to flee to Canada because of his political beliefs. But it is clear, from the references to his poverty, his tax and alimony debts, that she is in for another stormy relationship, not unlike the one that caused her to become an expatriate in the first place. Undoubtedly, the sociologist in her is still very much alive, for it is his hardships and Trotskyite political beliefs she is in love with, and to this extent he emerges appropriately as an extension of her professor's thesis, for here again is one of the underprivileged of British Columbia that she can continue to study.

Gallant maintains an ambivalent attitude towards Canadian girls like Sarah, Laurie Bennett in "Potter," or Lottie Benz and Vera Rodna in "Virus X"; certainly they are not the vacuous girls she depicts in a 1957 story, "Jeux d'été," who, "being clucked through Europe by a Miss Baxter . . . had been looking at things in Italy and were shortly to be looking at things in Greece." Sometimes it is the situation behind the girls' predicament that is being satirized, rather than the girls themselves, and one of her targets here seems to be the academic world. Sarah's professor, for example, is referred to only by the name her father gives him, "Professor Downcast," and in "Virus X," Lottie's research for her thesis about "the integration of minority groups without a loss of ethnic characteristics" brings her to France from, of all places, multi-ethnic Winnipeg, for no better reason than that her professor is from Alsace. French academics do not escape, either, in Gallant's vision: in "Things Overlooked Before," an interpretive essay about *The Affair of Gabrielle Russier,* the subject figure is described as reflecting "the intellectual sheep's profile that for some reason abounds in academic circles" (*AGR,* 7), and indeed, the entire French academic system comes in for severe criticism in that book.

But though the Canadian girls may not occupy any special niche in Gallant's classification of expatriates, we are able to observe them in a number of juxtapositions—against the English, continental Europeans, and Americans—and thus to measure them with some degree of thoroughness. It is of course individuals rather than national types that Gallant is concerned with, and therefore it is risky to generalize about types; at the most, we can only observe that there is a degree of consistency in the characteristics that individuals of various nationalities reflect: "cautious" or "reticent" frequently characterize the Canadians, "loud voices" the English, "assurance" the Americans, and so on, but they are all more complex than these epithets suggest. Many of the Canadian girls are what Gallant calls those in "Potter" who come to the parties given by Piotr's cousin—"hesitant fiancées" or "restless daughters"—confused and uncertain about the value of family ties or emotional commitment to anyone, and very much, in fact, part of the general malaise that informs the post-war world at large.

Against exiles from totalitarian Europe, it is the elements of casualness and spontaneity that set the Canadian apart. As the Polish poet, Piotr, observes, Laurie Bennett "simply picked up her world and took it with her. He resented his exile . . . . He could almost have made himself hate her, because of her unthinking, pointless freedom, her casual way with frontiers" (*FD,* 175). Unlike the other Canadian girls discussed here, Laurie has no particular reason to be in Europe—no past to drive her there, no issue or prospect to entice her—for she is a girl who, at the outset at any rate, lives exclusively in the present. "Her idea of history began with the Vietnam war," we are told, and "Genesis was her own Canadian childhood" (*FD*, 169), and it is this clean slate that attracts Piotr, whose own life is filled with dark experiences and heavy legacies of suffering and guilt. But Laurie ultimately discovers the price of this kind of freedom, for her Italian excursion with another of her lovers turns to bitterness and mutual rejection. "We weren't really together," she rationalizes to Piotr on her return to him. "We were just two travellers who happened to be sharing a room" (*FD*, 208).

Vera Rodna of "Virus X" is, like both Sarah and Laurie, a bit of an *amoureuse*, though considerably more gauche and aggressive, but unlike Laurie, she had come to Europe for a very tangible reason: "No one here could know that Vera was only a girl from Winnipeg who had flunked out of high school and, on a suspicion of pregnancy, been shipped abroad to an exile without glamour" (*HT,* 176). She thus illustrates a reverse situation to that of the remittance man, who was sent in the other direction for his transgressions, and like him, she receives money from home to ensure that she does not return. Unlike the remittance man, however, Vera seems absolutely indifferent towards her past and her native country; she seems content to wander across Europe, maintaining a somewhat shadowy affair with a Canadian who has apparently transformed himself into a kind of permanent refugee. Since he never appears in the story, however, he lacks tangibility, compared, for example, to Felix of "The Other Paris," and the little we can surmise about him suggests that he is as parasitic and selfish as Roy Cooper of "In the Tunnel."

Within this perspective, Vera has a much heavier burden to carry than Lottie Benz, the victim of the disease referred to in the title, but whose total physiological ailments are not nearly so serious as her intellectual and psychological limitations. Vera in fact is, if Lottie could but see it, the subject of her thesis, for she has not lost any of her Ukrainian ethnic characteristics, and how better to integrate oneself into a society than by becoming pregnant in it? But like Carol Frazier, Lottie is essentially unimaginative and literal, doomed to marry a cautious and conservative man, and in the end, her exposure to Europe will count for nothing. In this story, Gallant directs a critical eye towards individuals from a number of nations, such as American servicemen and French taxi drivers, waiters, and hotel people, but her most withering glance is reserved for a Canadian couple Lottie has met on the plane, and who had subsequently invited her to an Ibsen revival:

The theatre reminded Lottie of Vera, although she could not think why. It was stuffy and hot, and had been redecorated, and it smelled of paint. "We may get a headache from this," Lottie warned. The new friends, whose name was Morrow, thought she had said something remarkable about the play. (*HT*, 186)

That neither Lottie nor the Morrows know anything about Ibsen seems irrelevant after this, and the Morrows' decision a few days later that they "did not want to spend too much time with Canadians over here" (*HT,* 188) can only work for the advantage of Lottie and other Canadians in Paris.

The theme of the Canadian girl abroad receives a thorough examination in Gallant's second novel, *A Fairly Good Time* (1970), where Shirley Perrigny attempts to resolve a disordered life that was further complicated, but not caused, by her husband's leaving her. In her earlier novel, *Green Water, Green Sky* (1959), Gallant had remarked that "nothing is more reassuring to a European than the national who fits his national character" (*GWGS,* 35), and Shirley is at one point tempted to acknowledge this:

> Perhaps Philippe was right and it was best to imagine other people only as they ought to be. Shirley would then be described by any of the Perrignys to survive her as naive, puritanical and alcoholic, for in their eyes that was the North American makeup. (*FGT,* 50-51)

Shirley, it is true, does reflect two of these traits in varying degrees, but she is hardly puritanical, and measured against such Old World families as the Perrignys and the incredible Maurels, she wins be default if by nothing else. The Maurels bear strong resemblances to Odile's family in "The Other Paris" and to Madame Pégurin of "The Picnic": they are narrow, selfish, vicious, and grasping, and one can only assume that Shirley maintains her relationship with them, not only to indulge her inherited generosity to all who stray into her life, but to regain a sense of personal worth that Philippe's family consistently denies her.

Though the resolution of this novel dictates that Shirley will remain in Europe, she is clearly caught between two worlds, reflected first of all by the fact that she has lost two husbands, one from Canada, through an accidental death, and now one from France, through desertion and eventual divorce. But sporadic letters from her mother in Montreal, and occasional visits and communications from an old family friend, Cat Castle, also serve to remind her of her New World roots: "I'm not American," Mrs. Castle berates her as they meet for lunch. "To the best of my knowledge you weren't born one. If you're going to be that way, forgetting your heritage, I don't want to hear any more" (*FGT,* 36). Correspondence between Shirley and her mother, described as "an uninterrupted dialogue of the deaf," rarely contains any news, but constitutes rather a kind of transatlantic sparring at one another, but Shirley, in her moments of despair, reflects on the moral certitude of her parents that stands in contrast to her own rootlessness and uncertainties:

> Eccentric, unconformable, entirely peculiar by Canadian standards,

they had never doubted themselves or questioned their origins or denied the rightness of their own conduct; they could be judged but never displaced. Whereas she, ordering breakfast in a café-restaurant in the middle of the afternoon, paying for it with borrowed money, was a refugee. *(FGT,* 65)

Gallant in this novel, as she did in *Green Water, Green Sky,* reflects an ambivalence about the New and Old Worlds that is dramatized in the way families and their peripheral acquaintances resolve, or fail to resolve, dilemmas which are not restricted to any particular society. The psychological dimensions of these dilemmas, however, are frequently complicated and aggravated by their social contexts, or by the characters' perceptions of the nature and importance of these contexts, though it is not unusual for them to be deluded in these perceptions. The more manipulative and unconscionable of Gallant's figures—her Walter Hendersons, her Roy Coopers, her Eric Wilkinsons— on the whole do not suffer from these situations, simply because they shift their ground as the necessity arises, and are not bound to any tangible moral or national principle that operates on other characters. Wishart in *Green Water, Green Sky,* who at forty-two "passed as an English gentleman in America, where he lived, and as an awfully decent American when he went to England" (*GWGS,* 88), emerges as one of Gallant's most chameleon-like creatures in this respect, but we are left in no doubt, through her biting irony, that even a rogue can get caught in his own machinery:

His life would probably have been easier if he had not felt obliged to be something special on two continents, but he was compelled to return to England now, every year, and make them accept him. They accepted him as an American, but that was part of the buried joke. Sometimes he ventured a few risks, such as "we were most frightfully poor when I was a child," but he knew he hadn't achieved the right tone. The most successful impostures are based on truth, but how poor is poor, and how closely should he approach this burning fact? (Particularly in England, where the whole structure could collapse for the sake of a vowel.) (*GWGS,* 91-92)

Florence McCarthy's denying her mother's wishes that she marry this gigolo is her first mature protest against her suffocating family relationship, and her subsequent decision to marry Bob Harris is her second, but neither act saves her from the schizophrenia that her constant love-resentment polarity finally produces. Rootless for too long, without a fixed society to provide her with a foundation for behaviour or an identity ("I might have been a person, but you made me a foreigner," she berates her mother at one point), she simply withdraws from the chaos that a decade of aimless wandering had produced. Clearly, exile in Gallant's vision is much more than the simple act of moving from one country to another: that is only the framework, as these two novels indicate, within which more tangible displacements occur, and these almost invariably involve some form of family rejection or disintegration. Bonnie and Florence are exiles from the New World, but their real problem is that they are exiles from the possibilities of permanent human relationships.

Nevertheless, if consistently recurring character types, their behaviour, and their opinions as expressed in their conversations can be said to reflect something of what a writer thinks, then Gallant makes little attempt to disguise the views she has of various national groups in the Old and New Worlds. There is no question, either, but that she is on the whole more severe towards certain aspects of French and English societies than she is towards their New World counterparts, though it must be kept in mind that in *A Fairly Good Time*, virtually all the observations that lead us to this conclusion are filtered through the consciousness of the Canadian protagonist. But even so, Shirley Perrigny, for all her chaotic personal eccentricities, reflects an integrity and a sense of being alive that seems to be totally missing in the self-consuming bourgeois existence that her husband's family and the Maurels incestuously protect, though admittedly, Philip's protest that he cannot understand what he calls the "Anglo-Saxon mysteries" is legitimate, considering that Shirley is in his experience their chief exponent.

There is a strong anti-English note, too, in Shirley's attitudes, occasioned in part by her mother's Anglomania, and seemingly by a residue of her exposure at an early age to a family of British refugees her mother had taken under her wing:

> By the time she was seven or eight she was heartily sick of the flaxen heads and adorable accents her mother admired; nor did she share Mrs. Norrington's delight in the four cases of precocious intelligence the Team-Browning children were said to constitute. It occurred to the child that four loud, finical, humorless voices were passing for brains, and she wondered whose fault it was that she had been taught nothing more piercing than a Canadian mumble. (*FGT,* 99)

But Shirley is both like and unlike her mother, and that is part of her dilemma, though in discarding her mother's tendency to communicate through literary quotations ("I didn't know they were quotations until I started reading," she confesses late in the novel. "I thought they were our family language."), she takes a substantial step towards a new reality about herself. But in her recollection of some of Mrs. Norrington's more positive qualities, she incidentally articulates criticisms of Canada that appear in one form or another through much of the exile literature examined in this study: "In a society where eccentricity was not encouraged, she had acted out her beliefs; native of a country that welcomed neither passion nor poetry, she was shown to be naturally endowed for both" (*FGT,* 98).

Gallant's examination of exile as it is manifested in Canadian situations or through Canadian characters receives a particularly thorough treatment in her *Home Truths,* as has been seen in my discussion of such stories as "The Ice Wagon Going Down the Street," "In the Tunnel," and "Virus X," and it is in the Linnet Muir stories which conclude this collection as well as in her "Introduction" that she for the moment has resolved this question. Her introductory remarks are in places needlessly defensive, I believe, but particularly important are her comments about the relationship between a writer and his native land, and about the role that language plays in the phenomenon of individual or institutional insecurity. Pointing out that with Canadian readers she has often felt "on trial," not because of the literary qualities of her work, but because of "what are taken to be [her] concealed intentions" (*HT*, xii), she comes out unequivocally for the autonomy of the artist, in what she calls an "old-fashioned, liberal, and humanist" statement:

> Unless he has rejected his native origin . . . a citizen obviously owes more to his own country than to any other. In a democracy most of his obligations are moral and voluntary, and all the more to be observed on that account. But where his work is concerned, the writer, like any other artist, owes no more and no less to his compatriots than to people at large. (*HT*, xiii)

Though this credo may have a readily identifiable applicability to the exile writer—and in this study it fits particularly well Duncan, Wilson, Moore, Lowry, as well as Gallant herself—it is really just another way of arguing for the universal in art, a goal that is obviously as legitimate and necessary for the indigenous writer as for the exile. If a nation or an individual feels cheated, because the art is not "particular" or "unique" enough, such as in the case of the Montreal art collector she cites, then, Gallant implies, that is not the artist's problem, but the beholder's.

Another form of national or individual insecurity derives from the question of language—which is perhaps stating the obvious in a nation like Canada—but for Gallant it is more than a constitutional bilingual situation. The anecdote she relates of an erroneous translation of an English title into French, and of her own punishment for making the correction, is similar to a fictional episode in Clark Blaise's "Snow People," one of his stories about the Thibidault family.[7] There, when the teacher talks about "cuebeck" and the

"Gasp" peninsula and the way the "Purse" rock got its name, Thibidault, in a kind of instinctive response to his ancestry, leaps to his feet and gives the class a rapid, accurate lesson in French, for which enlightenment he is promptly punished. In both of these cases, it is the comprehension of language that separates the outsider from the insider, but in both situations it is paradoxically the indigenous people who are the exiles, the ones who fail to understand the reality being defined by the language in question. What Gallant realizes in retrospect is precisely what operated between Thibidault and his teacher, and which accounted for the "deadlock . . . between a grown woman and a child over a word and its meaning. I knew the meaning; she was led astray by the sound" (*HT*, xvi).

Insecurity in one form or another operates in many of the stories collected in *Home Truths,* and generally it is an element that separates the outsider from the natives, the intruder from the established order, the exile from the indigenous society, though it is not consistently the exclusive attribute of one or the other of these opposing forces. Sometimes it is portrayed in a humorous vein, as in "Jorinda and Jorindel," where the English Mrs. Queen has never taken to Canada because "she cannot get used to a place . . . where the working people are as tall as anyone else" (*HT*, 20). At other times, it allows Gallant to display a mild satire, as in "Ice Wagon," where Peter feels threatened by the newcomer Agnes, and does not know how to respond to her: "If she had been foreign, ill-favored though she was, he might have flirted a little, just to show that he was friendly; but their being Canadian, and suddenly left together, was a sexual damper" (*HT*, 116). (There are echoes here of Duncan's American girls in *The Voyage of Consolation* who vacated a coach because the Canadian girls in it were "not foreign enough.") And occasionally, Gallant is openly contemptuous towards social behaviour that derives from a tradition of insecurity, as in "The Doctor," where Linnet Muir questions "the right-and-wrong" principle formalized "in European social fiddle-faddle—the trivial yardsticks that measure a man's character by the way he eats a boiled egg" (*HT*, 300).

Canadians are charged occasionally with a national case of insecurity in the face of their more confident American neighbours, and as in Duncan, this theme receives some credible dramatizations in Gallant. She draws distinctions between Canadians and Americans, not to uphold the superiority of one or the other, but rather to wryly keep pointing out that they are not the same thing, much as Duncan did in *The Imperialist* and *Cousin Cinderella.* In "Jorinda and Jorindel," she inserts a parenthetical explanation to distinguish Irmgard from her American cousin, Bradley: "(Bradley is not required to think of answers; he is American, and that does. But in Canada you have to keep saying what you are.)" *(HT,* 21), but this theme is more fully examined in "In Youth Is Pleasure," which in large part explores Linnet's repatriation from New York to her native Montreal. As an exile in New York, she in effect had been without an identity, a fact which only in retrospect underscored for her the vast and comfortable confidence of the Americans:

> In those days there was almost no such thing as a "Canadian." You were Canadian-born, and a British subject, too, and you had a third label with no consular reality . . . . In Canada you were also whatever your father happened to be, which in my case was English . . . . I did not feel a scrap British or English, but I was not an American either . . . . Americans then were accustomed to gratitude from foreigners but did not demand it; they quite innocently could not imagine any country fit to live in except their own. (*HT*, 220)

Linnet's return to Canada is prompted partly by her feeling out of place in New York, where she was not even considered a proper refugee, but "just someone from the backwoods," but more fundamentally by her need to resolve the uncertainties she felt about herself and her origins. New York she is always to regard as her "deliverance" from her temporary Ontario home, "a place full of mean judgments and grudging minds, of paranoid Protestants and slovenly Catholics" (*HT*, 223), for its open attitudes and examples of spontaneous and healthy behaviour leave an indelible mark on her. But again this is one of her retrospective observations; for the youthful Linnet, a return to Montreal took on the urgency of a highly charged personal mission.

What she actually experiences as she returns to her country, however, falls far short of her expectations, and illustrates one of the inevitable prices the exile pays for trying to reverse what is fundamentally an irreversible process. As we saw earlier, Laura Salverson underwent much the same kind of experience, though Linnet draws more explicitly the relationship between the physical and the spiritual aspects of the country:

> As my own train crossed the border to Canada I expected to sense at once an air of calm and grit and dedication but the only changes were from prosperous to shabby, from painted to unpainted, from smiling to dour. I was entering a poorer and a curiously empty country, where the faces of the people gave nothing away (*HT*, 222)

But as she points out, the return home also constitutes her "sea change," that will allow her to proclaim her own independence, for in her residence in exile she had acquired the components of a moral vision that would permit her to live in Canada from now on on her own terms.

It is appropriate to conclude my discussion of Mavis Gallant with her "Varieties of Exile," not only because of its happily chosen title, but also because of the resolution it convincingly offers to Linnet's own involvement with the experiences of exile. Interestingly, too, it links Linnet, in her idealistic obsession with refugees, to Shirley's mother in *A Fairly Good Time*, for neither "could get enough of them," and of course, as mentioned in an earlier chapter, its depiction of the remittance man constitutes a link with such writers as Sara Jeannette Duncan and Stephen Leacock. Gallant had earlier, in "The Prodigal Parent," presented a kind of parody of the remittance man, for here the father in question is sponging off his offspring, rather than the other way round, and none of the family can afford to send him abroad. And of course he is a fake Briton: he has the regimental tie, the gestures and phrases, the accent, but all these merely serve to sustain the pose he assumed long before, in order to rationalize his rootlessness and philandering in Canada. He is closer in conception and execution to Gallant's Riviera parasites than he is to Frank Cairns in the present story, for the latter is the real thing, whose origins Gallant is merciless in describing:

> The institution of the remittance man was British, its genesis a chemical structure of family pride, class insanity, and imperial holdings that seemed impervious to fission but in the end turned out to be more fragile than anyone thought. Like all superfluous and marginal persons, remittance men were characters in a plot . . . . Hordes of young men who had somehow offended their parents were shipped out, golden deportees, to Canada, South Africa, New Zealand, Singapore. They were reluctant pioneers, totally lacking any sense of adventure or desire to see that particular world. (*HT*, 266)

This generalized portrait evokes the youthful Carysthwaite we met in Duncan's *A Social Departure*, but within this story the interesting thing is that it stands in juxtaposition to the idealized portrait of the refugee that Linnet subscribes to as the story opens, who "came straight out of the twilit Socialist-literary landscape of my reading and my desires" (*HT*, 261). It is a manifestation of Gallant's art and her irony that, with the introduction of the flesh-and-blood Frank Cairns, both portraits prove to be wrong, or at least deficient, for he is more complex than the stereotypes suggest, and for Linnet at any rate, he poses a disturbing moral dilemma. Though her deft sizing him up the moment she meets him—"stamped, labelled, ticketed by his tie . . . by his voice, manner, haircut, suit; by the impression he gave of being stranded in a jungle, waiting for a rescue party—from England, of course" (*HT*, 265)—is seemingly accurate, she could also be drawing here on her recollections of her own remittance man father in the stance she instinctively assumes against Frank. And this seems to be particularly true in the long and somewhat bitter tirade that follows for the next half dozen pages, which reflects both the intensity of the hostility she feels against her father and her inability to forgive him, though undoubtedly this extended analysis possesses a large degree of sociological truth as well. But Cairns is more than a representative of this phenomenon—"if he had been only the person I have described I'd have started taking an earlier train to be rid of him," Linnet confesses (*HT*, 272)—and it is in working out her puzzles about him that she in part resolves her own dilemmas.

Frank and Linnet of course share the lonely role of being exiles in a society that fundamentally distrusts them, and that they are both socialists constitutes another bond between them. But essentially, they are only momentarily travelling along parallel paths that will never meet, separated as they are not only by age, but by deep-rooted disparities in the way they view their moral obligations. When Frank enlists as a lieutenant, Linnet wonders why it is not as a private; and when he berates Canada over a trivial incident in the restaurant, her immediate reaction is to wonder why he is in a Canadian regiment, and immediately provides her own answer, not unlike that of Levine's Winnipeg academic: "They pay more than the Brits" (*HT*, 277). Frank's officer rank provides his passport back to England, and his subsequent death in action verifies Linnet's earlier observation that by 8 May 1945 the remittance man as a phenomenon would be extinct, but nevertheless she is left sad and confused by the way this relationship concluded.

Linnet ultimately begins to grow weary of refugees, for "they were going through a process called 'integrating' " (*HT*, 281), and thus ceasing to be foreigners, with whom at the outset she had felt very much at home only, she concedes, because "the home was all in my head" (*HT*, 262). Her earlier remark that "remittance men were characters in a plot" comes back to her now in another sense than she originally meant, for she discovers a novel she had written "about a man from somewhere, living elsewhere, confident that another world was entirely possible" (*HT*, 281), obviously about Frank Cairns, but also about a person very much like herself. That she destroys this manuscript with some reluctance is a measure both of her new maturity and of her lingering regret that something is over; her realization that "all this business of putting life through a sieve and then discarding it was another variety of exile" (*HT*, 281) is her affirmation of the reality that writing is both a liberating and an isolating process, a conclusion, as we will see in the next chapter, that is more painfully arrived at by a number of Moore's and Lowry's characters. Though Linnet is the only one of Gallant's exiles who is a writer, the kind of epiphany she experiences is common to many of her sensitive female protagonists, as we have seen, for their transition from innocence to experience is characteristically a low-key and subtle event.

7

Birds of Passage

For the most part, the exiles from the Old World discussed in earlier chapters were exiles out of personal, domestic, or economic necessity, viewing the New World in terms of its opportunities for a new mode of life, or for a station in life no longer tenable in their native land. They were not only celebrators of the literal possibilities of their new land, but believers as well in the moral superiority of a world that in part at least was seen in paradisal terms. Only occasionally did these exiles manifest any fundamental opposition between what they beheld in the external world they came into and their own internal vision of reality, and more rarely still did they give vent to any metaphysical, intellectual, or artistic impulses that might challenge what on the surface appeared to be a benign world. In short, they came to stay, to integrate themselves as much as possible into the fabric of Canadian society, to proclaim, in effect, the triumph of this world over their previous one.

By contrast, the three writers I examine in this chapter became exiles out of an intellectual and artistic compulsion rather than out of economic necessity, though this is not to imply that the problem of survival was not a factor in their decision. Their coming to Canada, however, was more a matter of accident than of any deliberate planning on their part, and on the whole they shared a distrust of some of the uncritical assumptions about the New World that were subscribed to by the earlier exiles, though as we will see, Malcolm Lowry celebrates in his own way their notion of its paradisal dimensions. Initially at any rate, neither Lowry, Wyndham Lewis, nor Brian Moore came to Canada with any a priori convictions about its long-term possibilities for them, but all three produced imaginative fiction about their Canadian experiences that ranks high in this country's stock of exile literature.

Of the three, Percy Wyndham Lewis is the most marginally Canadian in terms of his overall artistic reputation, for virtually all his literary and artistic output reflects attitudes and ideas that derive from his Old World experiences.

Yet his Canadian connections, though somewhat accidental and fleeting, were legitimate enough both for him and for Canada to exploit: he was born on his father's yacht moored at Amherst, Nova Scotia; he carried a Canadian passport all his life; he was an official Canadian war artist with the Canadian forces in France early in 1918; and he spent virtually all of World War II in Canada, most of the time in Toronto and Windsor. Just these factors alone, however, would not qualify him for inclusion among the three birds of passage being discussed in this chapter had he not left a legacy of over a hundred letters written while an unhappy exile in the New World and, after his return to England, one of his most powerful novels, *Self Condemned*, the only one of his two dozen or so works concerned with his Canadian experiences. While it may be tempting to read this novel as thinly disguised autobiography, it is in its own right a disturbing novel of exile that constitutes far more than a mere contrasting of Old and New World situations or an account of Lewis's own experiences, for on one level it represents the culmination of attitudes and visions that attended Lewis all his life. It is in his letters that he communicates his literal opinions about Canada, the United States, and England, and as we will see, he was inconsistent in his attitudes and ill at ease no matter where he lived in the world, though on balance he was intellectually and temperamentally more suited to the Old World than to the New. Interestingly enough, however, he remarked quite late in his life that his extensive experience in North America "tended to transform [him] from a good European into an excellent internationalist."[1]

Long before he even contemplated a return visit to the New World, Lewis was demonstrating a spirit and an attitude that reflected his uneasiness with many aspects of England and the Old World in general. In part, this outlook may represent a vestigial response to his North American roots and a residual but ambivalent loyalty to his American father, himself something of an outsider, and from whom his English mother separated in 1893 to raise her son in England; indeed, according to a reminiscence by Mrs. Anne Wyndham Lewis,[2] one of the reasons for their coming to Canada at all at the beginning of the war was for Lewis to explore his father's French-Canadian ancestry, though it was a mission that for various reasons he failed to pursue. There is no doubt that the greater part of Lewis's exilic and unconventional spirit was simply a reflection of the dichotomy that always separates the artist or the intellectual from the world around him, manifested in Lewis's case in his early experiments with Vorticism, and in his controversial opinions expressed in the two issues of *Blast* that he edited along with Ezra Pound and other members of the avant-garde.

Ironically, it was probably because he remained with his English mother rather than with his American father that Lewis was to develop a permanent ambivalence towards England, though it remained his actual as well as his spiritual home for most of his life. For his mother encouraged his early aesthetic impulses by enrolling him in the Slade School of Art after a disastrous year at Rugby, where his final standing was twenty-sixth in a class of twenty-six. His three years at Slade followed by some eight years on the continent helped to consolidate an intellectual propensity, if not towards exile at this point,[3] then certainly towards an impatience with propriety and convention, and towards a distrust of the values of a country that he nevertheless preferred over all others. That he chose to remain in England despite Ezra Pound's exhortations that he should live abroad did not blind him to that nation's shortcomings and inconsistencies, a situation he commented upon in a 1919 letter to the American art collector John Quinn: "As you know, in England one is up against the least imaginative and the most self-satisfied public in the world . . . . Yet they have a certain fairness, much more than the French" (*LWL*, 103-4). This ambivalence towards England was very much to shape many of his subsequent essays and novels, and as we will see, it was an issue that he inconsistently addressed in the many letters he wrote during his exile in North America. A specific tendency to exile is whimsically manifested in his 1932 travel book, *Filibusters in Barbary*, where it nevertheless assumes some credibility when it is set against the underlying weariness that he feels with European society in general and with the English in particular: "England, my England!" he apostrophizes. "Shall I return; or, like so many of your sons, become from henceforth an exile? I wished frankly to escape for ever from this expiring Octopus, that held me to it by my mother-tongue" (*FB*, 15).

His actual going into his self-imposed exile some seven years later was necessitated on the immediate level by his recognition that he could no longer live comfortably by his art in England and by his belief that such a possibility existed in the New World, reflecting, in this respect, the misconceptions held by many of his predecessors from the Old World. But in a larger sense his self-exile marks the culmination of some three decades of intellectual and artistic discomfort in the Old World, and can be seen as the kind of obligatory retreat to the wilderness that marks the responses of such fictional exiles as Grove's Philip Branden or Lowry's Sigbjørn Wilderness, who also manifested a weariness with the European scene. It constitutes a nice irony, too, that in his exile he took the reverse direction from the eastward pilgrimage of his early literary companions, Ezra Pound and T.S. Eliot, both of whom elected to remain in the Old World, a situation he generalizes about in a 1942 letter to Lady Waterhouse where he concedes that "it is far easier (experience seems to show) to bring an American to England, than to transplant an Englishman to America" (*LWL*, 316).

But of course, unlike those earlier exiles I discussed and unlike the two other birds of passage examined in this chapter, Lewis had no intention of making the New World his permanent residence. Whether by design or by accident, his six years of unhappy exile were precisely framed by the beginning and the end of the global holocaust that in one sense his own violent writing had anticipated: he sailed from Britain the day before war was declared in 1939 (escaping, by a fluke decision, passage on the ill-fated *Athenia*, the first allied ship sunk in World War II), and he returned to England on the first passenger ship to leave Montreal after VJ-day in 1945. This convenient escape and return seems in retrospect to constitute a calculated and selfish plan of action on his part, but it should be remembered, as he proclaims tediously in letter after letter, that he would have returned to England much sooner had he been able to earn enough money to do so.

At times, Lewis on the shores of the Great Lakes sounds like Ovid on the shores of the Black Sea, describing his place of exile in such unflattering but memorable epithets as "this misbegotten continent," "this god forsaken city," "this bush metropolis," "this sanctimonious ice-box," and "that really unspeakable national zero, Canada." The ambivalences and the inconsistencies he had characteristically reflected towards England now begin to shape his responses to both the United States and Canada, and as with many fictional exiles examined in this study, his attitudes towards the New World at times vary according to his own personal prospects. "I am thoroughly sick of the Stars and Stripes and all they stand for," he complains to his English agent in April 1941 (*LWL*, 287), yet by the following January, as his letter to Sir Nicholas Waterhouse makes clear, he reflects a complete volte-face: "I am awaiting news from the States about an appointment I believe I am getting. This place [Toronto] bores me in the most fearful way and I shall be glad when I find myself among Americans again" (*LWL*, 314). Like Ovid, too, he was not averse to importuning others on his behalf, and he wrote to such influential people as Noel Coward, Archibald MacLeish, John Crowe Ransom, and Edmund Wilson begging for appointments. At one particularly low point during his exile, he even convinces himself that all in all, he really preferred South Africa to America, as he desperately rationalized in a December 1941 letter to a casual acquaintance, I.W. Way:

> It may surprise you that anybody should wish to exchange the American continent, with all it possibilities—its wealth and its power—for what is certainly a less *central* scene. I like many things about America, and have had a certain measure of success here, too. But Africa is I feel sociologically a *prolongation* of Europe, whereas America is a *substitute* for Europe. I prefer Europe. And the *idea* of Africa appeals to me.[4]

That most of his anticipated appointments failed to materialize only sharpened Lewis's attacks on the country in question; like Frederick Philip

Grove, Lewis was never hesitant to ascribe his failure to be recognized to some deficiency within the particular society he was for the moment occupying, rarely seeing his own inconsistent and somewhat abrasive nature as a contributing factor. Undoubtedly, for an unwilling and uneasy exile like Lewis, shaped as he was by a number of different national influences and characteristics, a defensive and aggressive stance was at times inevitable, so it is not surprising that his fellow intellectuals in New York and Toronto tended to ignore or criticize him. There is probably, therefore, more than meets the eye behind his complaint in 1943 to Naomi Mitchison that because of the "provincialism" of Toronto and Ontario," it is impossible . . . to obtain a post in a university here, because they tell you that only Canadians can occupy such posts" (*LWL*, 354); a number of Canadian academics knew him at the time, including Northrop Frye, who has expressed the opinion that if "his career in Canada was a failure, I think it was the result of a rather perverse determination to make it so."[5] The history of academic appointments in Canada certainly does not support Lewis's contention: Canadians like Hugh MacLennan found that any vacant posts were frequently filled by Englishmen, and of course that Lewis himself secured a position at Assumption College in Windsor shortly after making this charge undermines his own argument.

Nevertheless, that Lewis's dilemma was at times personally difficult and painful cannot be doubted, and occasionally his letters communicate sensitively and evocatively the genuine afflictions of exile rather than mere self-pity, like the one he wrote to James Sweeney of the Museum of Modern Art a bare six weeks after arriving in the New World:

When you read me that letter the other night I found myself envying James Joyce at Vichy—so much nearer the centre of his world and of mine: with so many more friends than I have too, within some sort of reach. I feel as if I were in some stony desert, full of shadows, in human form. I have never imagined the likes of it, in my worst nightmares. (*LWL*, 277)

We have heard laments of this nature before, from Anna Jameson, from Susanna Moodie, and even from such committed exiles as Niven's Angus Munro and Grove's Philip Branden; clearly W.K. Rose's observation about Lewis's North American letters is relevant to all these situations: "a stranger in the land, as all expatriates discover, must needs be at the best of times a stranger" (*LWL*, 265).

Up to a point, the attitudes Lewis expressed towards the three nations that had some part in shaping him depended on who his correspondents were and where they were living. The unflattering epithets about Canada quoted earlier, for example, all came from letters written to acquaintances living in the United States or England, and Lewis cautioned his English correspondent that his comments about "the Stars and Stripes" were "needless to say . . . not for publication." To Lorne Pierce, on the other hand, at that time Editor-in-Chief of Ryerson Press in Toronto, his judgements of Canada were more guarded. "Between England and the States," he wrote in 1941, "—England distant, aloof, and snooty; the States near, dynamic, and a bit snooty too—poor Canada has not had much chance to find itself. It is trebly divided—between a West and an East, and a French and an English, in addition to the New World and the Old World division of loyalty" (*LWL*, 288). His hope initially was that Canada, because of its English connections, would be a better place for him than the "malignant blank wall" of New York, but as time passed, he found this was not to be; like Malcolm Lowry, he became increasingly hostile towards the "asphyxiating godliness" of his presbyterian surroundings.

To Lorne Pierce, too, he expressed a severer condemnation of England than he customarily did in his letters to his English acquaintances: "I should go on to point out that England is only *half* a nation or a fraction of a nation, so long as the majority of its citizens start life under such a fearful social handicap that they are debarred from contributing their quota of intelligence and energy to the general effort."[6] In part, this observation constitutes a continuation of Lewis's life-long antipathy towards the Arnoldian education system, which ignored anyone who was not born into the middle or upper classes: undoubtedly, he would applaud Philip Branden's action in *A Search for America* of hurling Arnold's "Essays in Criticism" into the fireplace. Yet Lewis himself stands clearly as a contradiction of this antipathy, or to express it another way, a verification of his own ambivalence, for after failing dismally at Rugby, that most Arnoldian of schools, he took on the world in his own terms and succeeded brilliantly. One cannot help thinking that Lewis always toyed a bit with the British even when, as during his New World exile, he was in his strongest Anglophile phase, a characteristic that is fictionally exploited in *Self Condemned*. But in an unfinished and unpublished 1941 fragment entitled "I can take it," he tentatively sounded out some of the ideas he would elaborate in that later novel. "The New World is a marvellous vantage-point for observation of the Old," he wrote, "provided you know the Old as well as I do," and he then proceeded to give a satirical analysis of a hypothetical British exile in Canada:

They tell me that the Englishman in Vancouver attains to a degree of Englishness—a broadness of A and an absence of R—that is unbelievable. The exile, certainly, tends to intensify the peculiarities of speech and appearance of his place of origin. I wonder what goes on *inside* these transplanted Britons—putting up their umbrellas to shield themselves from an almost-English rain? Or does *nothing* go on—just to achieve a perfect Britishness?[7]

On balance, Lewis was much more positive towards the United States than towards Canada, and his protest to Naomi Mitchison in 1942 that "both I and my wife loathe this place and the States so heartily that nothing would ever persuade either of us to set foot on American soil again" (*LWL*, 329), must be measured against his many favourable comments in other letters, and most importantly, against the praises he sings of that country in his *America and Cosmic Man*. Published three years after he returned to England, this book took shape during his exile, growing out of a series of lectures he delivered at Assumption College, and in effect argues the proposition that America, because of its demographic and political nature, is ideally suited to lead the way towards one world. Sounding a bit like O. Henry's "cosmopolitan in a café," Lewis proclaims, "I am just as much at home, if not more so, in Casablanca as in Kensington; feel in no way strange in Barcelona— like equally Paris, London, or New York," but feels most at home in America because, paradoxically, "no one really belongs there any more than I do. We are all there together in its wholly excellent vacuum" (*ACM*, 165). His cautious admiration derives in part from his recognition of the unique nature of that nation, for America, he argues, "is much more a psychological something than a territorial something" (*ACM*, 22) and in part from his apprehensiveness of the formidable possessiveness and energy of the Americans. "Theirs is the spirit of the spectator: one who has paid a great deal for his seat and brought with him a profuse supply of rotten eggs and bouquets large and small" (*ACM*, 21)—a portrait not unlike the one Sara Jeannette Duncan presented of the American Evelyn Dicey in *Cousin Cinderella* who, we recall, spoke of England "exactly as if she had shares in it."

It is likely, however, that Lewis never did come to understand the true nature of Canada or the United States, a process that, as he conceded in the unfinished fragment referred to earlier, he saw as "a birth-to-death matter . . . and pretty hard work, too." Perhaps—for an American at any rate—the ultimate proof of his basic incompatibility with the American ethos is revealed in the letter he wrote in St. Louis to a Marion Trowell, just as the World Series of 1944 between the St. Louis Cardinals and the St. Louis Browns was getting under way:

> We found this place in a state of feverish expectancy, in preparation for the orgy of sport which is now proceeding. Who the Cardinals are I don't know, but they've been licked by the Brown Socks. [sic]. That's our St. Louis team. Everybody is drunk.[8]

Lewis's uneasy attachment to Canada that we saw reflected in his letters is fictionally exploited in his powerful novel of exile, *Self Condemned* (1954), the writing of which, significantly, was not begun until some six years after his return from his exile. Like much literature of exile, it conveys a highly subjective and painful vision of experience, but clearly, too, it is a separate, imaginative work of art that has a life and a justification of its own, quite distinct from the literal experiences of Lewis himself. It is a novel that dramatizes the consequences of a self-exile that is both generated and resolved within the narrowest meaning of that term; since only the self was involved in making the initial decision, then only that same self can ultimately be condemned for that action and its tragic aftermath. But the novel's title ironically extends itself to suggest the possibility, though by no means the certainty, that the reborn René Harding deliberately condemns himself for his precipitous and costly decisions, for it is this point, the way the novel's conclusion should be interpreted, that has generated the most controversy among readers over the years.

As a historian who discovers that he can no longer teach history, Harding transforms abstractions and theories into acute personal moral issues, a process which not only compels him to condemn the world at large for its disregard of truth, but which also necessitates his own perpetual condemnation of himself for being a failed interpreter of those truths, a double dilemma that thrusts him into a state of permanent isolation and exile. His precipitous resignation from the university and decision to depart for Canada represent, from a domestic and social point of view, an inexcusably selfish course of action, but these actions translate intellectually into an existential self-accounting for which only he is answerable, though one can at the same time pity or censure him for his failure to recognize that in a world on the brink of global disaster no man can ever be an island unto himself. Harding's friend and intellectual disciple, Rotter Parkinson, can for the moment be, but he is "the last of a species," ensconced in a large private library that "was really a fragment of paradise where one of our species lived embedded in his books, decently fed, moderately taxed, snug and unmolested" (*SC*, 76). By withdrawing further into a corner of the world that is on the point of destruction, Rotter can survive in complete disregard of the larger world; Harding, on the other hand, is very much part of this larger world, and his private course of action has as a result far-reaching human consequences.

The tri-partite structure of *Self Condemned* allows us to follow logically the course of Harding's exile from its theoretical to its practical manifestations, through the three stages reflecting his protest, his withdrawal from the world, and his emergence into another world, a ritual not unlike that experienced by Gallant's Peter and Sheilah Frazier as they went through a process of being "disgraced, forgotten, and rehabilitated." In the first section,

"The Resignation," we not only have an opportunity to assess Harding's rationalizations and explanations for his decision, but in his various confrontations with members of his family and other individuals we also learn much about the nature of the world that he is giving up. We never do see René in an academic situation as a professor of history, and Rotter's long analysis of his intellectual stance does not quite compensate for what could have been a more effective way of dramatizing the crisis that precipitated his resignation. Indeed, university crisis or not, Lewis suggests in his depiction of the relationship between Harding and Rotter that a way of life was coming to an end anyway, with death or exile the only recourse:

> Both of them knew that this was the last year of an epoch, and that such men as themselves would never exist on earth again, unless there were, after thousands of millennia, a return to the same point in a cosmic cycle. They knew that as far as that quiet, intelligent, unmolested elect life was concerned, they were both condemned to death: that the chronological future was, in fact, *a future life,* about which they both felt very dubious. They might survive as phantoms in a future England: or they might learn to live in some other way. (*SC*, 78)

Measured against this gloomy possibility, René's decision at novel's end to remain in the New World reflects a realistic view of the state of the world, rather than a capitulation to expediency or a selling out of himself, a point supported by Rotter's analysis that Harding saw life as "a half-way house, a place of obligatory compromise" (*SC*, 96). It is appropriate that it is to his mother that René first announces his decision, for being French, she seems to understand his unconventional action more than do his English brothers-in-law, who reflect the expediency and hypocrisy that characterize the English society that Harding is rejecting. Because of the unpopular views he expressed in his book, *The Secret History of World War II*, he is perceived as a threat to his society, and relegated to the status of outsider or pariah, and in this respect he simply fulfils the historical pattern wherein anyone who posed a threat to conventional thinking or established order had to become an exile. In Harding's case, of course, it is a deliberate self-exile, rather than one enforced directly by the authorities, but it is no less painful for that. "I have shut the door behind me," he informs his mother. "There is no going back upon what I have said . . . . There has been no levity in the action I have taken. I took it secretly because there can be no consultation with others in a matter of conscience" (*SC*, 16, 17).

It is in depicting Harding's visit to his favourite sister Helen and her husband that Lewis becomes most outspoken in his criticism of English society; compared to Robert Kerridge, René's other brothers-in-law, Victor

Painter and Percy Lamport, are merely deluded opportunists beset by the notions of class or of British superiority. Victor, an "Ersatz gentleman," has exploited his connections with his eminent brother-in-law to elevate himself in his own esteem so he can pass himself off as the social equivalent of a duke, and "the curious thing," Lewis observes, "was that England still swarmed with Dukes of this sort in 1939" (*SC*, 72). Harding's visit to the Kerridges takes him to Rugby, and here Lewis is at his most vitriolic in his castigation of his former school, and of the processes condoned by Dr. Arnold that shaped generations of little "Christian Gentlemen," a portrait quite at odds with Ethel Wilson's benign evocation of the other Arnold in *The Innocent Traveller:*

> The sight of a mud-caked Christian Gentleman tearing down a field hugging a dirty ball, and a dozen dirty Christians, as gentle as himself, at his heels, seemed to [Dr. Arnold] entirely as it should be. Did it not harden muscle: and did it not add hardiness to a Christian Gentleman's moral uprightness? . . . The canes of the prefects, as well as those of the masters, would harden this Christian Gentleman-in-the-making in other ways: and fagging toughen the little rat who was to become a Christian Gentleman, and teach him the beauties of Authority. His learning to fear his redoubtable headmaster would be good practice for fearing God. (*SC*, 108-9)

This tirade is not entirely gratuitous, though it may constitute a getting even on the part of Lewis for his own dismal experiences at Rugby, for we are soon to meet, in the person of the clergyman Kerridge a modern "Christian Gentleman" and, in the person of Dr. Grattan-Brock, one of the current Rugby housemasters, both of whom spend the evening attacking Harding for his views, exhibiting very little Christian charity in the process. Grattan-Brock, "one of that numerous class of more or less learned English men (and in this class may be included a few literate Americans too) who believe they are Dr. Johnson" (*SC*, 126), sees Canada as an "extraordinary place to go to," and largely on the basis of his involvement in the Spanish Civil War, is prepared to condemn Harding as a Fascist because he "had made a remark of an unenthusiastic kind about communism" (*SC*, 128). In their narrowness and inflexibility not unlike the fellow-travellers Richler depicted in *A Choice of Enemies*, Grattan-Brock and Kerridge are incapable of seeing beyond the fashionable opinions of the day, and represent for Harding simply one more of the obstacles to truth that helped bring about his irrevocable step.

René's relationship with Helen, like the one with his mother and to a lesser extent with his two other sisters, is solidly predicated on a mutual trust and understanding, a reflection of their Gallic family bond that excludes his

English wife, Hester, and his three brothers-in-law, for Harding feels that he
and his sisters have all married intellectually incompatible spouses. Thus, his
intellectual rejection of England has its personal and emotional equivalent
in this division within his family, so it is appropriate that in this final farewell
it is to Helen that he communicates the personal agony that exile really
involves:

> "Sadness, you know, at parting . . . . At leaving everything, at going
> away into a wilderness among so very solid a mass of strangers. And
> never to come back. Never to come back . . . . Then the fact that
> Canada is four-fifths an authentic wilderness does not matter. It would
> be the same emptiness anywhere. The same ghastly void, next door to
> nothingness." (*SC*, 137)

Harding's observation that "to get out of the world I have always known"
is tantamount to getting "out of the world" entirely, begins to be verified as
he and Hester find themselves aboard "the last boat out of Europe." Here, in
transit between the Old World that they know and the New World that is for
the moment unknown, they are in a state of social and psychological limbo,
much like the passengers on the emigrant ship in Norman Levine's *Canada
Made Me*, or the Edgeworth women in Wilson's *The Innocent Traveller*,
though clearly without the latters' buoyant anticipation of what the New
World promises for them. Indeed, the American academics René meets on
board the *Empress of Labrador* fill him with despair because of what he
perceives as their intellectual limitations, and these encounters foreshadow
the even greater isolation that he is to be thrust into once he reaches Canada:

> This first conversation in limbo, where the same language had been
> spoken, where (at one point) the same interests had been invoked, but
> no contact had been made, was ominous. America had reached a very
> different level of consciousness, but it was completely cut off from life,
> and a kind of cold smartness presided at the new elevation . . . . He
> was approaching a land of sterilized thinking, and reflections of another
> life. (*SC*, 155)

In part, René's attitude here must be written off as an a priori prejudice
against Americans, not unlike that reflected by his brother-in-law Percy
Lamport who, "like many of his countrymen, took up a very rigid position
regarding the Yahoo on the other side of the Atlantic" (*SC*, 57). But it
reflects, too, a defensive stance on his part that is characteristic of the exile:
if he fails to understand or appreciate the world he is moving into he can
always ridicule or criticize it, and quite clearly at this self-imposed nadir of

his academic and social life he does not seem inclined to be charitable towards others. Only in his domestic life at this point does he begin to demonstrate concern: largely ignored in his original decisions, Hester now causes René to regard her for the first time as a human being, for her despair at leaving everything she is familiar with very precisely echoes his own lament he made to Helen. Nevertheless, though his concern "was the beginning of a new way of thinking about Hester" (*SC*, 147), she essentially retains for him throughout their exile the role of vacuous but sensuous sexual companion that René makes sure she does not abandon. It takes her suicide to jolt him into a realization of the fact that she had much more substance to her than he had allowed.

In the second part of the novel, "The Room," the tangible implications of exile in Canada are dramatized, and here Lewis draws extensively on his own experiences in Toronto's Tudor Hotel in the early 1940's. But Momaco is not precisely Toronto any more than Lowry's Eridanus is Dollarton, but rather a composite of the physical and social features of a number of Canadian cities: we learn, for example, that a river divides the city in two, and that its French-Canadian population exceeds it English-Canadian segment, that it is closer to Canada's bush land than is Ottawa, and so on. Where it does more closely approximate the Toronto of the 1940's is in its "formidable sabbaths": Lewis observes that "there are Ten Commandments in Momaco, as in no other city in the world" (*SC*, 187), and in his description of its archaic drinking regulations he sounds very much like Lowry in his comments on Enochvilleport in "The Bravest Boat."

That this section of the novel opens some three years after the Hardings arrive in the New World emphasizes not only the permanence of their exile but also its unvarying nature: in effect, as foreshadowed by the arctic manifestations during their voyage on the appropriately named *Empress of Labrador*, an immense freeze has rendered them immobile in their "twenty-five feet by twelve" room that does not relent until their hotel is destroyed by fire. Appropriately, therefore, the first description of their exile in Canada is couched in imagery that confirms both the nature of the country and the cold intellectuality of René that caused the exile in the first place:

> They were as isolated as are the men of the police-posts on Coronation Gulf or Baffin Bay. They were surrounded by a coldness as great as that of the ice-pack; but this was a human pack upon the edge of which they lived . . . . They were hermits in this horrid place. They were pioneers in this kind of cold, in this new sort of human refrigeration; and no equivalent of a central heat system had, of course, as yet been developed for the human nature in question . . . . They had grown used to communicating only with themselves; to being friendless, in an inhuman voice. (*SC*, 170)

In effect, the entire course of the Hardings' exile is played out within a
"fire and ice" pattern, for regularly relieving their glacial existence are their
passionate sexual encounters that always seem to eliminate the problems
and arguments of the moment—verifying in a whimsical way, incidentally,
Lewis's prophecy about the cultural ice-age he made in his *America and
Cosmic Man*: "In the end I suppose women will come to the rescue—indeed
they will have to: that is how the ice-age will slowly be made to recede"
(*ACM*, 227). But within the Hotel Blundell there are other human passions as
well—intrigues, adulteries, fights, prostitution, and even murder—which
anticipate the literal conflagration that eventually destroys it, propelling its
inhabitants from their garrison existence into the larger world. That this
experience is both painful and necessary for the Hardings was foreshadowed
by René's earlier fight in the hotel's beer parlour, a confrontation occasioned
by the offence that his English accent gave the local patrons, but also one
that served as an important revelation for him: "We have had our baptism of
fire, have we not, in the violent life of this hotel. It is an astonishingly violent
place, but no more violent than the world of which it is so perfect a
microcosm" (*SC*, 231). Thus his earlier argument about getting "out of the
world" receives an ironic verification, for even in a garrison exile he is very
much in the world of violence he was trying to escape.

It is after this confrontation, however, that René begins to sense a growing
integration with the New World, a feeling that is counterbalanced by Hester's
increasing concern that they will never return to England. Thus the intellectual-
emotional division that had always separated these two, but that could
always be bridged by "amorous treatment, vigorously administered," takes
on, after the fire, the aspect of a more profound incompatibility:

> So the passionate solidarity of the two lonely exiles practically confined
> to "the Room" . . . had begun to crumble. The destruction of their
> prison had resulted in their coming out of their seclusion into a more
> normal existence. Momaco began to relent. But Hester retained the
> spirit of the disregarded intruder in a most jealously exclusive society:
> and, as she saw it, René had in fact broken away, and, in however
> qualified a manner, gone over to the side of the enemy—had made his
> peace with Momaco. (*SC*, 310)

Hester's violent suicide, precipitated by René's intention to accept a university post in Momaco, reflects convincingly the measure of her extreme
isolation: in England, though intellectually estranged from René, she had
her family for support and comfort, whereas in Momaco the only English
woman who has befriended her is more loyal to Canada than to England, and
Hester thus feels doubly betrayed. *"I can only go out of the world"* (*SC*, 392),

is her posthumous message to René, and thus she joins the refugee writers Stefan Zweig and Ernst Toller in the ultimate response to unhappy exile, while ironically providing René with a fulfilment of what he saw as *his* solution.

On one level, the solution that René chooses both to justify and alleviate his exile brings him back to where he started: occupying a chair of history at a university. But of course he has changed, and so has the world, and long before he was offered any academic post "he knew that he could never return to London, now or when the war ended" (*SC*, 310), and he thus has already confirmed his commitment to the New World. His present situation parallels his earlier one, too, in that he has written another book, one that his colleagues McKenzie and Trevelyan think very highly of, but one that he has some qualms of conscience about, for he feels that it reflects "an insidious softening of the core" and an absence of "the old integrity and belief." As with the earlier book, we have no concrete evidence as to its intrinsic value; the judgement of McKenzie seems on balance to be more dependable than that of Rotter, for his world is not the closed one that Rotter's was, and René's relationship with McKenzie is that of equal colleagues rather than the master-disciple pattern of the earlier one. The transition in Harding from integrity to expediency is difficult to verify or trace, for his contention that it is there could be as much a reflection of his abiding cynicism towards academics as it is a genuine product of conscience: it is perhaps more to the point to see his emptiness as an emotional one deriving from the lingering shock of Hester's suicide rather than an intellectual one.

Our final view of Harding, therefore, as he settles in at a prestigious American university, is an ironic one, for it seems to reflect a complete integration of this "glacial shell of a man" into a world whose inhabitants, we are led to believe, are also hollow men, though his characterizing of them as "unfilled with anything more than a little academic stuffing" (*SC*, 407) seems gratuitous at best, and, in light of Professor McKenzie's integrity and intelligence, even insulting. This bleak concluding scene of *Self Condemned* undoubtedly reflects Lewis's bitterness over his own failure to be appropriately recognized in the New World, and his unrelieved despair during his long winter of discontent in Canada. But it fulfils in an ironic way, too, his prophecy in *America and Cosmic Man* that when the inevitable cultural ice-age does settle down upon the United States, cultural manifestations will survive mainly in the universities, and within this perspective Harding seems particularly well qualified to survive his immersion.

As far as any lasting or positive relationship with Canada is concerned, Wyndham Lewis was, in spite of his birth and other legitimate connections, a more fleeting bird of passage than either Malcolm Lowry or Brian Moore, neither of whom had originally any legal or family connections with Canada.

Yet it is these two who elected to remain in the New World, and to exploit
their Canadian experiences quite extensively in their fiction, with the result
that their status as exiles is more of a mixed quantity than Lewis's: though a
willing exile from Great Britain, he became an exile by compulsion within
Canada, and as a result his fiction never really transcended the bitterness
that was generated. Lowry and Moore, on the other hand, while sharing
Lewis's lifelong tendency to be an outsider, saw their relationship with the
New World in less simplistic terms, in part, at any rate, because the world in
which they attained their intellectual and artistic maturity was a more
complex one than that experienced by Lewis.

For Malcolm Lowry Canada was in the first instance merely an accidental
stop-over in a series of travels that from his youth onwards constituted his
own "voyage that never ends," but though he came to Canada out of
expediency, he remained out of devotion. Unlike Lewis and Moore, he came
to this part of the New World in stages, following upon a number of earlier
voyages that in a sense were romantic quests: after his journey round the
world on a freighter at eighteen, he sailed to Boston in 1929 to meet one of
his literary mentors, Conrad Aiken, and to Oslo in 1930 to find another,
Nordahl Grieg, both of whom very crucially influenced his first novel,
Ultramarine (1933). But both literally and imaginatively for Lowry, it seemed,
heaven and hell always followed close upon one another, and these paradisal
voyages were counterbalanced in the mid-1930's by his return journey to the
New World in ill-fated attempts to cure his alcoholism and to save his first
marriage; his brief incarceration in New York's Bellevue Hospital (1935) and
his initial visit to Mexico (1936) served instead as background experiences
for his two most disturbing works, the posthumously published *Lunar Caus-
tic* (1963) and his masterpiece, *Under the Volcano* (1947). Within the geographical framework of the New World and within the perspective of Lowry's
personal tribulations, Canada emerges as a paradisal extension of the Cordil-
leran skeleton of North America that has its demonic manifestations in the
volcanic Mexican portion; in simplified terms, this is the vision that Lowry
articulates in the seven stories that make up *Hear Us O Lord from Heaven
Thy Dwelling Place* (1961) and, in a less polished and unified manner, in
October Ferry to Gabriola (1970), the last major novel he was working on at
his death, though a work he began as early as 1946.

Like Wyndham Lewis, Lowry was a prolific letter-writer, and he has left
us, mainly in his correspondence with Conrad Aiken, a legacy of comments
about Canada that complement his fictional expressions of exile. Relatively
few of these reflect the obligatory negative remarks that visitors from abroad
have been prone to make about the New World, and the most memorable of
these—"the bottom of a stinking well in Vancouver," "this Godawful environment of rain and fear," "the most hopeless of all cities of the lost," "this

damned hostile and ugly country"—were written during Lowry's first six
months or so in Canada, when he was suffering under a restrictive guardian-
ship arranged by his father. Significantly, his attitude undergoes a complete
reversal when he and Margerie Bonner, soon to become his second wife,
discover in the late summer of 1940 the small hamlet of Dollarton on Burrard
Inlet that is to become his Eridanus. "Note new address!" he rejoices to
Aiken in a letter dated 6 September 1940. "We live in a shack on the
sea . . . . Outside the window, a vast white calm where sea is confused with
sky and the Rockies [sic] . . . . Anyhow it is a wierd [sic] and wonderful
place and we love it."[9] (Though misspellings of any sort were uncharacteristic
of Lowry, he continued to confuse British Columbia's Coast Range with the
Rockies.)

From this stage of his exile on, though he frequently makes adverse
comments about Canada's social and cultural shortcomings, he consistently
and exuberantly celebrates its physical realities and climatic extremities,
even though their home is literally ravaged by fire and threatened by flood
and storm. Only near the end of his fourteen-year retreat in these primitive
surroundings does he express concern, not about the hardships, but about
the possibility of eviction, with his self-built shack and pier standing precari-
ously against the encroachments of a polluted civilization:

> Our oasis still stands, we still even add to it, our well gives forth pure
> mountain water still, the sea between oil-slicks is still marvellous to swim
> in . . . . To abandon the place, the house in its peril seemed, seems,
> traitorous but to stay simply inviting madness: how both to abandon it
> without treason and remain without going cuckoo but at the same time
> go—and by the way where? . . . All this, which has been brutally
> aggravated for the last years by the fact that I've been trying to write
> about this very thing—I mean specifically here, the life, the wonderful
> wonderful life, the approaching eviction, the horrible horrible evic-
> tion . . . .[10]

About Canada as a human landscape he has more reservations, though
his characteristic sense of humour allows him to avoid the bitterness that was
frequently present in the observations of Wyndham Lewis. Like Lewis, he
rails mercilessly against Canada's puritanical drinking laws—with possibly
more reason, given his own propensities—but even so he on one occasion, in
a letter to his literary agent, celebrates the moment by penning a spontaneous ditty on Canada's cold and uncharitable spirit:

> Old Blake was right, and got down to the hub
> When he said we should worship in the pub,

> Save only in Canada, where I'm told
> The churches and taverns both are cold.[11]

But he is frequently serious, too, in his condemnation of what he sees as dangerous tendencies in Canada, such as the "power and ubiquity" of the Mounted Police (in 1953 yet!) and the "quasi-totalitarian" nature of the emerging Social Credit party in British Columbia. But his most heartfelt concern was directed towards what was threatening Canada's natural and human resources, in which respect this sudden exile seemed in retrospect to have been far in advance of Canada's indigenous writers; it is a concern, too, that constitutes, as we will see, the backdrop to many of the stories in his *Hear Us O Lord*. In an otherwise self-indulgent letter to his brother in England, he touches on this aspect of the life he and Margerie were experiencing in Dollarton ("—or perhaps I should spell it Dolorton," he adds):

> We only live here by grace of being pioneers, and Canada, alas, is forgetting that it is its pioneers who built this country and made it what it was: now it wants to be like everyone else and have autocamps instead of trees and Coca-cola stands instead of human beings. In that way, for it has little culture at all, it could destroy its soul . . . . (*SL*, 218)[12]

Lowry's claim to be a Canadian—and Canada's claim on him— is predicated on his fourteen-year residency in this country, for which he was granted "landed immigrant" status; he was neither born in Canada, like Lewis, nor did he, like Moore, become a Canadian citizen. In a sense, he felt at home everywhere except in the England of his birth and education, but there it was a familial, rather than a cultural or intellectual, incompatibility that operated, though like Lewis, he sensed increasingly that England pointed to the end of an era rather than to any kind of renaissance. Yet paradoxically, he was also never certain that he belonged anywhere, disturbed as he was by the dual forces of his own impulse towards exile and what he at times sensed was a cosmic plot to keep him perpetually dispossessed: perhaps what Sigbjørn Wilderness meant by "the billows of inexhaustible anguish haunted by the insatiable albatross of self" (*Hear Us*, 31). Characteristically, he qualified his opinions about being a Canadian with comments about Canada's shortcomings, and it is clear that he never took too seriously the possibility of establishing legal and permanent connections with this country. "I like Canada anyway," he writes to his father in 1942. "Who knows but that I might not become a Canadian Ibsen or Dostoievsky? They certainly need one,"[13] and over a decade later he explains to Albert Erskine that while he "could in good conscience swear allegiance to Canada itself," the current political situation in his province does not really encourage it: "all in all it seems to me

British Columbia is a hell of a paradoxical place to ask any Englishman to give up his English passport in, with all that means, no matter how one might believe in or love Canada per se" (*SL*, 336, 337).

It becomes clear, therefore, that Lowry had long recognized that he was destined for permanent exile, and perhaps his most definitive word on this matter was that expressed in his letter to Robert Giroux early in 1952:

> From the personal point of view I had travelled about the world as a sailor so extensively without a passport before I was twenty that I had practically lost all sense of national barriers and had almost come to look on the world as a citizen thereof and its inhabitants as one happy or unhappy family. Devoted since boyhood to America, and married now to an American, I practically think—and thought of myself—as a kind of American, though Canadian, English and what-not.[14]

This outlook receives formal expression in much of Lowry's fiction, for both thematically and structurally, the voyage motif, with its attendant echoes of eviction and dispossession, constitutes a dominant strain. It is an appropriate touch, of course, that his monumentally conceived opus bore the title of *The Voyage that Never Ends*, for that refrain of the perpetual exile applies with precise relevance not only to Lowry himself, but to the many representations of his multiple protagonists. This predicament is whimsically described by the archetypal Sigbjørn Wilderness in "Through the Panama" as the

> plight of an Englishman who is a Scotchman who is Norwegian who is a Canadian who is a Negro at heart from Dahomey who is married to an American who is on a French ship in distress which has been built by Americans and who finds at last that he is a Mexican dreaming of the White Cliffs of Dover. (*Hear Us*, 96)

Whether one reads *Hear Us O Lord* as a series of unconnected stories or as a novel of the kind he described in a letter to James Stern (*SL*, 151), it gives rise to many interpretations, not the least significant of which involves the concept of exile. Within this perspective, it chronicles a series of voyages and experiences of exile figures who, dispossessed of a natural and untested Eden in the opening story, "The Bravest Boat," eventually repossess an experiential, man-controlled one in the triumphant concluding story, "The Forest Path to the Spring." That the exiles have different names from story to story—Sigurd and Astrid Storlesen, Sigbjørn and Primrose Wilderness, Kennish and Lovey Cosnahan, Roderick and Tansy Fairhaven—reflects the fact that it is not only the world at large that sees individuals differently in different situations, but that the individuals themselves do, and in this

respect these multiple protagonists provide some answers to the question
"—Who am I?—" set off typographically in "Through the Panama" (47).
These questions of identity and of how one responds to different worlds and
different experiences, as we have seen in a number of writers, are central to
the dilemma of the exile; Lowry's particular contribution to this paradigm is
that he brings to it a kind of cosmic overview, for his characters, particularly
the Wildernesses, who appear in or are mentioned in five of these stories,
very readily assume allegorical as well as realistic dimensions.

Strictly speaking, the two inhabitants we meet in "The Bravest Boat" are
not as yet exiles, but only on the point of so becoming, since, like Adam and
Eve, they have come to the limits of their static paradise, and are about to
enter the "loud world" represented by Enochvilleport across the fjord. A
measure of Lowry's unrelenting hatred of Vancouver's hypocrisy, narrowness,
and spiritual ugliness is reflected in the long and convoluted sentence (over
500 words) he constructs to describe Enochvilleport, a city resonating with
the echoes of Cain and the underworld: this extended tirade, as the following
excerpt illustrates, underscores, too, the kind of immersion into an experiential world that lies in store for Sigurd and Astrid:

> but for the fact that some of these were churches, you would be sure you
> were in hell: despite that anyone who had ever really been in hell must
> have given Enochvilleport a nod of recognition, further affirmed by the
> spectacle, at first not unpicturesque, of the numerous sawmills relent-
> lessly smoking and champing away like demons, Molochs fed by whole
> mountain-sides of forests that never grew again, or by trees that made
> way for grinning regiments of villas in the background of "our fair and
> expanding city," mills that shook the very earth with their tumult, filling
> the windy air with their sound as of a wailing and gnashing of teeth.
> (*Hear Us*, 17)

Disappearing into the chaos of the storm at the conclusion of this story,
Sigurd and Astrid are resurrected in the opening scene of "Through the
Panama" as Sigbjørn and Primrose Wilderness; here, as "the sole passengers"
boarding the *S.S. Diderot*, they assume allegorically the roles of an Adam
and an Eve exiled from Eden, ready to undertake their obligatory descent
into experience. During their voyage to the Old World via the Panama
Canal, we become witnesses to human accomplishments and adversities
hinted at in the earlier story, and occasionally faint echoes remind us of that
earlier existence, echoes that undergo modulations throughout these stories
until they are reassembled, so to speak, into the resonant harmony of "The
Forest Path to the Spring." Early on in his voyage, Sigbjørn becomes conscious of the agony of exile, intuiting that his own highly subjective feeling,

"the inenarrable inconceivably desolate sense of having no right to be where you are" is really a manifestation of the larger cosmic "universal sense of dispossession" (*Hear Us*, 31). This dilemma is shared by other characters in these stories, particularly Roderick Fairhaven in "Present Estate of Pompeii," who observes wryly at one point in his tour of the ruins that "this, pre-eminently, is where you don't belong" (*Hear Us,* 177), as well as by the Llewelyns in *October Ferry to Gabriola*. All these individuals, like the Wildernesses, are exiled from Eridanus, and yet, if they return, they face the constant threat of eviction, a quandary that Ethan Llewelyn succinctly grasps: "to be evicted out of exile: where then?" (*OF*, 4).

Lowry is not always cosmic, however, in his articulation of the exile state of mind, for occasionally he has his characters express opinions about Old World-New World distinctions that clearly derive from personal and local experience. At times, in an aphoristic comment like "Canada, whose heart is England but whose soul is Labrador" (*Hear Us*, 32), he evokes other exile writers as separated in time and attitudes as Frances Brooke and Wyndham Lewis; at other times, his trenchant observations are uniquely his own, as reflected, for example, in Sigbjørn's seething recollections of English schoolmasters:

> —Tragedy of someone who got out of England to put a few thousand miles of ocean between himself and the non-creative bully-boys and homosapient schoolmasters of English literature only to find them so firmly entrenched in even greater power within America . . . and responsible for exactly the same dictatorship of opinion, an opinion that is not based on shared personal or felt experience or identity with a given writer, or love of literature, or even any intrinsic knowledge of *writing*, and is not even formed independently, but is entirely a matter of cliques who have the auxiliary object of nipping in the bud any competitive flowering of contemporary and original genius, which however they wouldn't recognize if they saw it. (*Hear Us*, 75)

Earlier he had characterized these unimaginative types as "public school boys fishing vicariously for Hemingway's trout" (*Hear Us*, 31), and it is in opinions like these that Lowry gives credence to the view that, like Wyndham Lewis, he saw England degenerating into a state of aesthetic and spiritual inertness.

Lowry remained, however, ambivalent towards England and his relationship with that country; that he should die there, all the while (as his final letters, with their repetition of "Dollarton Grasmere" suggest) dreaming of the Eridanus from which he is exiled, constitutes the kind of ironic irresolution that attended him throughout his life. Sigbjørn Wilderness is troubled

by dilemmas of this sort as his ship passes Acapulco, port of entry to another
landscape that helped shape Lowry's vision:

> A sense of exile oppresses me. A sense of something else, beyond
> injustice and misery, extramundane, oppresses, more than desolates,
> more than confounds me. To pass this place like this. Would I, one day,
> pass England, home, like this, on this voyage perhaps by some quirk of
> fortune not to be able to set foot on it, what is worse, not want to set foot
> on it? (*Hear Us*, 41-42)

This acknowledgment that return is impossible is normally one of the
characteristics of the committed exile, and in Lowry's case it is buttressed by
his convicton that aesthetic salvation also lay in other directions, particularly in those directions taken by Joyce, Aiken, and Faulkner. On one level,
"Through the Panama" can be viewed as an attempt to resolve the relationship between these two tendencies, for Sigbjørn is as much exercised by his
literary legacies as he is by the question of where he belongs; his geographical and mythological voyages are in a sense paralleled by an exploration of
the intellectual and aesthetic labyrinths from which he is trying to emerge as
a writer with integrity and a unique personal vision.

The marginal gloss in "Through the Panama" from Coleridge's *Rime of
the Ancient Mariner* allows us to trace the progress of Sigbjørn's physical
and spiritual descent into perilous experience, for with him, as with the
Mariner, "an agony constraineth him to travel from land to land." The gloss
begins as his ship reaches the Mexican coast, the demonic landscape of his
own eschatological universe; it intensifies its supernatural omens and threats
as he reaches the Panama Canal, the nadir of his descent, where it gives way
to a secular, prosaic gloss about the human cost of this project; and then it is
briefly cited again as the ship, having survived the fury of the Atlantic storm,
comes to safety off the headlands of England where Sigbjørn, like the
Mariner, "beholdeth his native country." His own penance, that every once
in a while "begins anew" as it did for the Mariner, leads ultimately not only to
an understanding of himself as an individual within his world—an answer, in
effect, to the two questions that have attended him all along, "Who am I?"
and "Where am I?"—but also, as he explains in terms of the protagonist
within his own novel, to a resolving of his literary dilemmas:

> Martin's blindness, isolation, anguish, is all for a reason. I can see that on
> that road to Damascus, when the scales drop from his eyes, he will be
> given the grace to understand the heroic strivings of other artists too.
> Meantime he must slug it out, as they say, in darkness, that being his
> penance. (*Hear Us*, 85-86)

Within this perspective, Sigbjørn and Primrose, though in the literal sense merely "passengers in transit," emerge as archetypes of the universal exile who is being taken "away inexorably from the only place on earth he has loved, and perhaps forever" (*Hear Us*, 38). The supernatural and mythological visitations, from a "lone black albatross" to a passenger ominously named Charon, attend them on their obligatory pilgrimage, as do threats of separation and the literal dangers of shipwreck. But they overcome all these obstacles—Charon turns out to be nothing more dangerous than acting Norwegian Consul in Tahiti—and eventually they find themselves "safe in the midst of chaos," thus continuing the life cycle that was initiated by Sigurd in "The Bravest Boat" when he launched his bottled message in the tempest of his primeval chaos, "all those years before Astrid was born" (*Hear Us*, 22).

The three Italian-based stories that follow, aside from offering comic relief from the anguish of "Through the Panama," depict the transfigured Lowry protagonist confronting those elements of reality that constitute the residue of man's creative contributions to the world: fame, immortality, memorabilia, ruins, and the like; in this respect they represent an ironic and deflative response to Sigbjørn's and Martin's obsessions—to say nothing of Lowry's—with their books and reputations. In "Strange Comfort Afforded by the Profession," Sigbjørn Wilderness has been metamorphosed into an American writer visiting Rome on a Guggenheim Fellowship, and he muses over his relationship with such dead writers as Keats, Shelley, and Poe. Happily, of course, the fact that his own literary remains are not housed in various museums proves that he is very much alive, and in this respect at least, he can derive "strange comfort" from his profession.

In "Elephant and Colosseum" the novelist Kennish Drumgold Cosnahan in a sense cannot prove to his Italian publisher that either he or his novel, *Ark from Singapore*, exists, because he is unable to find the promised Italian edition of the book. But he does discover by chance Rosemary, the elephant that inspired his novel years earlier: she clearly has more reality than the art that she provoked. But the story is also about love: Cosnahan's love for his absent wife, Lovey L'Hirondelle, for his mother, dead on the Isle of Man, and for Rosemary herself, the kind of love William Carlos Williams (or Wilderness Carlos Wilderness, as he is parodied in "Through the Panama") celebrates in "The Sea Elephant." It appears, too, that there might be a bit of a spoof in this story on Fitzgerald's *Tender Is the Night* (for which Lowry had once written a film script), for Cosnahan recalls "that felicitous meeting in Rome by the hero of a book he'd been reading with a girl named Rosemary" (*Hear Us*, 134).

This story gives support, too, to the idea raised earlier about the nature of Lowry's multiple protagonists: that all these individuals are really different facets of the same persona. Kennish encounters this situation in a very

tangible way when he meets his Italian publisher, but he plays whimsically on
this theme, too, in his imaginary conversations, where he has Drumgold and
Cosnahan confront each other on a number of occasions in a kind of literary
catechism. Kennish also puts a number of unanswerable questions to himself
that in effect constitute variations on the "Who am I?" question posed by a
number of individuals in these stories:

> What did man know of his own nature? How many people went through
> life thinking they were other than they were? Not even the evidence of
> his own essential being right under his red nose would convince him.
> How many lives were necessary to find out? Heroic old Quattras, now a
> Canadian, had never lost the illusion that he was a writer—and who was
> Cosnahan to say him nay? . . . Yet what did he, Cosnahan, know of
> himself? Was he a writer? What *was* a writer? (*Hear Us*, 146)

"Present Estate of Pompeii" serves as a transitional story between the
other two Old World tales and the concluding two set in the New World,
juxtaposing three levels of reality: the immediate present (the ruins of
Pompeii), the remote past (the eruption of Vesuvius), and the immediate
past (life in Eridanus). The protagonist here is the Scottish-Canadian schoolmaster Roderick McGregor Fairhaven who, facetiously comparing the ruins
of Pompeii to Liverpool or Vancouver, senses "the strange and utter
meaninglessness, to him, of his surroundings," and meditates instead upon
the paradise he had left behind in Eridanus. Yet he is realist enough to
acknowledge that modern man is in a sense doomed to remain a perpetual
exile, that his goal of an "unevictable happiness" is unattainable, a point he
expands on to his wife, Tansy:

> "The traveler has worked long hours and exchanged good money for
> this. And what is this? This, pre-eminently, is where you don't belong. [It
> is] some great ruin that brings upon you this migraine of alienation—and
> almost inescapably these days there seems a ruin of some kind involved—
> but it is also something that slips through the hands of your mind, as it
> were, and that, seen without seeing, you can make nothing of: and
> behind you, thousands of miles away, it is as if you could hear your own
> real life plunging to its doom." (*Hear Us*, 177)

In the most literal sense, this story offers a pessimistic comment on the
exile's longing for an unevictable paradise, whatever its geographical setting,
very much the same kind of comment, as we have seen, that was provided by
the long opening section of Laura Salverson's *The Viking Heart*. Whether
through natural or man-made causes, man's self-built worlds seem ultimately

doomed to destruction, to assume a condition that at best is merely a variation on the present state of Pompeii, and it is this realization that has so exercised the protagonists of many of Lowry's works. Yet Fairhaven is above all a pragmatic realist, and this cosmic awareness of man's ultimate doom cannot dampen his celebration of the present state of Eridanus; in particular, he proclaims the importance of man's own creative obligations in the building of an inhabitable paradise:

> Until a man has built (or helped to build—for he had helped the Wildernesses build their house) a house with his own hands, Roderick thought, he may feel a sense of inferiority before such things as Greek columns. But if he happens to have helped build so much as a summer shack upon the beach he will not feel inferiority, even if he does not understand in the aggregate the entire meaning of a Doric temple. (*Hear Us*, 198)

In practical terms, this credo celebrates the priority of New World pragmatism over an attitude or response to reality conditioned by Old World cultural legacies and values, a position taken, as we have already seen, by such earlier exiles as Moodie, Niven, and Grove. It illustrates, too, what the Llewelyns in *October Ferry* suddenly realized about the meaning of the proverb, "as a bird wandereth from his nest, so is man who wandereth from his place": if man, like the bird, *builds* his own house with his own native craft, he is dispossessed and alienated forever if he leaves it. And of course, that Roderick and Tansy are enjoined, in their guided tour of Pompeii, to visit brothels, and ruined brothels at that, underscores the unreality of their temporary Old World experiences as juxtaposed against life in Eridanus.

In that the final two stories of *Hear Us O Lord* depict the exiles back in their paradise of Eridanus, they constitute a resolution of the parenthetical thoughts and fears that attended Sigbjørn Wilderness on that distant day when he emerged from the storm to board the *S.S. Diderot*:

> (This morning, walking through the forest, a moment of intense emotion: the path, sodden, a morass of mud, the sad dripping trees and ocherous fallen leaves; here it all is. I cannot believe I won't be walking down the path tomorrow.) (*Hear Us*, 29)

He does walk the path again: as Sigbjørn in "Gin and Goldenrod," as he leads Primrose through a dimly remembered maze of paths in order to pay his debt to a local bootlegger; and as a nameless composer in the final story who continually traverses the forest path as he composes his opera entitled "The Forest Path to the Spring." In the earlier story, the paradise has been despoiled by developers, and Sigbjørn is overcome with anguish and hatred, perhaps recalling his earlier definition of a Canadian as "a conservationist divided against himself" (*Hear Us*, 95), a point he expands on here: "But man was not a bird, or a wild animal, however much he might live in the wilderness. The conquering of wilderness whether in fact or in his mind, was part of his own process of self-determination" (*Hear Us*, 204).

Wilderness conquering wilderness: obviously Lowry cannot resist the pun here any more than he can avoid linking "Primrose" and "path" in tracing Sigbjørn's route to "dalliance." But in a more serious sense, this statement argues for the complete integration of man with all aspects of himself and with his physical environment, the kind of resolution that is dramatized in "Forest Path," a work that in his enthusiasm for it, Lowry saw as "the only short novel of its type that brings the kind of majesty usually reserved for tragedy . . . to bear on human integration and all that kind of thing" (*SL*, 266). The movement in this eight-part novella is from a simple factual description of Eridanus to a complex examination of the narrator's relationship with the components of this paradise. In keeping with the narrator's musical background, the movement builds through an accumulation of tones, details, modulations, and repetitions, as first the physical landscape, then the inhabitants, and finally the shacks which constitute the community are all brought into harmonious focus and relationship with each other. Juxtaposed against these details of physical setting are a number of other meanings of Eridanus— nautical, astronomical, and mythological—a device that not only helps to link this story to the rest of *Hear Us O Lord*, but that also allows us to see its nameless narrator in increasingly cosmic and allegorical terms.

From this point of view, all the exiled protagonists of the preceding stories are metamorphosed here into the persona of this Everyman figure who, in the act of creating his opera, resolves all their residual tensions about eviction, dispossession, separation, and guilts: the concept of exile as a result, therefore, ceases to exist. The narrator becomes at once the first inhabitant of this paradise and the descendant of countless generations, and at one point after a brief excursion to a particularly idyllic corner of Eridanus, he experiences a kind of epiphany wherein he senses this relationship to eternity:

> And some shadow of the truth that was later to come to me, seemed to steal over my soul, the feeling of something that man had lost, of which these shacks and cabins, brave against the elements, but at the mercy of the destroyer, were the helpless yet stalwart symbol, of man's hunger and need for beauty, for the stars and the sunrise. (*Hear Us*, 232)

Ironically, if we look at this story in terms of Lowry's total vision, the voyage that was not supposed to end does in fact do so, and one can readily see the appropriateness of Lowry's decision to have this story constitute the concluding movement of his magnum opus. And it is entirely fitting that the narrator of "The Forest Path to the Spring" work in the language of music, for only in such a protean, non-verbal art form can an experience of total and harmonious integration be realized.

Within the perspective of the journey theme that is central to so much of Lowry's works—not only in the stories here, but in two of his posthumous novels, *Dark as the Grave Wherein My Friend Is Laid* and *October Ferry to Gabriola*—the operating motif in this final story is that of the return: a return to one's own place, to one's human commitments, to an existential paradise where one is prepared to accept mortality. In a very real sense, the story provides an answer to the question that Yvonne posed to Geoffrey Firmin in *Under the Volcano*, "In what far place do we still walk, hand in hand? (*UTV*, 366), his answer to which she never did read, for it was in his unmailed letter to her: "I seem to see us living in some northern country, of mountains and hills and blue water; our house is built on an inlet and one evening we are standing, happy in one another, on the balcony of this house, looking over the water." (*UTV*, 36-37)

But a return to one place involves also a departure from another, a situation that always involves a process of reconciliation, and Lowry's entire life can be viewed as an unsuccessful attempt to resolve the conflicts that arose as a result of his many voyages and temporary homes. At one point in "Elephant and Colosseum" Cosnahan reflects on his own assumption of an American identity, and then poses a question that is not only difficult to answer in a general sense, but in Lowry's own particular case, was rendered forever unanswerable by his untimely death: "But there was still this much of the European left in him, that he could ask the old question: how can a European feel himself American without first making his peace with Europe, without becoming, however deviously, reconciled with his home?" (*Hear Us*, 142). Such a question, we recall, had no bearing on how Wyndham Lewis viewed himself, but as we will see, it is a crucial one, in terms of his fiction to date, for the third of our birds of passage, Brian Moore.

Born in Belfast, Brian Moore has been an exile from his native Ulster since the early 1940's, when his service with the British Ministry of War Transport took him to North Africa, Italy, and southern France. After the war, he served in Poland with a United Nations agency, free-lanced as a journalist in Scandinavia, and after a brief stay in England emigrated to Canada in 1948, a country whose citizenship he still holds, despite his residency in the United States since 1959. "Having acquired the habit of expatriation," he recalled in 1976, "I found I did not want to go home to

Ireland. In Ireland I saw my past, but no future,"[15] and in terms of his physical residencies he has thoroughly vindicated this decision, having lived in, or travelled extensively in, some seventeen different countries during his lifetime.

To a greater extent, therefore, than either Lewis of Lowry, Moore is a writer who has deliberately severed his links with his past, but like Lowry's Cosnahan, he has not found it an easy process to discard the Old World, for it constitutes a very large component in the majority of his novels to date, even in the half dozen that have New World settings and characters. Visiting Belfast in 1976, he saw the house of his birth as "a monument, to a time, and a life, which is gone forever and will never be again," but this experience produced in him the kind of ambivalent vision that is central to any exile:

> I know only that once again, as has happened so often in my years of self exile, in countries far from the land of my birth—I stood balanced on that seesaw of emotion and memory which has been the fulcrum of my novels—the confrontation between now and then, between there and here, which was and is the fruit of my decision to choose exile.[16]

When he did begin to write his serious fiction in the early 1950's, it was that Irish home and that Irish past that constituted his subject-matter, rather than the superficially more dramatic events he had experienced by going into exile. And his first two serious fictional protagonists, Judith Hearne and Diarmuid Devine, locked forever in the restrictive and uncharitable world of deterministic Belfast, not only remain as two of Moore's most powerfully evoked and sensitively portrayed characters, but in their status as more or less normal representatives of that world, offer convincing justification for his going into exile in the first place. As far as making a personal commitment, therefore, about where and how to live, it was probably not difficult for Moore to sever his ties with Belfast, but in his artistic creations of his various fictional worlds, the protagonists who experience the strongest sense of dislocation and who have the most disturbing moral doubts are those exiled figures who in their pilgrimages to the New World have also abandoned the forces and values that shaped their early lives. This dilemma is central to a number of his North American novels, particularly *An Answer from Limbo* (1962) and *Fergus* (1970), and in such finely wrought short stories as "Grieve for the Dear Departed" and "Uncle T," published in 1959 and 1960 respectively.

The first of these stories is set in Dublin, where a family is grieving for the dead father Daniel Kelleher, but its most important character is the absent son Michael who had gone off to America some sixteen years earlier because of irreconcilable differences with his father. For this, his father had never forgiven him, but the grieving wife and mother knows that "Dan's hate was mixed with pride" and on this belief she faked a telegram from Dan that would ensure Michael's return. The mother's grief is a double one: for her dead husband, but also for the absent son, the other "dear departed" of this title, and added to her grief is the guilt she feels over the betrayal she subsequently feels she has committed:

> I wrote out that cable never thinking, thinking only of me, of Michael, a child I wanted to see again, cold to my husband, cold to his paralyzed face, writing down what he could no longer stop me writing, taking from him the only thing he had left, his pride, his right to hate.[17]

This is not an exile story in the sense that it juxtaposes the Old World against the New in any specific scenes or situations, but rather in the sense that exile has divided a family against itself. Michael had attempted over the years to reconcile himself with his father, but one foresees in this story only the kind of delayed forgiveness that Fergus convinces himself he receives during the visitation of his dead parents. Throughout Moore's fiction, father-son conflicts constitute a recurring theme, and frequently, in novels like *The Emperor of Ice-Cream* and *The Doctor's Wife,* the accumulating levels of such conflicts suggest that not only households but entire societies turn this kind of hatred in on themselves.

Moore's strongest short story, "Uncle T," grows out of a situation similar to that which informed "Grieve for the Dear Departed." Here both Turlough Carnahan and his nephew, Vincent Bishop, are in exile in the United States and Canada respectively, and in both cases their anticlericalism and generally rebellious nature had caused their fathers to repudiate them. Strangers to each other until they meet in New York, they nevertheless had formed mutually positive impressions of each other, and a belief in their likeness, through a three-year exchange of letters. "I have long thought that you—a rebel, a wanderer and a lover of literature—must be very much like me when I was your age," Uncle T had written[18] and it is this bond, along with the possibility of working in his publishing firm, that Vincent had exploited to convince his new Canadian bride to accompany him to New York.

Barbara immediately detects and articulates truths about Uncle T's phoney character that Vincent is not willing to acknowledge, and as the evening drags on, both Irish husbands increasingly find themselves on the defensive against the realities about their situations mercilessly being revealed by their North American wives. "I know you," Bernadette scolds Turlough as he makes one last desperate attempt to salvage the evening, "it's your own fault, it's an old story, making yourself out to be something you never were" (*TS,* 51). Barbara and Bernadette are obviously more in touch with reality than their husbands are, but though they have logic and experience on their side, their attitudes nevertheless seem selfish and uncharitable. Vincent makes a response to his uncle at the end that his own father was unwilling to make to him, and perhaps because Turlough is such a loser, Moore convinces us that he deserves this acknowledgment. Vincent is clearly more like his uncle than he was prepared to admit at the outset, and for that reason his sudden glimpse of him from the taxi is a deeply troubling one:

> There, half-drunk on the pavement, stood a fat old man with dyed hair. Where was the boy who once wrote poems, the young iconoclast who once spoke out against the priests? What had done this to him? Was it drink, or exile, or this marriage to a woman twenty years his junior? Or had that boy never been? (*TS*, 55-56)

The power of this scene derives from our realization that the questions Vincent meditates on might well one day be asked about himself, as foreshadowed by his dismissing Barbara and his joining his uncle in "one for the road." The story does not unequivocally lead to this conclusion, for Vincent and Barbara seem better equipped for life in the New World than Turlough and Bernadette; that a final resolution is left in abeyance is one measure of the skill and honesty with which Moore handles the realities of exile, a talent that becomes increasingly visible in his three main novels of exile set in the New World.

Turlough Carnahan's importance in Moore's vision of the New World at this time is suggested by the fact that the title figure of *The Luck of Ginger Coffey* (1960) is at the outset of that novel very much like him: James Francis Coffey, too, is a loser and an inveterate bluffer about the reality of his own personal situation. But Moore catches Ginger early enough (though in his crucial fortieth year) that he can make moves to offset the fact that his luck has just about run out, provided he is willing "to abandon the facts of his life for the facts of the world" (*GC*, 118). His exile in the New World, deliberately chosen as an alternative to the dead ends of his existence in Dublin and Cork, provides him with the opportunity to do this, though it is not an easy process for him, and his basic mediocrity makes any spectacular improvement in his fortunes unlikely. For Carnahan, it is pathetically too late, and like James Madden of *Judith Hearne* (1955), he appears doomed to fade into insignificance through alcoholism and bitterness; exile for him simply provided the opportunity to perpetuate his delusions in a world where he is virtually anonymous but where, without the talent and drive of a Brendan Tierney, he will very quickly go under.

For most of Moore's exiles in the New World, the process of self-discovery and self-realization is a grim and somewhat frightening one, with only Ginger, near the end of his ordeal, reflecting the kind of rhapsodic acceptance of this world that frequently attended such earlier exiles from the Old

World as Niven's Angus Munro, Grove's Philip Branden, and Lowry's Sigbjørn Wilderness. Moore, unlike those writers, is exclusively an urban novelist, and thus there is little evidence in his works of the idea of the New World as paradise, which seems largely to be tied to Canada's wilderness and rural aspects. For him, such cities as Montreal, New York, and Los Angeles may provide opportunities that are unrealizable in Belfast or Dublin, but they are also centres of corruption, favouritism, and hypocrisy, though on the whole the determinism that operates in these New World cities seems less pervasive and less inflexible than it is in the Old World.

In his carefully preserved image of a Dublin squire, Ginger walks blindly into this kind of situation on that first working day of a new year when he sets out, down to his last fifteen dollars and three cents, to make his mark on Montreal. That "there wasn't a soul in Montreal who would say There goes a man who's out of work" (*GC*, 7), on the one hand reflects the kind of anonymity that protected Carnahan in New York, but on the other hand, it suggests that this city is prepared to honour this illusion while Ginger takes the opportunity to transform it into reality. For most of this first day, he tries to do just that, clinging to his belief in the "rags to riches" cliché about the New World as opposed to the Old World, where, he muses, it "was Chinese boxes, one inside the other, and whatever you started off as, you would probably end up as" (*GC*, 12). That he fails in all his attempts on that first day is due partly to his inflated opinion of himself, but also to the ingrained hostility of the officials he meets, who together constitute the entrenchment of class and privilege in Montreal. As a New Canadian, therefore, Ginger had not only to manipulate "the facts of his life," but also to suffer the establishment's suspicions and prejudices barely disguised beneath the veneer of time-worn labels and clichés about the Irish.

It is not until he is faced with the prospect of losing his wife and daughter that he is prepared to surrender his illusion about immediate success in the New World or his inflated image of himself. This process involves his inexorable descent from *Executive & Professional* of the Unemployment Office and from the editorial floor of the *Tribune* to the subterranean proofreading room, and, as he loses Veronica and Paulie, to a basement room of the YMCA. By the time he has exchanged his Dublin squire's clothing for the "anonymous and humiliating" delivery driver's uniform which, significantly, "fitted him perfectly," he has attained the exile's ultimate position of isolation and anonymity, very much as Philip Branden did when he took on the lowly waiter's job in *A Search for America*. This point marks the beginning of Ginger's true self-awareness, and for the moment, since "no one in the world knew where Ginger Coffey was," he is tempted, like the hermit in *Emily Montague*, to assume the ultimate state of exile: "to retire from the struggle, live like a hermit, unknown and unloved in this faraway land" (*GC*, 104), but he is too much a man of the flesh to pursue this notion seriously.

Ginger cannot remain anonymous for long, and his new identity is threatened when he is recognized by some former Dublin residents, but this recognition scene, where past reputation and present reality converge, produces an epiphany-like awareness in Ginger about his commitment to his exile: "What did it matter? What did they matter, so long as he was not going home? And in that moment he knew that, sink or swim, Canada was home now, for better or for worse, for richer or for poorer, until death" (*GC*, 133). His formalizing of his commitment in the language of the marriage ceremony emphasizes the relationship between his two abiding concerns, the preserving of his family and the justifying of his exile to Canada in the first place; it also suggests that his exile represented an existential protest against the closed order of the Old World, and a belief that one can only find his true nature through an individual and pragmatic testing of experience rather than through following prescribed rules and routines.

To dramatize Ginger's commitment to his exile and at the same time his lingering doubts and uncertainties about his action, Moore exploits a number of obligatory situations where we witness Ginger moving from private rationalizing through a grotesque initiation ceremony to a final legal vindication of his new status. On that first day when he was still optimistic about his chances, he enters a church, ostensibly to keep warm, but in reality to justify his anti-clericalism: "one of his secret reasons for wanting to get away to the New World was that, in Ireland, church attendance was not a matter of choice. Bloody well go, or else, tinker, tailor, soldier, sailor, rich man, poor man, you were made to suffer in a worldly sense. Here, he was free . . . " (*GC*, 21). And yet, he recalls the thunderous sermons of Father Cogley that seemed directed specifically at him, wherein he prophesied that unbelievers and adventurers would end up "in some hell on earth, some place of sun and rot or snow and ice that no sensible man would be seen dead in" (*GC*, 18). His rejection of the church, therefore, is not entirely a comfortable decision, and certainly not an intellectual one, but rather, in keeping with his blustering optimism of that day, an impulsive and boastful manifestation of his pride.

But the next day he hits bottom as he joins a group of misfits who constitute his proofreading companions, and it is here, in a local tavern, where he undergoes a grotesque initiation ceremony into his Canadian experience, as the drunken Fox, in a bitter parody of the exile's dream, gives his vision of Canada as seen from the bottom:

> "I have to explain the facts of life to our immigrant brother. Do you want to be remembered, Paddy? . . . Then you must bear in mind that in this great country of ours the surest way to immortality is to have a

hospital wing called after you. Or better still, a bridge. We're just a clutch of little Ozymandiases in this great land. Nobody here but us builders . . . . Remember that in this fair city of Montreal the owner of a department store is a more important citizen than any judge of the Superior Court. Never forget that, Paddy boy. Money is the root of all good here. One nation, indivisible, under Mammon that's our heritage." (*GC*, 70)

That the judge at Ginger's trial is humane and charitable in the sentence he hands down suggests that Fox is not entirely correct in his analysis of the Canadian dream, but Ginger, already having met such petty, self-serving individuals as Beauchemin, Kahn, and MacGregor undoubtedly has some of his worst fears confirmed by this tirade. And as his fellow proofreaders hint that Ginger's promised promotion might never materialize, he begins to have serious doubts about his exile: "Was it for this he had traveled across half a frozen continent and the whole Atlantic Ocean? To finish up as a galley slave among the lame, the odd, the halt, the old" (*GC*, 72).

Appropriately, the courtroom scene where he is finally recognized and vindicated follows immediately upon his self-confession in his cell, where he firmly acknowledges that whatever has happened to him is exclusively his fault, "not God's, not Vera's, not even Canada's (*GC*, 223). This *mea culpa* stance reflects the fundamental integrity that has always resided within Ginger (as we see, for example, in the Melody Ward episode), but that was frequently compromised because, in his concern for his family, he was always too eager to see himself as someone greater than he really was. It is this same concern that the judge takes into account as he sentences Ginger: "I am dealing with you leniently, Coffey, because I am sorry for your family. To be alone in a new country, with their breadwinner in jail, seems to me a fate which your wife and child do not deserve" (*GC*, 233). The reconciliation with Veronica that follows constitutes a logical consequence both of his moral rebirth and of this legal recognition by Canada as a person deserving a further chance, a situation that stands in sharp contrast, for example, to the deterministic resolving of Judith Hearne's and Diarmuid Devine's personal dilemmas in their Belfast worlds.

The "luck" of Ginger Coffey in this process of transformation and reconciliation lies, ironically, in the fact that he is able to overcome that very stereotype of the Irish that various individuals parrot at him during that first long day of job-seeking. It is the Old World that has shaped him into the Dublin squire persona we meet initially, but it is the pragmatic New World that allows him to discard that image; therefore his "luck" resides in the fact that *Executive & Professional* and the *Tribune*'s editor *did* turn him down, for from this moment on he can no longer rely on being "at present a praiser of his own past," to borrow Stephen Dedalus's phrase about his father. From a sociological point of view, Ginger emerges as a valid representative of the post-war Irish immigrants, whom Moore described in an early interview as "people who weren't doing very well at home . . . and got a terrible shock because they met a society that really wanted . . . work for money. And you had to know how to do something."[19] Ginger unconsciously acknowledges that he is one of these people as he waits in a movie theatre to go through with the prearranged assignation with the call-girl—people who took on menial jobs for the sake of their families, just as he has done for Veronica and Paulie. "Wasn't he one of them? Wasn't he a stranger here, never at home in this land where he had not grown up. Yes: he too" (*GC*, 170).

Clearly, for the person who does "know how to do something," the New World in Moore's view, with its resilient pragmatism, offers unlimited opportunities, and within this perspective, A.K. Brott and the eccentric W.K. Wilson, both of whom unselfishly extend a helping hand to Ginger, represent respectively its conventional and its bizarre possibilities. Gerry Grosvenor, on the other hand, emerges as the self-seeking opportunist of this world, for though he offers to help Ginger, he is of course after Veronica, and it is evident that he sets up that disastrous interview with MacGregor of the *Tribune*, knowing that Ginger's failure will enhance his own chances with her. All in all, he is merely one of the near-caricatures that Moore has drawn from his Canadian experiences, not unlike R.M. MacKinnon of *Mary Dunne*, who is even more unflatteringly depicted as the "Warm Brown Turd," so Ginger quite justifiably is amazed that Veronica should be attracted to this "self-satisfied sausage." Though he plays a considerable role in the lives of Ginger and Veronica, Grosvenor is not developed in sufficient depth to stand as any kind of mean against which Ginger can be measured, and indeed, neither one of them can be said to constitute substantial representatives of their respective worlds. As a result, it is not as valid in this novel to try to assess Moore's attitudes towards his two worlds as it is in *Limbo*, or *Fergus*, where characters from both sides of the Atlantic are drawn with more complexity.

Moore quite properly emphasizes Ginger's isolation throughout this novel, for as with all exiles, he is an outsider as far as both his worlds are concerned. Father Cogley's tirade against those who desert Ireland has its New World counterpart in the prejudices and hostility of those petty officials who see any immigrants as threats to their own secure world, so in both cases, Ginger has only himself to fall back on. Though he is by no means as articulate as Lewis's René Harding, he intuitively recognizes that "there can be no consultation with others in a matter of conscience," and therefore he makes all his honest decisions about his fate in total isolation. He confronts in his imagination a terrifying void in these situations, for haunting him until the very end is his fear that Veronica will remain with Grosvenor, abandoning him to a lonely existence in his new land; this spectre receives tangible shape when he goes to visit the sick proofreader, old Billy Davis who, he learns, also left Ireland to seek his fortunes in the larger world:

> Irish. *An immigrant, same as you.* A young wanderer, once traveling through this land of ice and snow, looking for the bluebird. ERIN GO BRAGH. But was it really ERIN FOREVER? What trace of Erin was left on William O'Brien Davis save that harp and shamrock, that motto, faded as the old reminder that BILL LOVES MIN? Would Ginger Coffey also end his days in some room, old and used, his voice nasal and reedy, all accent gone? (*GC*, 207)

Much as Vincent Bishop was disturbed by his vision of his Uncle T metamorphosed into a pathetic loser, so Ginger here is haunted by the spectacle of youthful hope betrayed, a situation obviously more frightening for the exile than for one secure in his own native land.

The Luck of Ginger Coffey is the only one of Moore's novels where the exile theme is played out within Canada, though he is to concern himself with other aspects of the Canadian experience in such novels as *I Am Mary Dunne* (1968), *The Great Victorian Collection* (1975), and *The Mangan Inheritance* (1979). In the larger perspective, however, *Ginger Coffey* marks the beginning of the exile's attempt to accommodate himself to increasingly bewildering aspects of the New World and to resolve his residual loyalties to the Old, processes that both Brendan Tierney and Fergus Fadden pursue in a more profound way than Ginger, but nevertheless are unable to complete satisfactorily. Largely because Ginger's severance from the Old World was more final than either Brendan's or Fergus's (unlike them, for example, he received visitations from neither the living nor the dead), his final resolution, in terms both of his own vision of the New World and of a reconciled domestic situation, is the strongest of the three.

The progression from *Ginger Coffey* through *Limbo* to *Fergus* involves not only an increasing complexity in character, but also a corresponding complexity in the total settings in which the protagonists work out their dilemmas. Or perhaps it is more accurate to say that because the cities in question reflect the nature and compulsions of the individuals within them, the realistically perceived Montreal gives way to the increasingly surrealistic cityscapes of New York and Los Angeles. Brendan and Fergus are not only exiles, but writers-in-exile, and their dilemmas take on layers of complexity that did not obtain for Ginger, who essentially wanted only to be able to preserve his family intact, even if that meant surviving "in humble circs." For him, therefore, Montreal, in contrast to Dublin, is seen as a benign world, where a flexible pragmatism will sustain him from crisis to crisis, and where in a pinch he could always follow Wilson to Blind River. No such easy solutions or alternatives appear to be available for either Brendan or Fergus, whose artistic compulsions keep them in a kind of bondage to the forces that recognized and encouraged them in the first place and the abandoning of which in effect would amount to the abandoning of their careers as novelists. "How easy it was to rationalize that first taste of corruption," Fergus recalls (*F*, 63), as he rues his involvement with Boweri and Redshields, and it is a similar moral dilemma that keeps on troubling Brendan as well, beside which Ginger's survival problems seem quite minor and relatively easy to solve.

In *An Answer from Limbo*, the Old World and the New World meet most dramatically in the scene surrounding Brendan's meeting his mother at the airport, a scene that both literally and symbolically fulfils one of Moore's concerns while writing this novel: "to put Irish Catholicism against the rootless wasteland of North America."[20] That these two worlds are fundamentally incompatible we have already surmised from our initial glimpses of Brendan and Mrs. Tierney in their separate worlds, and it is reinforced by the reservations of Ted Ormsby who, among other roles, acts out the remnants of Brendan's conscience back in Belfast: "He was conscious . . . of the dangers to this woman in rejoining a son whose world and whose ways were so opposed to her own" (*AL*, 16). That they barely recognize each other at the airport after seven years apart is in the literal sense not all that surprising, but it anticipates the gulf between them that grows wider as time goes on, for Brendan has, in spite of some lingering reservations, totally committed himself to his exile in the New World:

> Did I come to America because of my need to write, my need of Jane, or simply my old need to run? I do not know. But this morning, as I got off the bus at the airport . . . I knew that it is this world I care about, this world of moving staircases, electric eyes, efficient loudspeakers. Exile now means exile from this. My island is no longer home. (*AL*, 30)

And, ironically, his earlier boast that he has escaped "the provincial mediocrity" of his native land means he has abandoned, too, the values represented by his mother, whose "lostness" as she enters the airport terminal is only the outward manifestation of how out of place she is in the New World.

But Brendan cannot entirely exorcise the forces of the Old World, any more than Ginger or Fergus can, for the paradox they all face is that it is these forces that have both shaped them and driven them into exile in the first place, and they all find themselves, to reverse the familiar epigram, between two worlds, one very much alive and the other powerless to die. "Limbo is the modern condition: a place, neither heaven nor hell, a place of oblivion," Moore said in his working notes for this novel,[21] but Brendan's isolation is not only cosmic, for his ambition and selfishness have made it a very human situation as well, as reflected in his inability to understand either Jane or his mother. By the end of *Limbo*, Brendan has fulfilled his primary reason for going into exile in the first place, for he *has* become a successful novelist, but in his personal relationships it has been a costly victory. Earlier we saw him asking himself about his real reason for exile, whether it was to pursue his ambitions to be a writer, or to pursue Jane, or simply to run away (reflecting Moore's own contention that it is frequently for mundane, rather than artistic, reasons that a writer goes into exile),[22] but the course he consistently followed in the New World leaves no doubt about the priority of that first reason.

Where Ginger Coffey failed in his anticipated career, but succeeded in saving his family, the reverse holds true for Brendan and this, suggests Moore, is one of the penalties that some exiles are compelled to pay. *An Answer from Limbo* makes the same point, too, that Lewis's *Self Condemned* did, that such a resolution does not elevate the exiled protagonist in any moral sense, but simply and unmistakably reminds him that the initial decision to go into exile produces all kinds of personal consequences that must at times seem to outweigh any artistic or professional advantages gained. Quite early in this novel, but after he has made his irreversible decision about the centrality of his novel, Brendan sincerely tries to resolve the human cost of what he is to do, in his poignant apostrophe to his dead father: "I know only that if I were granted the wish to bring back to this world for one hour any human being I have known or read of, I would put in the call tonight for my father . . . I wanted to prove to him that he was wrong, that I, of all his children, will do him honour. O, Father, forgive me as I forgive you. Father, I am your son" (*AL*, 67).

This lament between father and son, as we have seen, constitutes a recurring note in Moore's exile fiction, and it is particularly important in *Fergus*, where it is Fergus's father who makes the first and the last of the visitations from the dead to break in upon his lonely existence on the Pacific. It is not only geographically that Fergus is isolated, for he also feels vulnerable in a number of crucial personal relationships: with his youthful mistress, whom he is afraid of losing, with his Hollywood producers, threatening to cut him off if he will not change his novel to their liking, with his former wife, bleeding him for alimony and child support. In short, he is at that impasse where nothing in his present life is working out, and thus he wills into his consciousness all those forces of his past life that at one time had significance for him. When that long ordeal is over, he has achieved some victories, costly though some of them are, and he is able to dismiss the ghosts of the past as dawn breaks over the New World. Just before he had seen his father for the first time, he had stood looking over the Pacific, hearing the breakers pounding on the shore, and as his father leaves at the end, he becomes conscious of this recurring beat again. Thus, his earlier recollection of the refrain from Xenophon, *"Thalassa, Thalassa, the loud resounding sea, our great mother, Thalassa"* (*F*, 4), takes on a new significance, giving Fergus a kind of cosmic comfort, for like the Greek exiles who long ago sang the lament, he too, acquires both sadness and sustenance from beholding the sea in a world so far from his homeland.

Fergus on one level depicts Moore's fascination with communications of various sorts—fake telegrams ("Grieve for the Dear Departed"), unmade telephone calls (*Limbo*), unreceived letters (*Mary Dunne*)—but in its unusual and unique way of showing how Fergus Fadden receives his messages from home, this novel dramatically personifies what the real cost of exile is. As a committed novelist, Fergus has to find out whether he, like Brendan Tierney, can get his revenge on the past "by transforming it into a world of words," but his succession of visitors, from beyond the grave as well as from his immediate world, make it impossible for him to find an easy or certain answer. He is misunderstood as an individual, harangued for his morals, berated for his selfishness, attitudes of the Old World that have been levelled, not only against such deliberate exiles as Ginger and Brendan, but against such accidental ones as Sheila Redden or such imminent ones as Gavin Burke of *The Emperor of Ice-Cream*. Reinforcing the doubts that all these familiar charges resurrect are the threats emanating from his present California world, ranging from the impulsive petulance of his mistress, Dani, to the deliberate and obscene ultimatums coming from the Hollywood producers, Redshields and Boweri. In his past world, Fergus *did* have a presence and a reality, even though he has tried to transform them, but in his present world, he is everyday aware of his insignificance. "I could live here for a year and leave no mark on anything," he realizes. "My presence would count for nothing" (*F*, 133).

Fergus tries on one occasion to explain to his angry visitors why he has changed, but his explanation also underscores the kind of penalties one incurs in choosing a life of exile:

> Let me try to explain? Most people live their lives in one place, and they meet, essentially, the same people, year after year. But I've lived in Ireland, worked as a newspaperman in England and France, came to America and worked on Long Island, then in New York, and now I'm here on the Pacific, I'm trying to say I've lived in so many places, it's impossible to remember— (*F*, 200-1)

Here Fergus and Elaine, respectively an exile to the New World and a girl born in the New World, stand alone against the fury of the mob, simply for the reason that Fergus in his selfishness had forgotten her name and forgotten an earlier role he had played in her life. The Old World's unforgivingness and lack of charity, personified in Father Allen's hostile diatribes, unmistakably constitute a justification for Fergus's exile in the first place, but one can also understand, by the mob's accumulated fury, why it is that Fergus was not easily free of that legacy.

But Moore is not simplistic about the relative virtues of moralities of the Old and New Worlds in the novel. That California produces such monstrous figures as Boweri and Redshields, and such pathetic manipulators as Dani's mother, Dusty, helps make us uneasy about Fergus's future. For the moment, however, he has achieved a limited personal and moral victory: Dani has returned to him, he has refused to compromise his artistic convictions, and he has in effect cut off all further communication with all those, whether dead or living, who have tried to transform his life and his art. That it is a new dawn, too, rather than continuing darkness, that greets him as "he walked towards the house" suggests his victory, though our final view of Fergus also spells out the kind of cosmic isolation that his exile has produced.

In none of these three North American novels does Moore impose a facile solution upon the dilemmas of his protagonists, and Brendan's agonizing questions at his mother's funeral—"Am I still my mother's son, my wife's husband, the father of my children? Or am I a stranger, strange even to myself?" (*AL*, 319)—apply with very little modification to Ginger and Fergus as well. Brendan's epiphany is not unlike the observation made by Moore about the lost generation expatriates, that when they returned to America, they experienced "a terrifying realisation that the country of their boyhood is lost forever." Doubts, fears, uncertainties—these are the emotions experienced by Moore's exiles in the New World, but at the same time they achieve an existential or experiential resolution of their dilemma that was not possible for such Old World protagonists as Judith or Devine. Only Moore's more recent Irish protagonists, like Sheila Redden of *The Doctor's Wife* (1976) or Eileen Hughes of *The Temptation of Eileen Hughes* (1981), seem to be able to say with Ginger Coffey that "a man's life was nobody's fault but his own," and act decisively on that conviction, a realization that undoubtedly Moore himself came to as he set out long ago on his own life of exile.

Unlike Lewis and Lowry, Moore has always been, in a personal sense, happily committed to exile, and indeed, his two self-exiles, from Ireland and from Canada, reflected none of the family or economic compulsions that operated with the other two, though he was eager to get free of the secular and spiritual strife that characterized his birthplace. Of these three exiles he is far and away the least committed to any one country, though as his rich and varied fiction reflects, he is thoroughly familiar with the particularities of many—Northern Ireland, Eire, England, Canada, the United States, and France. He has on a number of occasions[23] made a useful distinction between the writer *in* exile, whom he sees operating largely from external compulsions, and the writer *as* exile, who is motivated more by artistic, intellectual, or moral reasons than by social or political conditions in his homeland. Within this framework, Lewis was temperamentally always a writer *in* exile, for he characteristically placed the blame for his situation on factors within English, American, or Canadian society. Lowry in a sense reflected both these definitions: though physically in exile from a hostile family and a nation manifesting various deficiencies, he was also in a state of permanent exile against himself, against his inner world whose fantasies and nightmares confirmed his literal, day-to-day fears of eviction and dispossession, making it difficult for him to know where he did and where he did not belong. Only Moore in an uncomplicated sense is a writer *as* exile, for confirmed by his realization that he never intends or wants "to go home again," he sees whatever society he is for the moment concerned with as an integral world with its own legitimate reality, shapable to the exile's own particular vision.

8

Emigrés and Academics

It has become clear in this book that exiles are not easily or consistently classifiable into airtight groups, and that where I have placed a number of writers in one general category I have done so as much for convenience as for any exclusive vision or aesthetic that they alone possess. In any study of this sort, there are inevitably many writers who are left out, in terms of the categories they could fit into, and many others whose achievements or historical importance do not warrant their receiving an entire chapter to themselves, even though, in such cases, some have contributed important disparate works to the literature of exile in Canada. It is a half dozen or so of these writers, whose background experiences and approaches to exile make them sufficiently different from those discussed so far, that I will be examining in this penultimate chapter.

Among the more important of such writers are those political refugees or émigrés who came not only out of the Old World, but from a part of that world that at the time of their exile was associated ideologically or militarily with the enslavement of humanity. Many of these are émigrés more than once, not infrequently having moved from their native country to other parts of Europe before ultimately emigrating to the New World, and in a number of cases they have escaped more than one form of totalitarianism. Clearly, a writer whose vision has in large part been shaped, for example, by a double onslaught of Nazism and Communism, will see both the Old World and the New in less simplistic terms than those whose exile derived from something less traumatic, with the frequent result that the standard responses we have come to expect from the Old World exiles are not always forthcoming. But sometimes, too, as I suggested in my opening chapter in connection with Josef Skvorecky, the sheer surprise at the differentness of the New World begins almost immediately to render the Old World quickly expendable, a situation that gave some concern to the Lithuanian émigré Czeslaw Milosz, now living in the United States: "A country or a state should endure longer than an individual . . . . Today, however, one is constantly running across survivors of various Atlantises. Their lands in the course of time are transformed in memory and take on outlines that are no longer verifiable."[1]

Of the first group of émigrés to arrive in Canada—those who had fled the Nazis—two individuals are relevant to this study, the German-born Eric Koch and the Austrian-born Henry Kreisel. Their experiences are similar: after escaping Nazi regimes during the 1930's they settled and studied in England, were deported to Canada in July 1940 as enemy aliens, and after their release from Canadian internment camps studied at the University of Toronto, and have become permanent residents and successful writers in Canada. Both have written about these experiences, Kreisel in his "Diary of an Internment"[2] and Koch more recently in a much fuller account, *Deemed Suspect: A Wartime Blunder,*[3] and both confessed to virtually a total ignorance about the country to which they were being deported. But as Koch points out, "with the Nazis on England's doorstep," their compulsory exile was not unwelcome, and their first look at Canada was described in terms we have become familiar with since Colonel Rivers first saw this country in 1769:

> Our voyage up the St. Lawrence River had been gorgeous. the magnificent river, the picturesque little villages along its banks with their silvery church steeples and, finally, the sight of the dramatic cliffs of Quebec cheered us tremendously. Everyone, with the exception of a few cynics, felt optimistic and in a good mood. (*DS*, 70)

These two writers have, however, taken quite different fictional directions since that time, with Kreisel examining in an essentially realistic style the moral and psychological manifestations of exile, while Koch has used the elements of fantasy and satire to create surrealistic worlds or to explore the complexities of international intrigue. In his four novels to date, it is exaggerated or fanciful cultural or political situations that are exploited, whether in Canada and France (*The French Kiss*, 1969), the United States (*The Leisure Riots,* 1973 and *The Last Thing You'd Want to Know,* 1976), or in the emerging African nation of Lalonga (*Good Night Little Spy,* 1979) with characters being little more than stereotypes or caricatures. His concern has not been, therefore, to measure one world in terms of another, though the fact that in three of his novels the first person narrator is a European does give him the opportunity to get in some predictable comments now and then. More important, however, is the fact that in those novels the narrator is also a "double" figure: a reincarnation of an earlier figure in *The French Kiss*, and a de-Nazified former assistant to Hermann Göring in the two novels about

America, and thus he acquires the ambiguity and elusiveness to transform himself as required and assume the appropriate roles for the fantasy in question.

In his role, for example, as General de Gaulle's "Canadian expert," the narrator Jo-Jo of *The French Kiss* was sent to Canada in the disguise of a history professor, and he was thus in a position to prepare the groundwork for de Gaulle's famous *Vive le Québec libre* speech. The novel's subtitle *A Tongue-in-Cheek Political Fantasy*, warns us, however, not to take Koch too seriously in the judgments he makes of Canada and France, and the following outburst from one of Jo-Jo's many mistresses in Montreal can be taken as typical of his view not only in this work, but throughout his fiction in general:

> You come here like some French Colonel Blimp; you sit in your campus canteen, or your faculty club, or wherever, and you believe everything your rabble-rousing friends tell you. I would have thought a Parisian intellectual, who allegedly played some role in the government for a while, would be a little more sophisticated. But you're just as gullible as some little virgin from Chicoutimi. (*FK*, 33)

What we can take more seriously in Koch, especially as revealed in his two satires on America, are society's obsessions with leisure and with death, and here he not so subtly links these American tendencies with the totalitarianism of the Nazis. The Washington-based institute that monitors society's transgressions is an all-powerful think tank called CRUPP, whose president, the ex-Göring assistant Friedrich Bierbaum, and staff control their world with a computerized efficiency that turns up situations that are at times disturbing and at other times hilarious. For example, in *The Leisure Riots* the narrator tells what happens to a man whose early and financially profitable retirement from Jupiter Aircraft involves a compulsory adult education scheme: "This is what the poor man has to do: read *War and Peace*, learn the violin, take paleontology, archaeology and history lectures at the Smithsonian, and learn Spanish . . . . [and] if he refuses, they stop the pension cheques" (*LR*, 43). And in *The Last Thing You'd Want to Know* the American people, in their fear of death, buy 16,000,000 Ouija boards annually, and elect a witch as Democratic president. Clearly, what Koch is interested in is not so much measuring one established culture against another, as it is in presenting situations that seem far-fetched, but which are logically possible, given society's current tendencies to allow itself to be unduly swayed by legislation, by technology, or by cults.

Like Eric Koch, Henry Kreisel maintained during his internment a strong sense of humour, and an acceptance of the fact that his world had permanently changed:

Very early on during my internment I decided that I would write in
English. I had known the language for less than two years . . . but I felt
it absolutely essential that I embrace English, since I knew that I would
never return to Austria and wanted to free myself from the linguistic and
psychological dependence on German.[4]

His eighteen months of internment, "in a kind of no man's land," he recalls,
allowed him to see the 1930's and his own future in a proper perspective, and
from the outset he remained faithful to his determination to be a writer. In
spite of his difficulties with the language, and with contacting sympathetic
readers and publishers, he did write during his internment a few short stories,
and some portions of a novel entitled *Miguel Amore*. After being released in
the fall of 1941, he prepared himself for admission to the University of
Toronto where he enrolled the following year. His internment undoubtedly
did much to establish the framework in which he was to express himself as a
novelist, for virtually all of his fiction to date, including *The Rich Man* (1948)
and *The Betrayal* (1964), as well as some of his short stories collected in *The
Almost Meeting* (1981), record the experiences of various exile figures
whose burdens derive both from their Jewishness and from the global effects
of the holocaust. In these works it is not so much the comparative values of
Canada and the Old World that are examined as it is the entire texture of a
life that has been profoundly shaped by events that are not clearly understood in either world. In his two novels, the standard exile motif of the
journey is central to the protagonists's dilemma, but their journeys have far
more ironic consequences than was the case with many of the individuals we
have examined so far, for in effect those quests cancel out whatever goal
inspired them in the first place.

Both Jacob Grossman of *The Rich Man* and Theodore Stappler of *The
Betrayal* believe that their journeys to the Old and the New Worlds respectively will bring about a vindication of an earlier action: for Jacob, his
decision thirty-three years previously to emigrate to Canada from his native
Austria, and for Theodore, the role he played in an ill-fated escape attempt
out of Nazi Germany. But the conventional New World-Old World polarities
of innocence and experience, honesty and cynicism, wealth and poverty,
freedom and involvement, undergo ironic and inconsistent reversals, and
both men are ultimately caught up in their own rationalizations, with their
missions, if not absolute failures, then certainly very much compromised. In
both these novels, Kreisel confirms the existential realization that an act can
be justified only at the moment of its execution, for its immediate and
long-term ramifications, as well as events in the world at large, ensure the
ongoing transformation of the act. And of course that it inevitably involves
other people, many of them totally innocent at the time of its enactment,

confirms the futility of maintaining a morally rigid position towards the rightness or wrongness of that action.

The Betrayal in particular verifies these observations, for in terms of its central action, what began as a somewhat convoluted and sordid series of human actions in the geographical and moral confusion of Europe receives its unfolding in the clear, cold, spacious, and seemingly uncomplicated world of Canada's far northwest. Edmonton on the North Saskatchewan takes over from Vienna on the Danube, and the initially innocent bit players in this drama, Katherine Held and Mark Lerner, increasingly assume their share of involvement from her father and Stappler, the original perpetrators of the betrayal. Except for Mark, all the participants are in the literal sense exiled from the holocaust and from the Old World; appropriately it is he, a professor of history, who is called upon to derive order and meaning from their experiences. That he cannot entirely do so is in part due to his own past involvement in that world, for he was wounded fighting the Nazis, and his own grandfather had many years earlier escaped from the Warsaw ghetto to settle in Toronto, but it is also due to the ultimate insolubility of this problem. Ironically, he is left in isolation to live with it, while the involved participants all go their own way: Joseph to immediate suicide, Theodore to assume a new identity and role as a medical man in the far north, and Katherine to a new life of the west coast. That Theodore was later killed in an avalanche while trying to save a man spells out on the one hand the purifying power of the pristine New World, but on the other, it also suggests that his guilt could be expiated, while Joseph's could not, for his was in human terms the greater betrayal.

In both *The Rich Man* and *The Betrayal,* one manifestation of exile is dramatized in man's vulnerability or ultimate isolation, for again and again he finds it impossible to communicate to others what seems to be an obvious truth about either himself or a particular situation. This kind of dilemma informs a number of his short stories as well, particularly "The Almost Meeting," "Two Sisters in Geneva," and "The Broken Globe," and again, as in his novels, neither Old World nor New World protagonists are seen in any way as being superior in avoiding or overcoming this problem. There is frequently a clash between individuals shaped by different cultures, as between Nick Solchuk and his Old World father in "The Broken Globe," or between the two English-born sisters, one from Canada and one from Italy, who unload their opposed visions of the world upon a reluctant Canadian narrator in Geneva. Nick's intellectual superiority over his father is undeniable, and his international reputation as a geophysicist has taken him far from the one-room school in Three Bear Hills, Alberta, where his curiosity about the earth was first aroused. But to the English narrator who visits the isolated old man, there is a majesty and a moral power about him as he stands outside his farm house and reaffirms his own ocular proof about the earth: "Look," he said, very slowly and very quietly, "she is flat, and she stands still."[5]

In "The Almost Meeting" a different kind of separation is dramatized, not unlike the "two solitudes" situation that Hugh MacLennan examined in his second novel. Kreisel employs the device of a story-within-a-story to depict how Old World legacies can surface with disastrous consequences in the New: Alexander Budak's novel tells of how family hatred engendered in Croatia destroys the marriage of Helena and Lukas in Edmonton, and how the son from that marriage undertakes an unsuccessful quest across North American to find his father. "Twice he almost found Lukas, only to have him vanish before he could meet him face to face" (17). And in Budak's own life, it is this kind of "almost meeting" that defines his relationship with his literary mentor David Lasker, who had written a number of novels and poems about immigrants in Canada. "Often in his writing," Budak recalls about these works, "people of different nationalities came together and almost touched, only to find themselves pulled apart again" (12), which is precisely what happened when Budak took a trip to Toronto to meet him. Twice Lasker failed to appear as promised, actions he subsequently rationalized in a letter to Budak:

> It was impossible for me to see you . . . . You wanted to ask me things. I have no answers. But you are in my heart. Let me be in your heart also. We had an almost meeting. Perhaps that is not much. And yet it is something. (21)

As many exiles discover, the common things they might share with others because of similar backgrounds are often undermined by their uncertainty as to how these elements apply in their new land, for they, as well as their worlds, have undergone transformations that are not always understood.

Such transformations are particularly evident in the works of the Czechoslovakian-born Josef Skvorecky, who fled his homeland after the Communist takeover of 1968, joining such earlier post-war émigrés as his fellow-Czech, Jan Drabek, and the Hungarian-born Stephen Vizinczey and George Jonas. Unlike Koch and Kreisel, these writers entered their Canadian exile shaped by an alienation that has a twofold derivation: from the Nazi occupations of their homelands during their adolescence, and from the later Communist regimes, whether domestically generated or imposed externally by the Soviets. In a more literal sense, therefore, than is true for exiles motivated purely by economic, social, or artistic reasons, these émigrés, in their political or military opposition to these totalitarian regimes, were internal exiles before they became exiles in the physical sense, with the result that their writings often reflect responses to their worlds that are neither simple, predictable, nor consistent.

Now teaching at Erindale College, University of Toronto, Skvorecky brought with him to this country his long-time interest in jazz, literature, and film, components that along with politics and the pursuit of love constitute the substance of his fiction. In spite of his own grim and dangerous experiences in his homeland, his view of the world is essentially optimistic, an attitude that has undoubtedly been strengthened by the personal and political freedom he has found in Canada. But even in his early fiction, his protagonists reflected a kind of black humour about their precarious situations ("My country could get along without my life," the youthful Danny Smiricky rationalizes in *The Cowards,* "but I couldn't"), and from that 1958 novel to *The Engineer of Human Souls* (1984)[6] Skvorecky characteristically communicates a vision that combines the comic and the melancholy with his strong sense of the ironic. Never far away, however, is the note of sadness and nostalgia, for the reality of what an exile loses is always strong in Skvorecky— what his protagonist refers to as "the essence of everything. Associations in time, in appearance, in theory, in the heart, omnipotent and omnipresent" (*EHS,* 107).

At the outset, Daniel Smiricky on one level is free of these associations, for he feels "utterly and dangerously wonderful in this wilderness land," and he does not at this point sense the paradox he creates by praising "this country of cities with no past" (*EHS,* 4). For of course *he* has a past, and this fact automatically gives his new city and all the roles he plays there—as novelist, as contact for Czechoslovakian émigrés, as professor of literature—a dimension that vastly complicates his existence as an exile. The youthful Danny of *The Cowards* and *The Swell Season* had relatively straightforward problems—to survive, to chase girls, to play the saxophone—but here, as he approaches fifty, he has to try to resolve the contradictions that exist not only between one country and another, but between one time and another and between shifting ideologies and versions of truth. The novel's formal structure ostensibly allows for a rational and intellectual attempt by Professor Smiricky to understand and communicate the essences of these worlds: the seven chapters, built around the subjects of his graduate seminars, address themselves to such topics as the irrational, guilt, pessimism, courage, fear, greed, betrayal, and love. But almost immediately, the exchanges between himself and his half dozen students (whom he amusingly refers to as "Anglo-Saxons with names like Bellissimo, Hakim, Svensson" (*EHS,* 10) dramatize the void that separates them: the students find nothing relevant to their times, for example, in Hawthorne's comments on pride, hatred, or fanatical thinking, abstractions that in Danny's life have been concrete and painful personal realities. "I despaired for those legions of students," he muses at one point, "who are taught American Literature from someone from Harvard who, lecturing on the function of colour in *The Scarlet Letter,* deals only with the function of colour in *The Scarlet Letter"* (*EHS,* 64).

Other aspects of the novel's formal structure, too, point to a non-simplistic resolution of meanings. Its long, whimsical subtitle, numerous epigraphs, frequent flashbacks, letters, songs, snatches of foreign languages, shifting eyes—all these devices dictate a discontinuity of experiences, and reinforce the complex musical structure of this novel that derives originally from Skvorecky's passion for Dixieland jazz but which goes far beyond the predictable improvisations of that simplistic form. Even the formal division into seven chapters has its built-in diminished interval, as it were: six of them are on the serious, major novelists like Hawthorne and Conrad, but the seventh combines a minor American writer, H.P. Lovecraft with a sex shop of the same name to suggest that not all important things are found in literature or the intellect. And indeed, the permanent relationship between the exile Smiricky and his New World is solidified in this final chapter, when he and Irene Svensson (his Nicole in the Fitzgerald chapter, loved but untouched; his determined seducer in the Conrad chapter) spend reading week in Paris in sexual bliss. Among other things, Skvorecky seems to be suggesting here, exile can bring about an unexpected fulfilment of a dream: the Danny-Irena sexual pursuit that began in *The Cowards* and constituted such brilliantly humorous episodes in *The Swell Season* has here come to a resolution. Appropriately, however, the aging Daniel is no longer the eager, active pursuer he was of Irena back in Kostelec, but he accepts his New World Irene as a kind of obligatory possibility within the framework of his professional relationship to her. "I really should start something up with Irene Svensson," he rationalizes during that first seminar on Poe. "She betrays all the signs of expecting it" (*EHS,* 11).

The juxtaposition of attitudes and visions in this novel is not unlike what we saw in Mavis Gallant's story, "Potter," where the innocence of the Canadian Laurie Bennett stood in sharp contrast to the experience and cynicism of the Polish poet, Piotr. Daniel, too, poses a problem to his students who looked at him "with curiosity," and he recognizes that "premature cynicism is not a characteristic of young Canadians" (*EHS,* 9). This innocence is reflected by the landscape in which Edenvale College is situated: "a wilderness," "a white, cold, windy Canadian landscape," "a white wasteland broken only by a few bare, blackened trees" (*EHS,* 3), descriptions of Canada that by this time are not unfamiliar. But it is a personal sadness, rather than exultation at discovering a new Paradise, or outright despair over its physical and cultural barrenness, that this scene generates for Smiricky, a sadness that comes in part from his realization that his students—and by implication, the world at large—will never understand his kinds of experience. The sounds of Russian poetry, the blend of beauty and terror he finds in Poe, a Czech singer's voice "echoing down the antiseptic college corridor"—

these resonances begin to fill the empty landscape for him, but he is compelled as an exile to savour them alone. Occasionally, when addressing other
exiles, he can sense their understanding, but he feels compelled, as he puts it,
to "sermonize unmarxistleninistically" to them about the intellectual emptiness that characterizes democracies like Canada:

> For you see, I also know about their real country, the one they carry in
> their hearts, about the light that seems to shine only in dictatorships, for
> in democracies it is outdone by the glare of glossy magazines. The real
> religion of life, the true idolatry of literature, can never flourish in
> democracies, in those vague boring kingdoms of the freedom not to
> read, not to suffer, not to desire, not to know, not to understand. (*EHS*,
> 279)

Smiricky's sadness over a lost youth, over a lost country, over lost dreams
is counterbalanced not only by his sense of physical well-being, of residing in
a place where no harm can come to him, but also by his realization that if
there is a paradise it can be defined in part by its existential possibilities.
"There is beauty everywhere on earth," he muses early in the novel, "but
there is greater beauty in those places where one feels that sense of ease
which comes from no longer having to put off one's dreams until some
improbable future" (*EHS*, 4). That the dreams might well be modified as the
exile's experiences change is inevitable, as we saw in the Danny-Irene
relationships, and of course new dreams constantly arise, as some of Danny's
fellow exiles realize: "because American reality is too different from their
dream of it . . . the dream now is Czechoslovakia" (*EHS*, 165). But also,
like Henry Kreisel, Josef Skvorecky dramatizes the relativity of human
actions, a point that evades not only most of Smiricky's graduate students at
Edenvale, but also a number of his earlier acquaintances from his totalitarian worlds. Daniel Smiricky has not always been prepared to accept that
notion of relativity, but by novel's end, when he can say "I have not lost the
meaning of life, merely the illusion that life has a meaning" (*EHS*, 533), he
has moved much closer to that existential position.

The Engineer of Human Souls is of course also an academic novel, a
genre that conveniently lends itself, both intellectually and emotionally, to a
comparative analysis of contrasting worlds. It is not only that many of the
particular components of the academic world are ready-made for fictional
dramatization; they are also easily adaptable to distortion and satire, approaches
that, for the insecure exile in particular, frequently constitute a first line of
defence. The North American academic world is for Europeans an easy and
convenient target, for one of the enduring myths on that side of the Atlantic
is the superiority of Old World educational systems, a belief, however, as we

have seen in Mavis Gallant and Wyndham Lewis, that is not universally upheld. Nevertheless, it is this aspect of the New World, and particularly of Canada, that continues to constitute the main target for a number of exile writers whose protagonists find themselves involved in an academic situation in this country.

We will recall that in *Canada Made Me,* Norman Levine commented on the Old World academic in Winnipeg who was there only for the money, and it is a similar situation, at a mythical western Canadian university, that informs *No Englishman Need Apply* (1965) by the English-born Denis Godfrey, who for many years was an English professor at the University of Alberta. The title reflects the strong and recurring Anglophobe attitude that has surfaced in Canada throughout much of this century, particularly during the depression years (and an ironic recollection of which, we remember, came to the English exile, Malcolm, in Gallant's "Malcolm and Bea" as he was in the process of picking up two Canadian girls). Godfrey plays his variation on this theme through his central character, Philip Brent, a newly hired Englishman who becomes a pawn in the academic power struggle between the English-trained and the American-trained factions at Marston University, with the Canadian faction, Wyndham Lewis notwithstanding, remaining largely invisible and silent. Paralleling this main plot line is the subsidiary and aesthetically weaker intrigue involving Lucy Brent and a young Canadian couple, Steve Horton and Debbie Kristenson, whom she uses, among other reasons (for she has also briefly been Steve's lover), in a kind of subconscious way to buttress her isolated pro-Canadian stand against her husband and other Marston academics who can hardly wait to get out of Canada.

Philip's failure to secure a British academic post had filled him with "a profound sense of rejection," and the dishonest manner in which he accepted Marston constituted the first of Lucy's misgivings about his moral stature:

> That Philip had come to western Canada reluctantly and as a last resort could not be disputed. In London, even after committing himself to Marston, he had continued to search for an English university appointment, not hesitating when the time approached to postpone his sailing date for a cool three weeks.[7]

In this initial scheming, Philip anticipates a number of academics we meet later at Marston, particularly Joseph Weinberg, a Czechoslovakian refugee turned British exile, who quite shamelessly uses Marston research money to seek a better position in California. Lucy's protest against this "academic skulduggery" is ridiculed by Philip and the Weinbergs, who believe that any means are justified to get them out of what Anita Weinberg calls "this awful frozen hold-in-the-ground," but Lucy's integrity is later vindicated: Weinberg, having resigned Marston in anticipation of a better American offer, loses that because of his wife's visa problems, and is forced to retire in "high academic disfavour." The Somervells, on the other hand, are academically honest, but are so thoroughly colonial in their attitude towards Canada that Lucy is more amazed than she is disturbed; in some respects, the Somervells, particularly in their total imperviousness to the reality of Canada, evoke such Sara Jeannette Duncan near-caricatures as Miss Game and Lady Doleford of *Cousin Cinderella:*

> In them the casual contempt for things Canadian, expressed by Philip and the various other newly-arrived English she had met, was not so much casual as axiomatic, a principle to be acted on. In Canada, according to the Somervells, one preserved one's superior Englishness, acted, spoke, dressed, ate, and thought as if in England . . . . The Somervell children were required to *speak* English. Any "Canadianism" uttered within the hearing of their parents, incurred a five-cent fine. (71-72)

The power struggle at Marston is appropriately dramatized in the workings of the administrative structure of the department, where the English-trained Professor Broddick is the actual head, but also where the American-trained Arthur Floyd assumes a number of decision-making duties on his own. This rivalry provides an element of tension to Broddick's explanation to Brent of the "Anglo-American compromise" that characterizes most Canadian universities, "with the emphasis, for better or worse, on the American side" (54), and also allows for the novel's ironic resolution: it is Floyd and his American appointee who lose out, while Philip is offered a full reinstatement, clearly a victory for the English faction. Whether Philip will accept this offer, or one in the Maritimes, is left somewhat in abeyance, but that Lucy experienced "a sense at last of reconciliation" suggests that Marston for the moment at any rate has won out.

No Englishman Need Apply therefore reflects the kind of irony that is not unusual in academic novels, and on the whole it provides a convincing dialectic on some of the more superficial issues of this kind of situation, though it makes no attempt to delve deeply into the intellectual nature of the contrasting worlds. By and large, it avoids the tendency mentioned earlier, to satirize the specific components of the academic setting, an approach that characterizes a large number of academic novels, not only those by indigenous Canadians like Jack MacLeod in his *Zinger and Me* (1979) and *Going Grand* (1982), but also those by such exiles as Saros Cowasjee in his *Goodbye to Elsa* (1974) and John Metcalf in both *Going Down Slow* (1972) and *General Ludd* (1980). Some of these, in their exploitation of all the predictable clichés, fail to convey any deep understanding of, or sympathy with, the real nature of the academic world, and all too often they rely unduly on caricature and illogical distortion of normal situations that fail to rise above the sophomoric recollections we all have of aspects of our education. Where writers like Lewis, Kreisel, Skvorecky, and Godfrey set up credible moral confrontations and dialectics engendered by a genuine academic situation, Metcalf, for example, tends to assign to most of his characters, except for his central protagonists, a kind of naïveté and intellectual limitation that on the whole is more annoying than it is amusing or convincing.

As a result, because we cannot believe sufficiently in the credibility of his characters or in his analysis of the academic world, his assessments of the Canada-England oppositions are also questionable. What do we learn, for example, about Canadian life or character when we are told in *General Ludd* that the only Canadian among the group of Canlit specialists is "that fat broad over there in the green dress"? Or about the English attitude towards North America when a bedraggled faculty wife, with "an excruciating Oxford accent," offers her predictable observation: "When my husband dragged me to America . . . I learned *they* had a literature and now he's brought me here I'm informed there's a Canadian one too"?[8] Perhaps because a novel about academics has as one of its sure audiences other academics, it seems to constitute for many writers an irresistible opportunity to indulge in forms of academic warfare, and hence the frequency of in-group jokes, caricatures, and other superficial volleys. At any rate, while Metcalf is in many of his non-exile works an entertaining humorist and a talented stylist, his satire in his two Canadian-based novels is on the whole too superficial and predictable to convey a convincing portrait of contrasting worlds.

A more substantial and consistent talent characterizes the last of the writers I wish to select from this large group of undifferentiated exiles, a writer whose life and work reflect the paradox of rootlessness even within the multiple worlds that shaped him. Born in North Dakota to an English-Canadian mother and a French-Canadian father, Clark Blaise grew up in America's deep south as well as in various parts of Canada, and to these shaping forces were later added, through his marriage to Bharati Mukherjee, the complexities of the vast Indian culture. His fiction ranges over this limitless territory, though of the stories I am concerned with here, only "Going to India" and "Continent of Strangers" take his protagonists beyond the confines of North America. It is the Canadian-American polarity that occupies his attention in most of his fiction, a situation, as he has pointed out, that demands a particularly sensitive aesthetic approach:

> When my first book came out, I was asked the differences (as an American-trained Canadian) between Canada and the States, and all I could say was "texture." The textures of American and Canadian life are

as proximate as separate societies can be, but if fiction has eyes and ears, attention to texture will disclose the difference . . . . Between Canada and the United States you [have] to stand very close; you [have] to take in everything.[9]

That first book was *A North American Education* (1973) which, like Lowry's *Hear Us O Lord*, depicts a multiple protagonist, variously named Norman Dyer, Paul Keeler, and Frank Thibidault, in the process of absorbing experiences that together reflect the pragmatic implications of its title. Characterizing these protagonists, much as was the case with Sigbjørn Wilderness, are recurring obsessions about who and where they are, and what their relationship with their world really is. "You jump into this business of a new country cautiously" (16), observes Dyer, while Keeler, who comes "from uncertain stock," realizes he will "never be quite at home here, though now even a citizen" (52), and Thibidault, from the most rootless background of all, wonders "what calamity made me a reader of back issues, defunct Atlases, and foreign grammars?" (155). As though verifying these existential manifestations of one's precarious position in the universe, occur sudden and uncontrollable threats that derive variously from both natural and supernatural causes: the peeping Tom in "Eyes," the boy floating to his doom on the Niagara in "Going to India," the crowded elevator in "Extractions and Contractions," the shredded mail and stolen keys in "Words for the Winter," and the mysteriously mangled fish in "Snow People." All these signs point to a world that is ultimately unknowable, and confirm that in Blaise's vision man's rational and logical attempts to order his life can at any time be undercut by the irrational.

Appropriately, *A North American Education* opens with a story that dramatizes one of the processes implicit in the title, but "A Class of New Canadians" goes well beyond mere instruction in the English language. Norman Dyer, an American academic, likes to think of himself as " a semi-permanent, semi-political exile" in the tradition of such famous exiles as Joyce, Nabokov, and Beckett, but in reality he is incapable of understanding the genuine motives of the exiles he is teaching. He wants to acquire a veneer of ethnicity by exploiting what he sees as their romantic and quaint attributes, or by frequenting Montreal's ethnic restaurants; when he tries to convince them that they should not rush into forsaking their ethnic characteristics, he is ungrammatically but firmly reminded, "two years in a country I don't learn the language means it isn't a country" (8). Dyer is in effect the incomplete person that his own "semi" epithets suggest, governed by appearances rather than substance, and able to dominate this group of assorted exiles only by virtue of his position, a role he sees as the equivalent of being "an omniscient, benevolent god." It is clear, in their determination to establish themselves in the New World and to forget their past, that they understand far better than Dyer does "the difference between the past continuous and the simple past" or "that simple futurity can be expressed in four different ways," concepts that he sees exclusively in grammatical contexts.

Dyer acquires a more sensitive and thorough comprehension of his Montreal world in "Eyes" and "Words for the Winter," though even there he cannot successfully resolve the dilemmas caused by his being an outsider, for paradoxically, even among the many foreigners who constitute that world, he remains an outsider. While the forces of a North American education are gradually transforming Dyer, that they cannot completely do so is suggested by the epigraph from Pascal that Blaise uses to counterbalance his belief in education's pragmatic necessities: "as we are always preparing to be happy, it is inevitable that we should never be so," an expression of the bittersweet determinism that informs all the stories in this collection. In "Going to India," for example, though on one level Paul Keeler celebrates the triumph of human love over language and culture (it is Anjali's sexuality rather than her eight languages that overwhelms him), on another level, as reflected in his panicky "*I'm not prepared*" realization on landing in India, it is clear, despite his protests to the contrary, that he *has* married "a culture and a subcontinent." That the story ends on a note of panic is aesthetically appropriate, for it picks up on the opening scene of horror of the boy on the Niagara; the question he posed at that point, "what kind of madman builds a raft in Niagara country?" (59), we can now apply with ironic relevance to what he himself has undertaken in the name of love, for who is to say that the boy's raft, too, was not built for love?

Though this story owes much to Forster, it also evokes Whitman's "Passage to India," particularly his stanza that celebrates the brotherhood of man:

> The earth to be spann'd connected by network,
> The races, neighbors, to marry and be given in marriage,
> The oceans to be cross'd, the distant brought near,
> The lands to be welded together.

And Whitman's celebration of modern technology finds an echo in the source of Keeler's complete confidence in the way their plane is being handled: "competence in the cockpit, the delicate fingers of Captain Mukherjee, the mathematical genius of Navigator Misra, the radar below, the gauges above" (77). Ultimately, however, the irony and scepticism of Forster are more relevant here than Whitman's celebratory optimism, a point reinforced by Keeler's recollection of appropriate lines from Eliot's *The Waste Land*.

Keeler's confession that "I'm afraid to start anything new in case I'll be a different person when I return" (64) constitutes on a general level a statement of what a North American education is all about if it is to be successful, for as we have seen with such exiles as Philip Branden and Ginger Coffey, it is this kind of transformation that they wish to undergo in the New World. But in its specific context in this story it applies to an earlier Keeler, who appears in "Continent of Strangers," but who recalls himself here as undergoing the kind of bohemian existence in Europe that we have seen in John Glassco:

> Five years ago I threw myself at Europe. For two summers I did things I'll never do again . . . wakening beside new women, wondering where I'd be spending the next night, with whom, how I'd get there, who would take me, and finally not caring . . . . Only living for the moment mattered . . . . It all reminded me that I was young and alive, a hitch-hiker over borders, heedless of languages . . . and feeling responsible to no one but myself for any jam I got into. (61-62)

That he is not quite this unbridled hedonist in "Continent of Strangers" is as much a product of his Boston upbringing as it is of Janet's sudden puritanism; in his Parisian escapades, having been saved from a Place Pigalle prostitute by the intervention of two more enterprising Americans, he sounds more like Morley Callaghan than Glassco: "His was a Europe of shrunken dimensions, and he was no bold discoverer. He was a writer, a creator; he would learn to satisfy himself with that" (105). Though he came to Europe for both culture and love, he gets neither, though at the end, as he prepares to join the nude Aino for some early morning swimming, he may finally achieve what he was deprived of in Place Pigalle. Clearly, on this continent he is the stranger, the exile, and in this respect, his North American education has been deficient.

The four stories that conclude this collection depict the protagonist progressively being exposed to situations that, if they can be divorced from the pain, mortification, sexual anguish, and fear that the youthful Frankie Thibidault experiences, in effect constitute pragmatic manifestations of what a North American education really means, and that ultimately lead him to an understanding both of his roots and of his present position in his world. This pragmatic dimension receives its bluntest and most perverse application in the title story, where Frankie is brought by his father to a circus tent to see Princess Hi-Yalla perform her simulated sexual acts, a lesson whose results mortify Frankie and infuriate his father, who nevertheless gives a fairly accurate explanation of what a pragmatic education really means:

> "Well, what in the name of God is wrong with two fathers getting together, eh? It was supposed to *show* you what it's like, about women, I mean. It's better than any drawing, isn't it? You want books all the time?

You want to *read* about it, or do you want to see it? At least now you
know, so go ahead and read." (172)

But sometimes, too, as in the episode about language in "Snow People"
referred to in an earlier chapter, a pragmatic action results in his confidently
taking possession of a truth about himself that no amount of dissimulation
and punishment can take away from him. His intuitive grasping here of the
importance of his heritage gives him a mastery over a sordid world that he is
not to duplicate again in these stories. At best, he arrives at a compromise in
most of these situations, but in one story, "The Salesman's Son Grows
Older," he gives a retrospective view that suggests he has achieved a kind of
peace for his son that his father was not able to provide for him. Was it
endurance, exile, or cunning, he wonders, in a slight modification of Stephen
Dedalus's formula, and in his recollection of the mindless police harassment
in Wisconsin that drove him back to Quebec, he quietly confirms the
existential possibilities inherent in his North American education:

> I'd thought of other places we could be, of taking the option my parents
> had accidentally left me. Nothing principled, nothing heroic, nothing
> even defiant. And so my son is skiing and learning French and someday
> he'll ask me why I made him do it, and he'll exercise the option we've
> accidentally left him. (161)

In Blaise's world, where the protagonist is psychologically and physically cut
off from the possibility of establishing permanent relationships, defining
exile as an "exercising of options" makes a great deal of experiential sense. It
is not, of course, only the North American landscape that is a perplexing one
for these protagonists, as we saw in "Going to India" and "Continent of
Strangers," but with its easy overlapping of Canadian and American experiences,
it renders such a definition particularly applicable.

9

The Legacy of Exile

Though the lamentations of Ovid occasionally echo in muted and modified form in some of our present-day exiles, the writers I have examined in this book on the whole reflect a rejection of the Ovidian vision of exile. With relatively few exceptions (notably Wyndham Lewis), they have taken as an enriching experience their immersion into their new worlds, and transformed their responses into positive and complex aesthetic expressions of the exile stance. The earlier writers in this tradition were generally content to limit themselves to fairly literal transcriptions of their exile experiences, but writers in this century, particularly those of the post-World War II era, have increasingly viewed exile as a psychological and intellectual state rather than as a purely physical one. But with all these exiles, the obligatory process of moving (even if only temporarily) into a state of isolation acts as a kind of synthesizing force that draws on the components of both worlds to create an entirely new reality that in some cases is benign and reassuring but more frequently, with the modern writers in particular, disturbing and chaotic.

The dramatic tension in exile literature derives from the conflict the protagonist experiences in his attempt to reconcile this new state of reality either with his impulse towards integration, or with his solipsistic belief that all worlds are wrong—the attitude that up to a point characterizes Lewis's René Harding. The exile writer is not necessarily any more afflicted with solipsism than the indigenous writer, but the latter is not quite so vulnerable, since he can usually count on the world around him to vindicate him, or at least to understand him. But it is not unusual for the exile writer, like Lewis or Lowry, whose protagonist seems perversely unable to reconcile his worlds, to perpetuate about himself a kind of personal mythology that is designed to justify or rationalize this aesthetic dilemma, or at least to explain his own sense of his uniqueness. Self-knowledge is transformed by the good writer, whether an exile or not, into a cosmic awareness of reality, but by a poor writer, merely into a kind of romantic solipsism.

All serious writers, of course, run the risk of not being understood, but the exile writer incurs a double risk, of alienating both the world he has rejected and the world he is moving into. Undoubtedly, this problem is more pronounced where one of the worlds in question constitutes an emerging rather than an established and widely recognized literary tradition, and Canada has in this respect occasionally been guilty of a double attack: on those who have come into the country, like Lowry and Moore, and on those who have gone abroad, like Richler and Gallant. At times, such attacks may simply be a reaction to an uncertainty as to how to categorize such writers, but frequently, too, they are generated by the explicit or implicit attacks these writers direct against their adopted or their rejected worlds: within this perspective, Gallant's earlier quoted caution about the obligations an artist has to any country seems to constitute the only sensible response.

But as Malcolm Cowley pointed out in his *Exile's Return*, one result of expatriation can also be the rediscovery of one's own literature, the existence or significance of which, for whatever reasons, the exile may originally have refused to acknowledge. With a nation like Canada, where loss of language is normally not a consequence of exile, the writer abroad and the indigenous writer do not lose touch with each other, though they may see both their nation and their literature in different terms. What is frequently involved, therefore, in this process of rediscovering one's literature is an acknowledgment on the part of the exile writer that he always has regarded himself as part of his nation's literary tradition, though he may proclaim this point a bit louder as he perceives that tradition growing stronger. The return from exile of a country's writers, as illustrated by Richler and Levine, reflects this acknowledgment, but this is not to say that they are more legitimately a part of Canada's literary tradition than is a permanent exile like Gallant. And of course a further spin-off of the works of these expatriates and exiles is that they compel the rest of the world to pay attention to Canadian literature, to the benefit of exile and indigenous writers alike.

In a heterogeneous nation like Canada, whose population includes an ongoing influx of immigrants, a study of the phenomenon of exile can never really be complete, for undoubtedly writers, like any other group, routinely constitute part of that larger component. For that reason among others, I found it necessary to impose a somewhat arbitrary framework around this study, and to concentrate my attention on the two groups of writers indicated in my opening chapter: those who have come to Canada from the Old World, mainly the British Isles and western Europe, and those native-born Canadians who have elected to become exiles or expatriates to the Old World. Obviously, even within these two groups, a rigid process of selection has been at work, governed both by chronology and by subjective taste, with the result that not only have the most recent writers been neglected, but also some that other readers might well see as being more important than I do.

Taken together, all these arbitrary limitations have disqualified a large number of writers from all over the world who have emigrated to Canada and written substantial fiction reflecting the various worlds they know. They come from the British Isles, from continental Europe, from South Africa, from India, from Australasia, from the Caribbean, from the United States: a catalogue of their names would vastly exceed the twenty or so writers I have examined here, so clearly a further volume of this sort would be required to give many of them the attention they deserve.[1] Without question, the phenomenon of exile that began almost as an accidental by-product of the British occupation of Canada has 200 years later expanded in importance to the point where it constitutes a major component of our national literature.

Whether exiles and expatriates discover their appropriate artistic ambience in other countries is the kind of question that in a sense can never be answered, for we can never know whether what was written abroad would have been better had it been written at home, or vice versa. In this respect, I cannot agree entirely with J.B. Priestley when he said in 1927 that writers "do not seem to realize that the best books are always written at home, that the writer should be the last of all people to sever his roots." I *can* agree with him completely, however, when, thinking of some of the lesser talents expressing their visions, he states: "Some of these exiles we can very well spare, reserving our sympathy for the Parisian quarter or Italian village horribly destined to receive them."[2]

If nothing else, Priestley as usual reminds us to maintain a perspective, and certainly not to presume anything uniquely special about writers in exile. Exile as a state of physical residency or as a state of mind can undoubtedly generate in some artists a strong impulse towards creativity, but others it might render absolutely barren. A character in James's story, "The Madonna of the Future"—an American artist in exile in Florence—was asked if he produced paintings fairly regularly. "Not in the vulgar sense," he replied. "I choose never to manifest myself in mediocrity."[3] Certainly not all the exile writers I have been concerned with in this study have been afflicted by that kind of modesty, but as a group, as is undoubtedly true of similar groups in all nations, they are in creative artistry more or less equal to any group of indigenous writers. That there are some genuine talents among them there is no disputing: we have only to think of Mavis Gallant's incisive analysis of the international realities of exile, or of Malcolm Lowry's endless manipulations of the theme of universal dispossession, or of Brian Moore's compassionate revelations of the marginal figure, self-exiled from the certainties of a number of worlds. All these manifestations of the exile condition seem to prefigure attitudes and visions of experience that are fundamentally different from those obtaining in earlier times. As the German exile, Thomas Mann, said not long before his death, "Exile has become something quite different from what it once was; it is no longer a condition of waiting programmed for an ultimate return, but rather [it] hints of the dissolution of nations and the unification of the world."[4] If that is true, then I think it is also true that the New World has helped to formulate and consolidate these shifting attitudes, and that Canada has played a significant role in this transition.

Within this perspective, it is fitting to give a final word to one of the most recent exiles to Canada, Josef Skvorecky, who in *The Bass Saxophone* expresses an enduring truth about exile and literature:

> To me literature is forever blowing a horn, singing about youth when youth is irretrievably gone, singing about your homeland when in a schizophrenia of the times you find yourself in a land that lies over the ocean, a land—no matter how hospitable and friendly—where your heart is not, because you landed on these shores too late.[5]

Though the note of lamentation here echoes Ovid's exiled state in *Tristia*, we have not really come full circle. Skvorecky's recognition that the world has permanently altered is the new component in the contemporary exile vision of the world. And it is the writer's realization that "in the schizophrenia of the times" he will always arrive too late wherever he goes that shapes the substance and the spirit of his resulting literature of and from exile.

Notes

NOTES TO CHAPTER ONE:
THE AMBIGUITIES OF EXILE

1. For example, see David Malouf, *An Imaginary Life* (New York 1978).
2. Ovid, *Tristia and Epistulae ex Ponto.* Translated by Arthur Leslie Wheeler (Cambridge 1953), 13, 143, 249.
3. *Ibid.*, 477.
4. David Williams, "The Exile as Uncreator," *Mosaic* 8:3 (Spring 1975):3.
5. Ernest Earnest, *Expatriates and Patriots* (Durham 1968), viii.
6. Malcolm Cowley, *Exile's Return: A Literary Odyssey of the 1920s* (New York 1956), 81.
7. Terry Eagleton, *Exiles and Emigrés* (New York 1970), 14, *passim*.
8. Josef Skvorecky, "A Country after My Own Heart," *Maclean's* (Mar. 1974), 24.
9. Vladimir Nabokov, *Speak Memory: An Autobiography Revisited* (New York 1966), 276.
10. John Matthews, *Tradition in Exile* (Toronto 1962), 48, *passim*.
11. Thomas Farley, *Exiles and Pioneers* (Ottawa 1975), 200.
12. Dennis Duffy, *Gardens, Covenants, Exiles* (Toronto 1982), 5.
13. Andrew Gurr, *Writers in Exile* (Sussex 1981), 13.
14. Brian Moore, "The Crazy Boatloads," *Spectator* (29 Sept. 1961), 430.
15. Mordecai Richler, "A Sense of the Ridiculous: Paris, 1951 and After," *New American Review* 4 (1968), 118.

NOTES TO CHAPTER TWO:
ROUGHING IT IN EXILE

1. Ovid, *Tristia and Epistulae ex Ponto,* 423.
2. Quoted in Clara Thomas, *Love and Work Enough: The Life of Anna Jameson* (Toronto 1967), 113, 114. The first half of the quotation is from a letter to Robert Noel in May 1837, and the second portion from one to her sister in Mar. 1837.
3. Margaret Atwood, "Afterword," *The Journals of Susanna Moodie* (Toronto 1970), 62.
4. Patrick A. Dunae, *Gentlemen Emigrants* (Vancouver 1981), 11.
5. John Howison, *Sketches of Upper Canada* (Toronto 1970), 1-2. Hereafter documented internally.
6. Catharine Parr Traill, *The Backwoods of Canada* (Toronto 1971), 5. Hereafter documented internally.
7. Susanna Moodie, *Roughing It in the Bush* (Toronto 1913), 7. Hereafter documented internally.
8. Carol Shields, *Susanna Moodie: Voice and Vision* (Ottawa 1977), 34.
9. Anna Jameson, *Winter Studies and Summer Rambles,* Vol. II (Toronto 1970, 1972), 184-85. Hereafter documented internally.
10. Thomas, *Love and Work Enough,* 101.
11. Frances Brooke, *The History of Emily Montague* (Toronto 1961), #135. Because both the four-volume Garland reprint of the 1769 edition and the 1931 Graphic edition reflect a misnumbering of letters, I am using the corrected New Canadian Library edition. Subsequent quotations are documents internally by letter number.
12. James Bacque, *The Lonely Ones* (Toronto 1969), 50.
13. Williams, "The Exile as Uncreator," 13.
14. W.H. New, "Frances Brooke's Chequered Gardens," *Canadian Literature* 52 (Spring 1972), 24-38.
15. John Galt, *Bogle Corbet* (Toronto 1977), 28. Hereafter documented internally.

NOTES TO CHAPTER THREE:
BETWEEN TWO WORLDS

1 Sara Jeannette Duncan, *The Imperialist*
(Toronto 1961), 118. The following abbre-
viations, hereafter documented internally,
are used for Duncan's books: *SD* for *A
Social Departure: How Orthodocia and I
Went Round the World by Ourselves* (New
York 1890); *AG* for *An American Girl in
London* (New York 1891); *VC* for *A Voyage of Consolation* (New York 1898); *DA*
for *Those Delightful Americans* (New York
1902); *I* for *The Imperialist* (Toronto 1961);
CC for *Cousin Cinderella: A Canadian
Girl in London* (Toronto 1908).
2 Marjory MacMurchy, "Mrs Everard Cotes
(Sara Jeannette Duncan)," *The Bookman*
48:284 (May 1915): 39.
3 Stephen Leacock, *The Boy I Left Behind
Me* (Garden City, N.Y., 1946), 19.
4 Sara Jeannette Duncan, *Selected Journalism,* ed. T.E. Tausky (Ottawa 1978), 58.
5 Frederick Philip Grove, *A Search for America* (Montreal 1928), 57.
6 Thomas E. Tausky, *Sara Jeannette Duncan:
Novelist of Empire* (Port Credit 1980), 132.

NOTES TO CHAPTER FOUR:
THE NEW WORLD TRIUMPHANT

1 Frederick Niven, *The Flying Years* (London
1935), 15. Hereafter documented internally.
2 Laura Salverson, *The Viking Heart* (Toronto
1923), 14. Hereafter documented internally.
3 Laura Salverson, *Confessions of an Immigrant's Daughter* (Toronto [1939]), 16. Hereafter documented internally.
4 Ethel Wilson, "The Bridge or the Stokehold?," *Canadian Literature* 5 (Summer
1960): 44.
5 Ethel Wilson, *Mrs Golightly and Other
Stories* (Toronto 1961), 25. Hereafter documented internally.
6 Ethel Wilson, *The Innocent Traveller*
(Toronto 1949), 68. Hereafter documented
internally.
7 Wilfrid Eggleston, *The Frontier and Canadian Letters* (Toronto 1957), 30.
8 Frederick Philip Grove, *It Needs to Be
Said* (Toronto 1929), 87.
9 Douglas Spettigue, *FPG: The European
Years* (Ottawa 1973), 64.
10 Frederick Philip Grove, *A Search for America* (Montreal 1928), 30. Hereafter documented internally. The New Canadian

Library Edition (Toronto 1974) has the same
pagination.
11 Frederick Philip Grove, *In Search of Myself*
(Toronto 1946), 160-61. Hereafter documented internally. The New Canadian
Library Edition (Toronto 1974) has the same
pagination.
12 In Frederick Philip Grove, *Tales from the
Margin,* edited by Desmond Pacey (Toronto
1971),206-15. See also Pacey's note on p. 310.
13 Frederick Philip Grove, *Settlers of the Marsh*
(Toronto 1925), 51. Hereafter documented
internally.

NOTES TO CHAPTER FIVE:
TOURISTS AND EXPATRIATES

1 Quoted in Malcolm Cowley, *Exile's Return*
(New York 1956), 20.
2 Leon Edel, "Introduction" to John Glassco,
Memoirs of Montparnasse (Toronto and
New York 1970), x. Glassco's book is hereafter documented internally as *MM.*
3 Morley Callaghan, *That Summer in Paris*
(Toronto 1963), 22. Hereafter documented
internally as *SP.*
4 Morley Callaghan, *Now that April's Here*
(Toronto 1936), 51. Hereafter documented
internally.
5 Leon Edel, "John Glassco and His Erotic
Muse," *Canadian Literature* 93 (Summer
1982): 108.
6 Leon Edel, "Introduction," x. Fraser Sutherland's recent monograph, *John Glassco:
An Essay and Bibliography* (1984) contains
information that questions these widely
accepted views about the composition of
Memoirs. See pp. 18-20.
7 Quoted in Ernest Earnest, *Expatriates and
Patriots* (Ithaca, N.Y. 1968), 24.
8 Norman Levine, " The Girl in the Drug
Store," *Canadian Literature* 41 (Summer
1969): 51.
9 Mordecai Richler, *The Acrobats* (New York
1954),66. The following abbreviations, hereafter documented internally, are used for
Richler's novels: *A* for *The Acrobats* (New
York 1954); *CE* for *A Choice of Enemies*
(London 1957); *H* for *St. Urbain's Horseman* (Toronto 1971).
10 Norman Levine, "The Girl in the Drug
Store," 51.
11 Mordecai Richler, "A Sense of the Ridiculous: Paris, 1951 and After," *New American Review* 4 (1968): 199.
12 George Woodcock, "Richler's Wheel of

Exile," *The Rejection of Politics* (Toronto 1972), 140-41.

13 Norman Levine, "Every Literature' Needs an Exile" *Saturday Night* (December 1976), 2.

14 Norman Levine, "Why I Am an Expatriate," *Canadian Literature* 5 (Summer 1960): 52.

15 Norman Levine, *The Angled Road* (Toronto 1952), 45. The following abbreviations, hereafter documented internally, are used for Levine's books: *AR* for *The Angled Road* (Toronto 1952); *CMM* for *Canada Made Me* (London 1958); *OWT* for *One Way Ticket* (Toronto 1981); *DWK* for *I Don't Want to Know Anyone Too Well* (Toronto 1971); *TI* for *Thin Ice* (Toronto 1979); *FST* for *From a Seaside Town* (London 1970).

16 The 1979 Deneau and Greenberg reissue of this book omits the original edition's final sentence: "Meanwhile the emigrant ship keeps coming over . . . and the tourist ship keeps going back." In addition, an early paragraph about the Irish woman journalist on board the emigrant ship (p. 20, 1958 edition), is omitted in the 1979 reissue, as well as in, puzzlingly, some reprintings of the first edition.

17 Norman Levine, "Letter from London," *The Tight-Rope Walker* (London 1950), 28, 29.

18 See, for example, "Something Happened Here" *The Canadian Forum* (May 1982): 12-15, 36.

NOTES TO CHAPTER SIX:
FROM THE OLD WORLD

1 Geoffrey Hancock, "An Interview with Mavis Gallant," *Canadian Fiction Magazine* 28 (1978): 32. Hereafter cited as "Interview."

2 Sara Jeannette Duncan, "Our Latent Loyalty," *Selected Journalism,* 58.

3 Mavis Gallant, *Home Truths* (Toronto 1981), xiii. The following abbreviations hereafter documented internally are used for Gallant's books: *OP* for *The Other Paris* (London 1957); *GWGS* for *Green Water, Green Sky* (Boston 1959); *MHB* for *My Heart Is Broken* (New York 1964); *FGT* for *A Fairly Good Time* (New York 1970); *EW* for *The End of the World and Other Stories* (Toronto 1971); *AGR* for *The Affair of Gabrielle Russier* (New York 1971); *FD* for *From the Fifteenth District* (Toronto 1979); *HT* for

Home Truths (Toronto 1981).

4 "Interview," 28.

5 "Interview," 29.

6 Ronald B. Hatch, "The Three Stages of Mavis Gallant's Short Fiction," *Canadian Fiction Magazine* 28 (1978): 92-114.

7 Clark Blaise, "Snow People," *A North American Education* (Toronto 1973), 185-230.

NOTES TO CHAPTER SEVEN:
BIRDS OF PASSAGE

1 Wyndham Lewis, *America and Cosmic Man* (London 1948), 7. The following abbreviations, documented internally, are used for Lewis's books: *FB* for *Filibusters in Barbary* (New York 1932); *ACM* for *America and Cosmic Man* (London 1948); *LWL* for *The Letters of Wyndham Lewis* (Norfolk 1963); *SC* for *Self Condemned* (Chicago 1955). The New Canadian Library Edition of *Self Condemned* (Toronto 1974) has the same pagination.

2 Anne Wyndham Lewis, "The Hotel," *Canadian Literature* 35 (Winter 1968): 26-28.

3 It is interesting to note, however, that his first story, "The Pole," published in Ford Madox Ford's *English Review* (May 1909), deals with expatriates from eastern Europe who survive by posing as artists among the gullible folk of Brittany.

4 Wyndham Lewis Archive, Cornell University.

5 Letter from Northrop Frye to Jeffrey Meyers, 2 Feb. 1979. Quoted in Jeffrey Meyers, *The Enemy: A Biography of Wyndham Lewis* (London and Henley 1980), 262.

6 Wyndham Lewis Archive.

7 *Ibid.*

8 *Ibid.*

9 Letter from Malcolm Lowry to Conrad Aiken, 6 Sept. 1940. Conrad Aiken Collection, Huntington Library, AIK 2516.

10 Lowry to Aiken, 16 July 1954, Conrad Aiken Collection, AIK, 2535.

11 Lowry to Harold Matson, 14 Aug. 1946. Malcolm Lowry Collection, The University of British Columbia Library.

12. The following abbreviations, hereafter documented internally, are used for Lowry's books: *UTV* for *Under the Volcano* (New York 1947); *Hear Us* for *Hear Us O Lord from Heaven Thy Dwelling Place* (New York and Philadelphia 1961); *SL* for *Selected Letters,* ed. Harvey Breit and Marg-

erie Bonner Lowry (New York and Philadelphia 1965); *OF* for *October Ferry to
Gabriola* (New York and Cleveland 1970).
13. Lowry to A.O. Lowry, 26 May 1942, Malcolm Lowry Collection, UBC.
14. Lowry to Robert Giroux, January 1952,
Malcolm Lowry Collection, UBC.
15. Brian Moore, "The Writer as Exile,"
Canadian Journal of Irish Studies 2:2 (Dec.
1976): 8.
16. "The Writer as Exile," 5, 6.
17. Brian Moore, "Grieve for the Dear Departed," *The Atlantic* (Aug. 1959), 46.
18. Brian Moore, "Uncle T," in *Two Stories*
(Northridge 1978), 25. The following abbreviations, hereafter documented internally, are used for Moore's books: *GC* for
The Luck of Ginger Coffey (Boston and
Toronto 1960); *AL* for *An Answer from
Limbo* (Boston and Toronto 1962); *F* for
Fergus (Toronto 1970); *TS* for *Two Stories* (Northridge 1978).
19. "Robert Fulford Interviews Brian Moore,
"*The Tamarack Review* 23 (Spring 1962):
17.
20. "David Watmough Interviews Brian
Moore," CBC Radio, 1 June 1963.
21. Box 16, Brian Moore Collection, University of Calgary.
22. "The Writer as Exile," 7.
23. For example, "The Writer as Exile," 6.

NOTES TO CHAPTER EIGHT:
EMIGRES AND ACADEMICS

1. Czeslaw Milosz, *Native Realm* (Los Angeles 1981), 106.
2. Henry Kreisel, "Diary of an Internment,"
White Pelican 4:3 (Summer 1974): 4-40.

3. Eric Koch, *Deemed Suspect: A Wartime
Blunder* (Toronto 1980). Documented
internally as *DS*. Other Koch works documented are *FK* for *The French Kiss* (Toronto 1969) and *LR* for *The Leisure Riots*
(Toronto 1973).
4. Kreisel, "Diary," 8.
5. Henry Kreisel, *The Almost Meeting* (Edmonton 1981), 147. Hereafter documented
internally.
6. Josef Skvorecky, *The Engineer of Human
Souls* (Toronto 1965), 33. Hereafter documented internally.
7. Denis Godfrey, *No Englishman Need Apply*
(Toronto 1965),33. Hereafter documented
internally.
8. John Metcalf, *General Ludd* (Toronto
1980), 16,10.
9. Clark Blaise and Bharati Mukherjee, *Days
and Nights in Calcutta* (Garden City, N.Y.
1977), 18. Subsequent references, documented internally, are to Clark Blaise, *A
North American Education* (Garden City
1973).

NOTES TO CHAPTER NINE:
THE LEGACY OF EXILE

1. For example, such writers as Austin Clarke,
Samuel Selvon, Bharati Mukherjee, Saros
Cowasjee, Neil Bissoondath.
2. J.B. Priestly, "A Voluntary Exile," *Open
House* (London 1927), 139-40.
3. Henry James, "The Madonna of the Future,"
The Novels and Tales of Henry James,
New York Edition, XIII (New York 1908,
1936), 444.
4. Quoted in Richard Exner, "*Exul Poeta:*
Theme and Variations," *Books Abroad*
50:2 (Spring 1976): 294.
5. Josef Skvorecky, *The Bass Saxophone*
(Toronto 1977), 29.

Bibliography

PRIMARY SOURCES

Bacque, James. *The Lonely Ones*. Toronto: McClelland and Stewart Limited, 1969.

Blaise, Clark. *A North American Education: A Book of Short Fiction*. Toronto: Doubleday Canada Ltd., and Garden City: Doubleday and Company, 1973.

_____.*Tribal Justice*. Toronto: Doubleday Canada Ltd., and Garden City: Doubleday and Company, 1974.

_____ and Mukherjee, Bharati. *Days and Nights in Calcutta*. Garden City: Doubleday and Company, Inc., 1977.

_____ *Lusts*. Garden City: Doubleday and Company, Inc., 1983.

Brooke, Frances. *The History of Emily Montague*. With Introduction and notes by Lawrence J. Burpee and an appendix by F.P. Grove. Ottawa: Graphic Publishers Limited, 1932.

Callaghan, Morley. "Now That April's Here" in *Now That April's Here and Other Stories*. Toronto: The Macmillan Company of Canada Limited, 1936, pp. 51-61.

_____.*That Summer in Paris: Memoirs of Tangled Friendships with Hemingway, Fitzgerald and Some Others*. Toronto: Macmillan of Canada, 1963.

Cowasjee, Saros. *Goodbye to Elsa*. London: The Bodley Head, 1974.

Drabek, Jan. *Whatever Happened to Wenceslas?* Toronto: Peter Martin Associates Limited, 1975.

_____.*Report on the Death of Rosenkavalier*. Toronto: McClelland and Stewart Limited, 1977.

_____.*The Statement*. Toronto: Musson Book Company, 1982.

Duncan, Sara Jeannette. *A Social Departure: How Orthodocia and I Went Round the World by Ourselves*. New York: D. Appleton and Company, 1890.

_____. *An American Girl in London*. New York: D. Appleton and Company, 1891.

_____.*A Daughter of Today*. New York: D. Appleton and Company, 1894.

_____.*A Voyage of Consolation*. New York: D. Appleton and Company, 1898.

_____.*Those Delightful Americans*. New York: D. Appleton and Company, 1902.

_____.*The Imperialist*. Introduction by Claude Bissell. Toronto: McClelland and Stewart Limited, 1961. [1904]

_____.*Cousin Cinderella: A Canadian Girl in London*. Toronto: The Macmillan Company of Canada Ltd., 1908.

_____.*Selected Journalism*, ed. T.E. Tausky. Ottawa: The Tecumseh Press, 1978.

Gallant, Mavis. *The Other Paris*. London: Andre Deutsch, 1957.

_____.*My Heart is Broken*. New York: Random House, 1964.

_____.*Green Water, Green Sky.* Boston: Houghton Mifflin Company, 1959.

_____.*A Fairly Good Time.* New York: Random House, 1970.

_____.*The Pegnitz Junction.* New York: Random House, 1973.

_____.*The End of the World and Other Stories.* Introduction by Robert Weaver. Toronto: McClelland and Stewart Limited, 1974.

_____.*From the Fifteenth District,* Toronto: Macmillan of Canada, 1979.

_____.*Home Truths.* Toronto: Macmillan of Canada, 1981.

Galt, John. *Bogle Corbet.* Introduction by Elizabeth Waterston. Toronto: McClelland and Stewart Limited, 1977. [1821]

Glassco, John. *Memoirs of Montparnasse.* Introduction by Leon Edel. Toronto and New York: Oxford University Press, 1970.

Godfrey, Dennis. *No Englishman Need Apply.* Toronto: Macmillan of Canada, 1965.

Grove, Frederick Philip. *Settlers of the Marsh.* Toronto. The Ryerson Press, 1925.

_____.*A Search for America.* Ottawa; The Graphic Publishers Limited, 1928.

_____.*It Needs to Be Said.* Toronto: The Macmillan Company of Canada Limited, 1929.

_____.*In Search of Myself.* Toronto: The Macmillan Company of Canada Limited, 1946.

_____.*The Letters of Frederick Philip Grove.* Introduction by Desmond Pacey. Toronto and Buffalo: University of Toronto Press, 1976.

Howison, John. *Sketches of Upper Canada* Toronto: Coles Canadiana Collection, Coles Publishing Company, 1970. [1821]

Jameson, Anna. *Winter Studies and Summer Rambles in Canada.* Toronto: McClelland and Stewart, 1923.

Koch, Eric. *The French Kiss.* Toronto and Montreal: McClelland and Stewart Limited, 1969.

_____.*The Leisure Riots.* Montreal: Tundra Books, 1973.

_____.*Deemed Suspect: A Wartime Blunder.* Toronto: Methuen, 1980.

Kreisel, Henry. *The Rich Man.* Toronto: McClelland and Stewart Limited, 1948.

_____.*The Betrayal.* Toronto: McClelland and Stewart Limited, 1964.

_____."Diary of an Internment." *White Pelican* 4:3 (Summer 1974) 4-40.

_____.*The Almost Meeting.* Edmonton. NeWest Press, 1981.

Levine, Norman. "Letter from London" *The Tight-Rope Walker.* London: Putnam, 1950.

_____.*The Angled Road.* Toronto: McClelland and Stewart Limited, 1952.

_____.*Canada Made Me.* London: Putnam, 1958.

_____.*One Way Ticket.* London: Secker and Warburg, 1961.

_____.*From a Seaside Town.* Toronto: Macmillan of Canada, 1970.

_____.*I Don't Want to Know Anyone Too Well.* Toronto: Macmillan of Canada, 1971.

_____.*Thin Ice* Ottawa: Deneau and Greenberg, 1979.

_____."Something Happened Here." *The Canadian Forum* (May 1982), 12-15, 36.

Lewis, Wyndham. *Filibusters in Barbary.* New York: National Travel Club, 1932.

_____.*America, I Presume.* New York: Howett, Soskin and Company, 1940.

_____.*America and Cosmic Man.* London and Brussels: Nicholson and Watson Limited, 1948.

_____.*Self Condemned.* Chicago: Henry Regnery Company, 1955.

_____.*The Letters of Wyndham Lewis.* ed. by W.K. Rose, Norfolk: New Directions, 1963.

Lowry, Malcolm. *Hear Uş O Lord From Heaven Thy Dwelling Place.* Philadelphia and New York: J.B. Lippincott Company, 1961.

_____. *Selected Letters,* ed. Harvey Breit and Marjorie Bonner Lowry. Philadelphia and New York: J.B. Lippincott Company, 1965.

_____. *October Ferry to Gabriola.* New York and Cleveland: The World Publishing Company, 1970.

Metcalf, John. *Going Down Slow.* Toronto: McClelland and Stewart Limited, 1972.

_____. *General Ludd.* Toronto, ECW Press, 1980.

Moodie, Susanna. *Roughing It in the Bush.* Toronto: Bell and Cockburn, 1913. [1852]

_____. *Life in the Clearings.* Introduction by Robert L. McDougall. Toronto: The Macmillan Company of Canada Limited, 1959.

Moore, Brian. "Grieve for the Dear Departed." *Atlantic* August 1959, pp. 43-46.

_____. "Uncle T" *Gentleman's Quarterly.* November 1960, pp. 118-19, 140, 142-54, 158.

_____. *The Luck of Ginger Coffey.* Boston and Toronto: Atlantic-Little, Brown and Company, 1960.

_____. *An Answer from Limbo.* Boston and Toronto: Atlantic-Little, Brown and Company, 1962.

_____. *Fergus.* Toronto: McClelland and Stewart Limited, 1970.

_____. *The Doctor's Wife.* Toronto: McClelland and Stewart Limited, 1976.

_____. *The Mangan Inheritance.* Toronto: McClelland and Stewart Limited, 1979.

Niven, Frederick. *The Flying Years.* London: Collins, 1935.

Ovid. *Tristia* and *Ex Ponto.* Translated by Arthur Leslie Wheeler. Cambridge: Harvard University Press, 1953. [1924]

Richler, Mordecai. *The Acrobats.* New York: G.P. Putnam's Sons, 1954.

_____. *A Choice of Enemies.* London: Andre Deutsch, 1957.

_____. *Cocksure.* Toronto: McClelland and Stewart Limited, 1968.

_____. *St. Urbain's Horseman.* Toronto: McClelland and Stewart Limited, 1971.

_____. *Joshua Then and Now.* Toronto: McClelland and Stewart Limited, 1981.

Salverson, Laura Goodman. *The Viking Heart.* Toronto: McClelland and Stewart, 1923.

_____. *Confessions of an Immigrant's Daughter.* Toronto: The Ryerson Press, [1939].

Skvorecky, Josef. *The Coward.* Translated from the Czech by Jeanne Nemcova. New York: Grove Press, Inc., 1970.

_____. *The Bass Saxophone.* Translated from the Czech by Kaca Polackova-Henley. Toronto: Anson-Cartwright Editions, 1977.

_____. *Miss Silver's Past.* Translated from the Czech by Peter Kussi. London: The Bodley Head Ltd. 1976.

_____. *The Swell Season.* Translated from the Czech by Paul Wilson. Toronto: Lester and Orpen Dennys, 1982.

_____. *The Engineer of Human Souls.* Translated from the Czech by Paul Wilson. Toronto: Lester and Orpen Limited, 1984.

Traill, Catharine Parr. *The Backwoods of Canada.* Toronto: Coles Publishing Company, 1971. [1836]

Wilson, Ethel. *The Innocent Traveller.* Toronto: The Macmillan Company of Canada Limited, 1949.

———. *Mrs. Golightly and Other Stories,* Toronto: The Macmillan Company of Canada Limited. 1961.

SECONDARY SOURCES

Aiken, Conrad. *Conrad Aiken Collection.* Huntington Library, San Marino, California.

Allen, Walter, ed. *Transatlantic Crossing: American Visitors to Britain and British Visitors to America in the Nineteenth Century.* London: Heinemann, 1971.

Atwood, Margaret. *The Journals of Susanna Moodie.* Toronto: Oxford University Press, 1970.

Ballstadt, Carl P.A. "Catharine Parr Traill" *Canadian Writers and Their Works* Fiction Series, Volume I, ed. Robert Lecker, Jack David, Ellen Quigley. Downsview: ECW Press, 1983, pp. 149-193.

Bradbrook, Muriel C. *Malcolm Lowry: His Art and Early Life.* Cambridge: Cambridge University Press, 1974.

Costa, Richard Hauer. *Malcolm Lowry.* New York: Twayne Publishers, Inc, 1972.

Cowley, Malcolm. *Exile's Return: A Literary Odyssey of the 1920s.* New York: The .Viking Press, 1951.

Dahlie, Hallvard. *Brian Moore.* Boston: G.K. Hall & Company, 1981.

Day, Douglas. *Malcolm Lowry: A Biography.* New York: Oxford University Press, 1973.

Denny, Margaret and Gilman, William, eds. *The American Writer and the European Tradition.* New York: Haskell House Publishers Ltd. 1968. [1950]

Duffy, Dennis. *Gardens, Covenants, Exiles.* Toronto. University of Toronto Press, 1982.

Dunae, Patrick A. *Gentlemen Emigrants; From the British Public Schools to the Canadian Frontier.* Vancouver and Toronto: Douglas and McIntyre, 1981.

Dunbar, Ernest. *The Black Expatriates: A Study of American Negroes in Exile.* New York: E.P. Dutton and Co. Inc., 1968.

Eagleton, Terry. *Exiles and Emigrés: Studies in Modern Literature.* New York: Schocken Books, 1972. [1970]

Earnest, Ernest. *Expatriates and Patriots: American Artists, Scholars, and Writers in Europe.* Durham: Duke University Press, 1968.

Edel, Leon. "John Glassco and his Erotic Muse." *Canadian Literature* 93 (Summer 1982) 108-117.

Eggleston, Wilfrid. *The Frontier and Canadian Letters.* Toronto: The Ryerson Press, 1957.

Exner, Richard. *"Exuel Poeta:* Theme and Variations," *Books Abroad* L No 2 (Spring 1976), 285-295.

Farley, T.E. *Exiles and Pioneers.* Ottawa: Borealis Press, 1975.

Fowler, Marian. *The Embroidered Tent: Five Gentlewomen in Early Canada.* Toronto: Anansi, 1982.

————. *Redney: A Life of Sara Jeannette Duncan.* Toronto: Anansi, 1983.

Fulford, Robert. "Robert Fulford Interviews Brian Moore," *The Tamarack Review* 23 (Spring 1962) 5-18.

Grace, Sherrill. *The Voyage That Never Ends: Malcolm Lowry's Fiction.* Vancouver, University of British Columbia Press, 1982.

Graham, W.H. *The Tiger of the Canadian West.* Toronto and Vancouver: Clarke, Irwin and Company Limited, 1962.

Gurr, Andrew: *Writers in Exile. The Identity of Home in Modern Literature.* Sussex: The Harvester Press and New Jersey: Humanities Press, 1981.

Hancock, Geoffrey. "An Interview with Mavis Gallant," *Canadian Fiction Magazine* 28 (1978), 19-67.

Hatch, Ronald B. "The Three Stages of Mavis Gallant's Short Fiction," *Canadian Fiction Magazine* 28 (1978) 92-114.

James, Henry. "The Madonna of the Future," *The Novels and Tales of Henry James.* New York Edition, Vol XIII. New York: Scribners, 1908, 1936, pp. 437-492.

Kenner, Hugh. *Wyndham Lewis.* Norfolk: New Directions, 1954.

Lamming, George. *The Pleasures of Exile.* London: Michael Joseph, 1960.

Lauber, John. "Liberty and the Pursuit of Pleasure: John Glassco's Quest," *Canadian Literature* 90 (Autumn, 1981) 61-72.

Leacock, Stephen. *The Boy I Left Behind Me.* Garden City: Doubleday and Company, Inc., 1946.

Lecker, Robert. *On the Line: Readings in the Short Fiction of Clark Blaise, John Metcalf and Hugh Hood.* Downsview: ECW Press, 1982.

Levin, Harry. "Literature and Exile." *Refractions: Essays in Comparative Literature.* London: Oxford University Press, 1968, pp. 62-81.

Levine, Norman. "Why I Am an Expatriate." *Canadian Literature* 5 (Summer, 1960), 49-54.

————. "The Girl in the Drugstore." *Canadian Literature* 41 (Summer, 1969).

————. "Every Literature Needs an Exile," *Saturday Night* (December 1976), 2.

Lewis, Anne Wyndham. "The Hotel," *Canadian Literature* 35 (Winter 1968), 26-28.

Lewis, Wyndham. *Wyndham Lewis Archive.* Cornell University, Ithaca, N.Y.

Lowry, Malcolm. *Malcolm Lowry Collection.* University of British Columbia Library, Vancouver, B.C.

MacDonald, R.D. "Canada in Lowry's Fiction," *Mosaic* XIV/2 (Spring 1981). 35-53.

MacMurchy, Marjory. "Mrs. Everard Cotes (Sara Jeannette Duncan)." *The Bookman* XLVIII, No 24 (May 1915), 39.

Malouf, David. *An Imaginary Life.* New York: George Braziller, 1978.

Materer, Timothy. *Wyndham Lewis the Novelist.* Detroit: Wayne State University Press, 1976.

Matthews, John. *Tradition in Exile.* Toronto: University of Toronto Press, 1962.

McCarthy, Mary. "A Guide to Exiles, Expatriates, and Internal Emigrés," *New York Review of Books,* Vol. XVIII, No. 4. (March 9, 1972), pp. 4-8.

McMullen, Lorraine. "Frances Brooke," *Canadian Writers and Their Works.* Fiction Series. Volume I, ed. Robert Lecker, Jack David, Ellen Quigley. Downsview: ECW Press, 1983. pp. 25-60.

Merler, Grazia. *Mavis Gallant: Narrative Patterns and Devices.* Ottawa: The Tecumseh Press, 1978.

Meyers, Jeffrey. *The Enemy: A Biography of Wyndham Lewis.* London and Henley: Routledge and Kegan Paul, 1980.

_____. ed. *Wyndham Lewis: A Revaluation.* London: The Athlone Press, 1980.

Milosz, Czeslow. *The Captive Mind.* Translated from the Polish by Jane Zieloneo. New York: Alfred A. Knopf, 1953.

Moore, Brian. "The Writer in Exile," *Canadian Journal of Irish Studies* 2:2 (December 1976). 5-17.

_____. *The Brian Moore Collection.* University of Calgary Library, Calgary, Alberta.

Morris, Audrey Y. *Gentle Pioneers: Five Nineteenth Century Canadians.* Toronto and London: Hodder and Stoughton, 1968.

Murdoch, Charles. "Essential Glassco." *Canadian Literature* 65 (Summer 1975) 28-41.

Nabokov, Vladimir. *Speak Memory: An Autobiography Revisited.* New York: G.P. Putnan's Sons, 1966.

New, W.H. "Frances Brooke's Chequered Gardens." *Canadian Literature* 52 (Spring 1972) 24-38.

Niven, Alastair, ed. *The Commonwealth Writer Overseas: Themes of Exile and Expatriation.* Liege: Revue des Langues Vivantes. 1976.

Pacey, Desmond. *Frederick Philip Grove.* Toronto. The Ryerson Press, 1945.

Peterman, Michael. "Susanna Moodie." *Canadian Writers and Their Works.* Fiction Series, Volume I. ed. Robert Lecker, Jack David, Ellen Quigley. Downsview: ECW Press. 1983. pp. 63-104.

Priestly, J.B. "A Voluntary Exile," *Open House.* London: William Heinemann Ltd., 1927, pp. 138-143.

Pritchard, William. *Wyndham Lewis.* New York: Twayne Publishers, 1968.

Richler, Mordecai. "A Sense of the Ridiculous: Paris, 1951 and After." *New American Review* 4 (1968), pp. 114-134.

Rose, W.R. *Wyndham Lewis at Cornell,* Ithaca: The Cornell University Library, 1961.

Shields, Carol. *Susanna Moodie: Voice and Vision.* Ottawa: Borealis Press, 1977.

Singer, Godfrey Frank. *The Epistolary Novel: Its Origin, Development, Decline, and Residuary Influence.* New York: Russell and Russell, Inc., [1933]

Skvorecky, Josef. "A Country After My Own Heart." *Macleans* (March 1974) 24, 25, 72, 74-76.

Spettigue, Douglas O. *Frederick Philip Grove.* Toronto: Copp Clark, 1969.

_____. *FPG: The European Years.* Ottawa: Oberon Press, 1973.

Stevens, Peter. "Perils of Compassion." *Canadian Literature* 56 (Spring 1973) 61-70.

Stobie, Margaret R. *Frederick Philip Grove.* New York: Twayne Publishers Inc., 1973.

Sutherland, Fraser. *John Glassco: An Essay and Bibliography.* Toronto: ECW Press, 1984.

Tabori, Paul, ed. *The PEN in Exile.* London: International P.E.N. Club Centre for Writers in Exile, 1954.

_____., ed. *The PEN in Exile II.* London, 1956.

_____. *The Anatomy of Exile: A Semantic and Historical Study.* London: Harrap, 1972.

Tausky, Thomas E. *Sara Jeannette Duncan: Novelist of Empire.* Port Credit: P.D. Meany Publishers, 1980.

Thomas, Clara. *Love and Work Enough: The Life of Anna Jameson.* Toronto: University of Toronto Press, 1967.

Wagner, Geoffrey. *Wyndham Lewis: A Portrait of the Artist as Enemy.* New Haven: Yale University Press, 1957.

Watmough, David. "Interview with Brian Moore," CBC Radio, June 1, 1963.

Wicks, Ulrich. "Onlyman." *Mosaic* VIII/3 (Spring 1975) 21-47.

Williams, David. "The Exile as Uncreator," *Mosaic* VIII/3 (Spring 1975) 1-14.

Wilson, Ethel. "The Bridge or the Stokehold?" *Canadian Literature* 5 (Summer 1960) 43-47.

Woodcock, George, ed. *Malcolm Lowry: The Man and His Work.* Vancouver: University of British Columbia Publications Centre, 1971.

_____, ed. *Wyndham Lewis in Canada.* Vancouver: University of British Columbia Publications Centre, 1971.

_____. "Richler's Wheel of Exile." *The Rejection of Politics.* Toronto: Newpress, 1972, pp. 138-145.

Index

Aiken, Conrad, 158, 159, 164
Atwood, Margaret, 12, 19, 119

Bacque, James, 28
Blaise, Clark, 35, 50, 139-40, 194-98
Brooke, Frances, 5, 8, 11, 12, 14, 15, 17, 18, 20, 23-31, 32, 33, 34, 49, 51, 62, 63, 71, 76, 82, 84, 125, 163, 173, 184

Callaghan, Morley, 7, 88-91, 93, 94, 197
Carr, Emily, 107, 108
Conrad, Joseph, 5, 190
Cowasjee, Saros, 193
Cowley, Malcolm, 4, 5, 7, 87, 88, 90, 91, 95, 200

Drabek, Jan, 188
Duffy, Dennis, 6
Dunae, Patrick, 13
Duncan, Sara Jeannette, 15, 20, 35-58, 69, 71, 76, 87, 93, 94, 100, 103, 115, 116, 120, 124, 139, 140, 142, 150, 193

Eagleton, Terry, 4, 5
Earnest, Ernest, 4, 5, 7
Edel, Leon, 88, 91
Eggleston, Wilfrid, 77

Farley, Thomas E., 4, 6
Fitzgerald, F. Scott, 7, 8, 89, 90, 109, 165, 190
Forster, E.M., 73, 196
Frye, Northrop, 148

Gallant, Mavis, 7, 35, 39, 44, 49, 50, 69, 90, 93, 102, 103, 107, 114, 115-43, 151, 190, 192, 200, 201
Galt, John, 6, 11, 12, 16, 21, 31-33, 35, 39, 76
Gissing, George, 87, 88, 90
Glassco, John, 7, 88-93, 94, 95, 100, 108, 109, 119, 197
Grieg, Nordahl, 158
Grove, Frederick Philip, 6, 11, 15, 20, 23, 30, 39, 49, 59, 69, 77-86, 105, 146, 148, 149, 167, 173

Gurr, Andrew, 6

Haliburton, Thomas, 8, 32
Hatch, Ronald, 120
Hawthorne, Nathaniel, 7, 189, 190
Hemingway, Ernest, 7, 90
Howe, Joseph, 8
Howells, William Dean, 36, 51
Howison, John, 13-14

Irving, Washington, 7, 92

James, Henry, 5, 7, 36, 45, 46, 49, 54, 56, 86, 120, 201
Jameson, Anna, 10, 11, 14, 20-23, 32, 148
Jonas, George, 188
Joyce, James, 89, 148, 164, 176, 195

Koch, Eric, 184-85, 188
Kreisel, Henry, 3, 107, 184-88, 191, 194

Leacock, Stephen, 27, 39, 142
Levine, Norman, 7, 8, 23, 50, 90, 93, 94, 102-14, 115, 143, 154, 192, 194, 200
Lewis, Anna Wyndham, 145
Lewis, Wyndham, 7, 8, 11, 16, 19, 20, 53, 66, 67, 82, 105, 144-58, 159, 160, 163, 169, 170, 176, 179, 181, 182, 192, 194, 199
Lowry, Malcolm, 7, 8, 11, 20, 23, 30, 49, 53, 60, 67, 72, 76, 80, 105, 109, 121, 139, 143, 144, 145, 149, 155, 157, 158-69, 170, 173, 181, 182, 195, 199, 200, 201

MacLennan, Hugh, 148, 188
Mann, Thomas, 92, 202
Marlyn, John, 66, 107
Matthews, John, 6
McClung, Nellie, 68, 87
McCulloch, Thomas, 32
Milosz, Czeslaw, 183-84
Mitchison, Naomi, 148, 150
Moodie, Susanna, 6, 8, 12, 13, 15-20, 22, 23, 26, 30, 31, 32, 33, 39, 60, 62, 65, 66, 76, 82, 105, 148, 167

Moore, Brian, 7, 15, 16, 49, 66, 67, 76, 103, 105, 128, 139, 143, 144, 157, 158, 160, 169-82, 200, 201

Nabokov, Vladimir, 5, 12, 195
New, William, 30
Niven, Frederick, 6, 16, 32, 59, 60-64, 65, 66, 67, 75, 76, 82, 148, 167, 173

Ovid, 1, 2, 3, 4, 10, 12, 17, 18, 21, 121, 147, 199, 202

Pacey, Desmond, 77, 78, 79
Pound, Ezra, 89, 145, 146
Priestley, J.B., 201

Richler, Mordecai, 7, 8, 50, 93-103, 110, 113, 115, 120, 153, 200
Rose, W.K., 148

Salverson, Laura, 6, 16, 30, 32, 59, 60, 64-70, 75, 76, 79, 84, 85, 107, 141, 166
Shields, Carol 18
Skvorecky, Josef, 1, 3, 5, 8, 183, 188-91, 194, 202
Spettigue, Douglas O., 77, 78, 79
Stobie, Margaret, 79

Tausky, Thomas, E., 54
Thomas, Clara, 20
Traill, Catharine Parr, 6, 12-18, 20, 22, 32, 71

Wharton, Edith, 7, 36, 49
Williams, David, 28
Wilson, Ethel, 6, 11, 16, 20, 35, 41, 45, 59, 60, 65, 69-77, 80, 105, 139, 153, 154
Woodcock, George, 101